Complete Horoscope

2024

Monthly astrological forecasts for every Zodiac sign for 2024

D1666156

TATIANA BORSCH

Translated from Russian by Sonja Swenson
Translation copyright © Coinflow Limited, Cyprus
AstraArt Books is an imprint of Coinflow limited, Cyprus
Published by Coinflow Limited, Cyprus
For queries please contact: tatianaborsch@yahoo.com

ISBN: 978-9925-609-56-7 (print)
ISBN: 978-9925-609-57-4 (ebook)

Contents

General Astrological Forecast for 2024

We are embarking on yet another difficult year, which can generally be divided into two very different periods. During the first half of the year, Jupiter, which is the most powerful planet in our solar system, will be in the sign of Taurus, creating a favorable aspect with Saturn. That means that both peoples' lives and events on the political stage will play out rather predictably.

This is a very good time for China – it will continue to expand its power, both economically and politically, which will of course impact its position in the global arena. We might see successful negotiations regarding Taiwan.

The first half of 2024 will also be very positive for India. Its economy is surging – over the next three to four years, it will be able to make significant investments in resolving problems such as poverty and develop its infrastructure and industry. It will become a global economic leader.

However, things are not so rosy in the Old World – Europe, where economic drivers such as Germany, are going through a troublesome astrological period. In India, this is known as Sade Sati (Saturn's transit through the sign of the Moon, which often includes the Moon's neighboring zodiac sign). Usually, this period lasts about three years. Each country will experience things its own way. For Germany, this most likely means an economic slowdown and domestic political and social turbulence. This is a trend that began in 2022 and will last for about three years.

The first half of 2024 is crucial for Russia, as presidential elections will take place in 2024. I predict that Putin will remain in power, despite the Russian opposition and meddling from the West, which will be unprecedented this time. Though Putin will remain in the Kremlin, his government will see a lot of turnover, as will other power structures.

The war in Ukraine will begin to slow down somewhat during the first half of the year, and though there will not be any major hostilities, skirmishes will break out in various spots on various fronts.

Ukraine's difficulties began with the Sade Sati in 2020. In 2024-2025, we will see this phenomenon reach its final phase. I believe that there is a very high chance of the country being divided into spheres of influence, with its very independence jeopardized. In 2024, and perhaps somewhat sooner, Poland might openly lay claim to Lviv and the western territories that were ceded to Ukraine following World War Two.

With regard to Ukraine's territories currently under Russian occupation – we will see a continuation of major construction and infrastructure restoration. I believe that in the first half of 2024, Russia's expansion may continue, as other Russian-speaking regions of Ukraine fall under its influence. May 2024 might be a very important time for this.

Economically, this is a hard time for Russia. Sanctions and trade limitations will make things significantly more difficult. There may not be enough budget for military operations, along with economic development, and major construction in the regions now impacted by war. But in the end, there will be an acceptable balance. Russia's economic recovery will be active enough, and as a result, we might see new companies created in regions around the country.

A major astrological event will take place from April 18-26, 2024. Two giants of the solar system – Jupiter and Uranus – will be in conjunction. This is one of the most unusual unions when it comes to finances. Depending on individual horoscopes, some people might see significant achievements here, while others will see unexpected changes for the worse. In principle, this is a neutral-positive aspect, but everything depends on individual information. This is an interesting time for cryptocurrency – we might see significant ups and downs with new financial instruments, which will seriously alter the currency markets, as Uranus in Taurus will lead to many financial shifts.

But also remember that during this time, we may see positive business propositions, career changes, promotions, salary raises, and successful investments!

In 2024, all businesses related to agriculture and produce might develop rapidly. More people might be noticeably more focused on eating a healthy diet.

The second half of 2024 will be much more troublesome for all countries, and far more difficult than the first half.

On May 25, Jupiter will transit to Gemini, and by June, we might start to see changes in plans and conflicts drag out, both in our interpersonal relationships and between countries. By mid-August, Jupiter will be forming a harsh aspect with Saturn, which promises a battle between old structures and the new world we live in. This aspect will repeat again in the fall and winter of 2024. Our world abounds with contradictions, and this will only become more apparent. The economic crisis will worsen, and almost no country will be spared.

The war in Ukraine will gain momentum once again. In the fall and winter of 2024, things will become difficult for Russia, as the hostilities take on a new intensity. This will continue into the first half of 2025, though gradually it will become clear that there is no military solution to this conflict, and things will start to die down. Sanctions will remain in place, though slowly but surely, things will head in a more constructive direction.

During the second half of the year, the European Union will see division among its member states. This trend will continue into 2025 as well. We might see some countries moving toward greater independence from Brussels. The reason may be the economic crisis, which will force many governments to work on behalf of their own countries.

Obviously we won't see any repeats of Brexit in 2024, though this may appear somewhat later. Over the next three to four years, the EU will undergo serious changes, and the European Commission might lose some of its powers, as dictating the rules of the game to the world will become much more difficult.

With regard to the United States, 2024 might be particularly difficult. Pluto is returning to its position in the US birth chart, and this is very important, as it will be in the sector of the sky responsible for the banking system, finances, and even society's emotional state.

Pluto is the planet responsible for purification and renewal, but it also brings the destruction of anything obsolete, which may trigger global crises, which are inevitable with any change in the system. That is why in 2024, economic strife may trigger demonstrations against the current government, as well as a serious struggle for power among members of the ruling class.

During the second half of the year, the United States may lose a lot of allies – this trend will continue into 2025. Perhaps this will be due to a stronger China, Russia, and India, or alternatively, growing economic problems. The US will weaken in its role as the hegemon.

The US presidential elections in 2024 may bring a repeat of what we saw in 2020. It is hard to imagine Joe Biden hanging onto the presidency. He will leave. But these elections will be full of scandal, most likely due to Trump's bombastic speeches.

During the second half of the year, Jupiter will be in Gemini, which supports Trump, as he himself is a Gemini. During the first half of the year, however, despite his histrionics, Trump will spend the first half of 2024 busy with legal troubles that began in 2023. But during the second half of the year, he will be at the center of society's attention – what more could a politician need? Both Trump and Ron de Santis have a good shot at the presidency. De Santis's birth time is unknown, but I think he has a good chance.

Another thorn in the US's side may be the situation in the Middle East, which is already unstable, but in 2024, some kind of military confrontation may break out.

Jupiter in Gemini creates a negative aspect with Saturn, which will close in mid-August, and which portends difficulties for the global economy. This means a situation that is highly unstable, with volatile markets and trouble in the banking sector.

We might, however, see scientific breakthroughs – perhaps new technology and discoveries await in the hands of the world's young and talented scientists.

Fashion will become more feminine and elegant during the first half of the year. Jupiter in Taurus means that we can expect more fitted silhouettes, and perhaps greater focus on traditional garb. Beige will be the color of the day, as will all hues of gold and brown. As always, black will be in demand. Clothing will be monochromatic.

During the second half of the year, we can expect light and dark blue, green, and unusual color combinations. The look will be unkempt and carefree, with a greater focus on youth fashions than the classics. Jupiter in Gemini also suggests flowing, translucent fabrics.

All year long, the weather will be unstable, with flooding affecting coastal countries and islands. We might see a more serious version of what has already happened in several regions of the world. During the second half of the year, many countries can expect to deal with strong winds and tornadoes.

While we can say that everyone has their own fate, global circumstances often are indirectly reflected in each of our lives.

Despite all the ups and downs, the first half of 2024 is the best time for getting married, having babies, or buying real estate.

During the second half of the year, I would not recommend any long-distance travel, starting any legal proceedings, or making important decisions about moving. During this time, many relationships will fall apart, if things were already on the rocks. But you can find out more about that in my forecast for each Zodiac sign.

Best of luck in 2024!

Astrologist Tatiana Borsch

2024 Overview for all Zodiac signs

ARIES

Overall, 2024 looks positive for you. It is a year designed to make you see life on a broader level and celebrate the successes you have already begun to see. This is a time to harvest the fruits of all your hard work.

Work

Generally speaking, you can divide 2024 into two vastly different periods. The first half of the year will be singularly successful when it comes to anything money- or work-related.

Business owners and managers will enjoy handsome profits from earlier projects, and they will put in the work to promote your latest ideas. Many Aries will work to expand their business, and they will find the money to make that happen.

Employees might count on a promotion, along with a salary raise to match. If there is nowhere for you to grow at your current job, there is nothing stopping you from finding something new or thinking about striking out alone. The stars will give you a lot of opportunities, and your job is to leverage them.

During the second half of the year (from June to December), things will be more difficult. Those planning on cooperation with someone in another city or abroad might run into a variety of obstacles.

That may include business partners from far away who keep changing conditions on you before breaking into outright hostilities and aggression. Alternatively, you will see worsening conditions on the world stage which will make any cooperation simply impossible. August, September, late November, and December are the grimmest times here.

Be ready for this and try to adjust your plans ahead of time.

Money

The first half of 2024 will be an unmistakably good time for your finances. During this time, most Aries will see significantly greater income, with January, late April, and all of May as the best periods.

During the second half of the year, your earnings will be more modest, but things will not become critical. You may have less money, but you will not end up bankrupt.

Love and family

The first half of 2024 looks like smooth sailing where your personal life is concerned. Many Aries will continue to improve their home, which they recently began. You can expect major repairs, construction, or to purchase a new apartment, home, or summer home. It all depends on your plans and financial abilities. Many will be thinking about welcoming a new family member, as well.

June and July are relatively calm months, though many families will face challenges in August, such as problems involving their relatives, and this trend will continue until the end of the year.

The best time for making new acquaintances is June and October, while July and November are the best times to reconnect with someone from your past. There's also no better time to find common ground with a loved one following a serious argument.

Health

In 2024, you are feeling rather energetic, but it is not worth putting your body to the test.

The stars recommend that you lead a healthy lifestyle and balance work and leisure.

During the second half of the year, the stars recommend that you remain vigilant when driving and traveling.

August, late November, and December are critical months.

TAURUS

2024 marks the beginning of a new cycle for you. Jupiter, the planet of luck, success, and new opportunities is spending most of the year in your sign, which means that a lot of doors will open, and your most important task is to select the right one!

Work

For most Taureans, 2024 is one of the best you have had in the last decade. The first half of the year will be particularly lucky for you, when business owners will receive new, attractive offers, while employees can expect a new job. Alternatively, you might run into new opportunities that weren't there in the past, and for many, that will mean a way out of the tricky situations you encountered in 2023.

During the first half of 2024, you will have an opportunity to correct any mistakes you made previously, for example, you will be able to reconnect with old friends, like-minded people, or someone influential.

Your opportunities in the first half of the year are highly unique, and it is worth taking maximum advantage of all of them, as the second half of the year will be much more difficult.

You might receive higher earnings along with these new professional prospects, or greater freedom in how you manage your money. At the same time, however, greater opportunities bring greater responsibility, and you can't lose sight of that, especially during the second half of the year. During this time, business owners and managers might disagree over money with a business partner or someone highly placed. The situation may grow serious, so keep that in mind and take steps in advance in order to save your skin.

The luck that will guide you through the first half of 2024 might make you over-confident or ambitious, which will cause issues where you least expect it.

The most difficult months will be August, late November, and December, when your troubles will come to a head, and you will spend 2025 dealing with it all.

Money

The first half of 2024 will be favorable for your bank account, as you will have regular income and somewhat more of it, as well.

The largest sums will come in May and June, though you will run into a roadblock after this period. For assorted reasons, your expenses will grow, perhaps due to business, or maybe your personal life.

Love and family

During the first half of 2024, your personal life will go surprisingly well, and you will make some new acquaintances. This is an exciting time for anyone single or who has been let down by previous entanglements. They might find a long-term or even permanent partner.

For those with a family already, this new love interest may become a sore spot, and during the second half of the year, this will become clear. If you want to keep your family together, it is worth thinking hard before embarking on a new romance.

During the second half of the year, most couples who have been together for a while will find their relationship put to the test, as well. If your relationship was already hanging by a thread, this may be the year that finally breaks it. Perhaps a new romance will replace the old one.

Couples who get along will make major changes to their home during the second half of the year. Perhaps they will purchase a new place to live or rehabilitate the old one. Construction and other difficult tasks are to be expected. You will have to dedicate a sizable portion of the family budget to this, and occasionally, the expenses will be overwhelming. You will not complete this project until next year, in 2025.

Health

In 2024, your energy levels are fairly high, and you have no reason to fear falling ill. However, in August and September, it is worth being cautious, especially if you have suffered from chronic illnesses in the past.

GEMINI

You are starting to see the results – both good and bad – of some important decisions you made recently. The stars recommend you joyfully celebrate the positive and fight off the negative. You will be spending the entire year facing off between these positions.

Work

The first half of 2024 is quiet, but not particularly productive. Business owners and managers at various levels will be reorganizing or maybe even expanding their business. You may have to deal with issues concerning land, real estate, construction, and other difficult administrative matters.

Things will go relatively smoothly and predictably during the first half of the year.

Employees should not count on seriously improving their position at work, but if you show some flexibility, you won't stagnate.

If you leverage the influence of your friends, or VIPs, you will be able to climb the totem pole, and late February and March are the best times for this.

During the second half of the year (especially from June to October), things will be more dynamic, but also more challenging. During this time, many Geminis will have to raise their voice to assert their rights, and it appears that there will be good reason for that.

But not everyone can think the same way. That is why starting in August, you will run into people who want to throw a wrench in the works for you.

Business owners and managers will have to face government agencies or someone influential and powerful.

Employees might see conflict with management, and closer to the end of the year, they might be thinking about a new job. During the first quarter of 2025, that might come to fruition.

Your relationship with colleagues in other cities or abroad is coming along with varying success and expect things to get particularly ugly here in November and December.

Money

Financially, 2024 is an overall neutral time for you. You will not spend your way into ruin, but your income is not particularly high. Late February and March are the happy exceptions here.

Love and family

Many Geminis will spend the first half of 2024 focused on their personal lives.

You might be busy with various real estate transactions, such as repair, construction, or purchasing an apartment, home, or summer home. If you already began that process in 2023, right now, it is continuing the way you had hoped.

During this time, your family life is peaceful and tranquil, and couples who get along will work together to deal with irritating household tasks. In many families, you will welcome new children or grandchildren.

During the second half of the year, however, things will shift. You may face trouble with your parents or an elderly family member. You might have a serious argument, or possibly someone will fall ill or experience other problems. Things might develop quickly after August and reach a crescendo in December.

Expect disagreements with relatives.

Those who are living far from home should be careful when it comes to foreign laws. They will become a real thorn in your side during the second half of the year, probably in November and December.

Despite all of these obstacles, remember that on May 25, 2024, Jupiter, the planet of success, will enter your sign and stay there all year long. That means that anything involving Fate will turn out in your favor.

Health

During the first half of the year, you are feeling a bit more tired than usual, so take care of yourself. You might have a tendency to gain weight, so follow a healthy diet and stick to it!

During the second half of the year, you will feel much more invigorated, and the stars recommend that you be sure to use this power for peaceful purposes only.

CANCER

2024 is a watershed for you, as you move from the past into the future. This is a year of harvesting what you deserve. You will reap what you have sown, no more, and no less.

Work

During the first half of the year, things will be going your way. You will be surrounded by friends, like-minded people, and those with influence and power. Thanks to their help, you will seriously shore up your position at work, and even become fairly well-known in your field.

Your contacts with business partners in other cities or abroad will also develop nicely, and you might reconnect with former associates or spend a lot of time traveling.

Employees can count on a promotion, which will go hand in hand with greater influence and possibly even a raise.

Those who work in the creative fields are in for particular success. This includes actors, musicians, artists, and anyone who works with words. They will see their popularity grow, as well as their income.

This winning streak might reach a crescendo in May. In March and April, you will be pleased with the way things are going.

During the second half of the year, things will become more difficult. Starting in June, you will see changes for the worse, and all Cancers will experience this differently.

Business owners and managers will have to deal with audits, a resurgence of old legal troubles, and all of this might take on a highly unpredictable hue.

You will not be able to resolve all of these difficulties in 2024, and some of them will continue into 2025.

Your relationship with colleagues in other cities or abroad will also become significantly more complex after June, and some business partners far away might begin behaving irresponsibly or even with hostilities. Alternatively, difficulties on the world stage will throw a monkey wrench into your cooperation.

Money

During the first half of 2024, your finances are looking stable, but things will take a turn. You will spend more than you make, so many Cancers will need to keep an eye on their bank accounts. But it is always darkest before dawn, and you are sure to recover by the second half of 2025.

Love and family

During the first half of the year, things will be peaceful, and loving couples will live together in harmony. Your children will be a source of joy, though you may spend the lion's share of the family budget on their needs.

You might get back in touch with old friends or a former flame. They may live far away now, or perhaps a little closer to home.

Single Cancers will have an excellent opportunity to meet a new partner, and that will probably happen among friends, while traveling, or among people from somewhere far away.

During the second half of 2024, that is, from June to December, expect a lot of psychological and emotional turbulence.

During this time, your relationships may grow more complicated, and you are not the culprit here. You may experience serious trouble involving relatives and gossip, and it will be difficult to see who is in the right and who is in the wrong.

This unpleasant trend will take place from August to December. In order to not let it spoil your life, hold onto your loved one and remember that the most important thing in life is love and family, and we can and must simply get through the rest.

Health

During the first half of the year, you are healthy, energetic, and leave great impressions on everyone Fate sends your way. After June, you will be more sluggish, and old chronic diseases may become aggravated, or perhaps new ones will appear. Be careful when driving and traveling, especially in August and December!

LEO

Jupiter, the planet of success, is calling you forward once again. The stars promise you new heights and new opportunities. However, they also warn you that as you gaze toward the sky, occasionally look under your feet, too. You must, in order to avoid making the same mistakes again.

Work

During the first half of 2024, you will be on an undeniably lucky streak. Business owners and managers will have a fantastic opportunity to take their business to a new level. You might see this growth begin during the second half of 2023, but right now, it is reaching a logical continuation.

Employees can count on a new job, and if you recently began one, you will strengthen your position or even see a promotion.

All of this will come to a peak in May 2024. However, after then, things will begin to clearly decline, and with each month, this trend will become more noticeable. In many cases, the culprit is a difficult relationship with a business partner or someone highly placed. You may end up dividing up your business, or dealing with financial and material demands. In some cases, these issues will all be intertwined.

Employees might encounter enemies and competitors, and this might sully your relationship with management or someone with influence.

You may come to realize that all of your recent achievements are under threat, and the earlier you open your eyes, the more quickly you will be able to take the necessary steps. Most likely, you will be unable to resolve all of these thorny issues in 2024, and they will continue into 2025.

Money

The first half of the year will be a boon for your bank account. You can expect a windfall in January, late April, and May.

During the second half of the month, things will worsen due to a financial disagreement with your partner or trouble involving your loved ones.

Love and family

During the first half of the year, you might put your personal life on the back burner, as you will be much more focused on work.

However, your relationship with your partner might start to fade or cool off, and the feeling is mutual. If you care for your family and loved ones, carefully analyze the situation, and take additional countermeasures. If not, then let the chips fall where they may.

If you are considering a divorce or recently initiated one, you will have to settle difficult issues involving real estate. Your partner will dig their heels into the ground here, and you can expect difficulties during the second half of the year, right when money troubles are most on your mind.

Alternatively, your partner may fall ill or go through a tough time, and you will have to help him or her with both words, deeds, and a hefty sum of money.

From August to December, couples will also face a roadblock. Suddenly, it will come to light that you do not share the same worldview or value system, and in general, you do not see this person as someone you want to be with for the long haul.

Health

All year long, you are healthy and energetic, and this will allow you to cope with all of the challenges of 2024.

VIRGO

2024 is a chance for you to leave the past behind and start life with a clean slate. You will have an extraordinary chance to reach the top of what you want, but you will have to put up a serious fight in order to make it happen.

Work

The favorable changes that began during the second half of 2023 will continue in 2024. Many Virgos will link their interests to business partners in other cities or abroad and cooperate to benefit both parties. Alternatively, you might move or open a business in another city or abroad.

2024 is a wonderful time for studies, as well as undertaking serious work on yourself, especially during the first half of the year.

Employees might see a 180-degree turn in their professional development – perhaps a job offer far from home, a move, or frequent travel.

During the first half of the year, from January to June, you will see anything work-related play out smoothly, without a hitch or any trouble.

During the second half of the year, however, things will become more difficult. Starting in August, business owners will have a serious disagreement with their partners. They may have clashing views over the direction their business should take, or perhaps over various financial matters. This sometimes happens when a business grows and starts earning serious money.

Expect things to come to a head in December, and maybe a business partner will leave. During this time, employees will run into competitors and foes, which will lead to a worsening of your relationship with management.

You are highly unlikely to manage all of this in 2024, and many of your troubles will continue into the future. However, Jupiter is high in the most crucial sector of your chart and will provide you with help and support all the way through.

Money

Your finances are looking up all year long. You can count on significant income in February, May, June, and October.

Your work-related troubles are largely over competition and ambition and are unlikely to be reflected in your bank account.

Love and family

Your personal life will see a continuation of the challenges that cropped up in the recent past. Divorcing spouses will be mulling over the last several years and understand what direction is worth taking in their relationship. You might try to rekindle your relationship, but in the end, this is just a merry-go-round unlikely to go anywhere. Of course, there are some exceptions.

Saturn, which is firmly in the sector of the sky responsible for marriage and long-term relationships, is forcing you to be as attentive to your partners as possible and will punish you harshly for any past mistakes. If you are both guilty of a tarnished record, then expect your relationship to cool off and worsen. If this happens to you, understand that life doesn't sit still, there is a big world out there, and there are many fish in the sea. You will find the right person.

Many will plan to move to another city or abroad, and closer to May, you will see that has become a reality.

Health

All year long, you are feeling energetic and have no reason to fear falling ill.

LIBRA

One chapter in your life is coming to a close by late 2024 – the transition from past to future, and it might not be an easy time at all. However, you are on the right track, and you will make it!

Work

During the first half of 2024, things at work will be relatively calm and predictable.

Business owners and managers of every level will be expanding their business and naturally, that involves many administrative and organizational tasks. You might be buying land or facilities and updating it for future work.

Employees will strengthen their position where they are now and be thinking about greener pastures. However, that is something for the future, and for now, it is best to remain in place.

The best months for anything work-related are March, May, and June.

During the second half of the year (from June to December), you will be busier, but also more stressed. Many Libras will be linking their interests to colleagues in other cities or abroad, but this will also bring a series of challenges.

Business partners from afar will unexpectedly change the terms of your cooperation, or perhaps behave inappropriately and even aggressively! You will already have faced this by late July or August, with things coming to a head in November and December.

You might also come to the interest of auditing agencies, or perhaps old legal troubles will resurface, adding to your woes.

Managers should keep an eye on their subordinates, who might prove themselves to be unscrupulous or incompetent, which is sure to cast a shadow on your business.

Employees would be wise to keep an eye on colleagues and stay out of any office gossip.

It is worth mentioning that during the second half of 2024, you will not be able to rush any solutions to these troubles, and they will continue into 2025.

Money

Financially, 2024 is difficult for you, but things will not be critical. You have a lot of expenses, but when the going gets tough, you will be able to count on your business partner for help. You may also receive favorable terms of credit or even sponsorship.

Those who are not part of the working world can count on support from a loved one who will be on a positive streak.

You may also enjoy profits from various real estate transactions.

Love and family

Many Libras will be immersed in the task of setting up their home. You may be dealing with major repairs, construction, or buying a new home, apartment, or summer home. In some cases, this might take place far from your current home.

Though the first half of the year will bring you administrative tasks that will all go as planned, without any setbacks or trouble, the second half is another story.

The stars advise all Libras who are moving to another country or planning to acquire real estate abroad to be incredibly careful with foreign laws, as during the entire period, and especially August to December, you may encounter a series of challenges here.

Your relationship with your spouse is harmonious and calm, and your loved one will support you during times of both happiness and sadness. You will be able to resolve problems much more easily together.

During the second half of 2024, many families will face problems involving relatives, and in some way or another, this will impact every member of the family.

During this time, parents will have to manage their children's affairs, and this may involve spending heavily.

Health

All year long, you are feeling less energetic than usual, and should keep an eye on your body especially if you are elderly or weakened by chronic illness.

Those who are young and healthy may also not feel like their usual, cheery selves, and many Libras will have to watch their weight during the first half of the year.

In any case, remember that right now is the time to quit bad habits and live a healthy lifestyle.

This, along with getting enough exercise, is the best protection against many diseases. From August to December, the stars recommend being attentive when traveling and driving.

SCORPIO

2024 will bring you new plans, which will then come to life. In the meantime, it is worth considering what you really need and what would be easy to give up.

Work

You will see varying levels of success at work. Many Scorpios will meet someone influential. Business owners and managers will be working on joint cooperation, which will benefit you, but also bring challenges when you run into people who are more influential than you.

Though you can expect to avoid nearly all problems during the first half of the year, during the second, you will run into a series of disagreements.

Perhaps your business partners will start behaving selfishly, which will reflect negatively on your relationship and business in general. Alternatively, he or she might make financial demands or become difficult when it comes to real estate. Perhaps that will take place somewhere far away, or closer to home.

During the second half of the year, employees can expect changes at work, which might continue into 2025. That may force you to adjust to changes in conditions or think about taking your talents to greener pastures. But Rome wasn't built in a day, so take your time in making any decisions and examine all the possibilities before you make a move.

The most difficult period is the second half of the year, especially December, when the challenges that began in August come at you, full force.

Money

In 2024, your bank account will see a lot of ups and downs. Your income is modest, but you will still have expenses, especially in the second half of the year. They may be related to weak spots in your business, or perhaps your personal life and your family's, or more likely, children's demands.

Love and family

You can expect significant shifts in your personal life. Jupiter, the planet of success, is in the sector of the sky responsible for marriage, love, and any long-term relationship.

Thanks to this, single people and those who have been let down by love in the past, can count on a fateful meeting, which will logically lead to living together or perhaps even marriage.

You can also expect relationship troubles, especially during the second half of the year, with the stormiest clouds gathering from August to December.

In the best-case scenario, this is just part of the normal hiccups we run into when getting to know one another, but in the worst cases, you will realize that your loved one's worldview or values system clashes with your own.

During this time, those with families can expect difficulties involving their children, and these issues may look different, depending on how old your children are, as well as past situations.

Spouses who have been together for a while can count on their loved one significantly strengthening his or her position at work.

Things are not perfect here, though, either – the arrival of someone on the sidelines is a real possibility, and this always makes our life more complicated. Skeletons always come out of the closet one way or another, and during the second half of the year, you will see just how true that is.

Health

In 2024, you will be feeling sluggish, especially from August to December. During this time, old, chronic illnesses may rear their ugly heads again, or perhaps new ones will appear.

Take care of yourself and remember that a healthy lifestyle will ward off most issues and protect you from many diseases.

SAGITTARIUS

Expect a difficult and tumultuous but also productive year. You will have to deal with constantly changing circumstances and to put in a lot of arduous work. In the end, though, it is worth it.

Work

During the first half of 2024, you will see immense success with anything professional. You will have no trouble finding work, no matter where you are. Things couldn't be better.

Business owners and managers will sign major contracts, which will take their business to the next level.

You can expect to strengthen your position at work, and employees might see a promotion in their current job, or perhaps a new, more promising job at a larger organization. In May 2024, this streak will reach its zenith.

During the second half of the year, the skies will begin to darken. Business owners and managers at every level will see new business partners and things might go very well as you embark on a new working relationship.

In many cases, you might also begin beneficial cooperation with partners in another city or abroad. However, there are problems looming on the horizon for August. Your relationship with partners will suddenly worsen, perhaps due to a disagreement over land, real estate, or other major property. In December, it will become clear that there is no way to resolve this peacefully, and you will have to wait until 2025 for it to go away.

Your relationship with colleagues from afar is also noticeably troubled, and that may be due to their behavior, or alternatively, difficult circumstances on the world stage, which might seriously hamper any cooperation.

Money

Financially, the first half of 2024 is booming. Expect the largest sums to come in late April and May, and this will be money you made honestly thanks to your own hard work from some time earlier. During the second half of the year, September is the best time, but overall, your earnings will be more modest, while your spending will grow.

Love and family

All year long, your personal life is looking messy. During the first half of the year, many Sagittarians will not have any romance on their minds – work before play! However, you may have a fateful romance, when a friendship with your colleague or a manager unexpectedly turns into something more.

For many married couples, the second half of 2024 will also be rather difficult. From August to December, all of your problems will come to a head.

By December, you will have to make a decision – stay together or go your separate ways, and many will realize that a thin peace is better than a good argument and try to find common ground.

Perhaps your children or a relative will mediate the situation. You will not see how it ends until 2025, but there is a chance of reconciliation.

In June, single people might meet someone new and intriguing. You might have a torrid romance, which will survive all of the difficulties life throws at you, and you can be assured there will be plenty.

Those with a family can also expect to meet someone new, and this encounter will present a direct threat to your existing relationship. The ball is in your court, but you're also the one responsible here.

If you are divorcing, you will have to deal with issues involving your shared property, especially real estate.

Health

In 2024, you are not feeling particularly energetic, so take care of yourself and be sure you lead a healthy lifestyle.

2024 is an ideal time to start a new exercise routine, drop bad habits, and get healthy.

Remember that only your health – or rather, problems with it – can prevent you from living the active, fun, productive life you want.

CAPRICORN

2024 is generally a good year for you. This is a time for hard work and well-deserved fun. The only thing you need to do is stay sharp, fresh, and think out of the box.

Work

During the first half of 2024, you will see a continuation of trends that began during the second half of 2023. You are not used to times like this when you can and should sit back and enjoy things. You will get a broader perspective on life and be pleased with your success and achievements.

However, that does not mean that you won't have to roll up your sleeves and get to work – quite the contrary! You will have a lot of work to do, but you will also have wonderful opportunities to demonstrate your success to others, and they will immediately give you a stellar rating.

You will reconnect with old ties, and you might renew cooperation with colleagues from other cities or abroad, or perhaps you will spend a lot of time traveling. This trend will reach a crescendo in late April and May.

During the second half of the year, the ball will suddenly end, and

Cinderella will have to rush back to her hard labor.

June to December will be an exceedingly tough time for you. You will see a series of successes, but you will also face a lot of trouble. Your innovative ideas and new projects will bring you success – and in fact, this will occupy business owners and managers of every level.

Employees will receive additional responsibilities, which will also lead to a nice raise. You will also encounter opportunities to try out a new job. June and October are the most dynamic times where this is a concern, and you can count on success here in the second half of the year.

It will not all be smooth sailing, however. In August, November, and December, you will have to accept that your collaboration with colleagues in other cities and abroad is on a negative spiral.

Your partners from afar might become hostile, aggressive, and any attempt to get back on the right track will be futile.

Alternatively, challenging international relations might mean that you won't get anywhere, anyway.

During the second half of 2024, visits from auditing agencies, or an unwelcome return of old legal problems will also be a thorn in your side. The astrologist suggests that you act accordingly and take preventive measures ahead of time.

Money

Financially, 2024 is not bad at all. You will have a regular income, and you might even have some pleasant surprises, such as a prize or bonus. You might also receive some unexpected gifts from Fate – such as a winning lottery ticket.

You will of course have some expenses, but most of them are related to your personal life and your children's or loved ones' needs.

Love and family

During the first half of 2024, many Capricorns will be fully immersed in personal matters. Parents will be pleased with their children's successes, and might be investing in their education, studies, or development, which will require a hefty sum. What's more, during the first half of the year may suddenly awaken a craving for love and romance in you. You may have encounters that are highly unlikely to end in marriage, but at least they will brighten your life for a while.

During the second half of the year, many families will face problems involving relatives, and that may look differently, depending on past circumstances. Most likely, you will see a resurgence of old problems, so you might already know where things are headed.

Health

During the first half of the year, you are healthy, energetic, and attractive, leading lasting impressions on everyone Fate sends your way.

During the second half of the year, the stars urge you to remain cautious when traveling or driving! The riskiest times are August, the last 10 days of November, and all of December.

AQUARIUS

In 2024, you will have to get both your business affairs and personal life in order. The time has come to shore up your defenses.

Work

2024 can be divided into two strikingly different periods. During the first half, business owners and managers will be expanding their business, and looking at real estate in order to make that happen.

Perhaps this is something you began in 2023, and now, it is reaching a logical continuation.

Buying land or facilities or perhaps major organizational tasks or repairs will set the stage for the first half of the year.

Employees might be thinking about opening a business or taking part in a family member's endeavor. For various reasons, some Aquarians will leave work altogether to focus on things more meaningful and interesting, such as academia or dealing with family matters.

During the second half of the year, the planets will shift their position, and you will feel changes in your mood and spirit.

In June and July, things will be calm and rather productive, though in August, you can expect clouds to gather on the horizon. That will most likely involve money trouble or material issues, which will become a hurdle with partners and like-minded individuals, and possibly someone influential. December will be the most challenging time here.

Money

The first half of 2024 is a blessing for your wallet. Aquarians will be able to count on support from business partners, help you may not have even asked for, and favorable terms of credit. You might also profit from successful real estate transactions, and in some cases, you will come into an inheritance.

The second half of the year will be more difficult, and you might feel like you are bleeding money, maybe because of issues at work, or possibly because of problems in your personal life!

Love and family

Many Aquarians will see the most important events of 2024 in their personal lives. Expect construction, major repairs, or buying a home, apartment, or summer home. Many will buy real estate either for their own use, or that of their children. And in some cases, that real estate will come in through an inheritance.

Many families will welcome children or grandchildren.

During the second half of the year, many Aquarians will face trouble involving their children. It is impossible to predict how this will look, but there will be cause for concern. In any case, your children's needs may have you spending through the nose.

Ding the second half of the year, especially from August to December, couples will find themselves in choppy waters. After a wonderful and romantic summer, you will have to accept that something in your relationship is off, and in some cases, the underlying issue may be financial in nature. It is a bad idea to mix love and money, as it usually leads to separation. Here, December will be the most difficult month.

Alternatively, couples might split over different interests and value systems.

Health

In 2024, you are feeling a bit sluggish. During the first half of the year, you might be fatigued or exhausted, and the best medicine is exercise and a good night's sleep. You might also have issues with your weight, especially if this has been a longstanding challenge for you.

After June, you will experience emotional stress, which will be reflected in your nervous system, which doctors believe is the root of all diseases. If that sounds like you, remember to relax and spend more time in nature, and to find someone you can trust with everything.

PISCES

The theme of 2024 is movement and change. Right now, you are able to reach all of the goals you have spent so long striving for.

Work

During the first half of 2024, you will see a continuation of trends that began in 2023. Your contacts with colleagues in other cities and abroad will take on particular importance, and you might continue your cooperation or spend a lot of time traveling.

You will find dependable allies here, and together, achieving the goals you have set for yourself will be much easier. You will also meet new business partners, and you might reconnect with former colleagues.

Many Pisceans will plan a move or to open a business or an affiliate in another city or abroad. These plans will come to life closer to May, and then you will have to deal with bothersome but necessary organizational tasks, such as acquiring real estate.

But all good things come to an end, and the second half of the year will be much more difficult.

You will start to see problems, which are difficult to predict.

Perhaps the laws of another country will get in the way of doing all your work, and getting all you need. Alternatively, you will face opposition from certain people. All of this will reach a crescendo in November and December, which may prove to be the most difficult months of the entire year.

During the first half of 2024, employees' positions are solid, and they may get a promotion, with the corresponding salary raise.

If you receive an invitation closer to May to work in another city or abroad, it is worth considering all of the risks that might bring. The astrologer believes there are sure to be many.

Money

You could call the first half of 2024 beneficial for your bank account. During this time, you will have a regular income, and you might have additional earnings as well, such as a bonus or support from loved ones.

During the second half of the year, however, things will be much more modest. Your expenses will increase while your income falls, and that may be due to business or perhaps your personal life.

Love and family

During the first half of the year, your personal life is also seeing a continuation of trends that began last year.

Those planning on a move to another city or abroad will get closer to bringing their plans to fruition. May will be particularly indicative where this is concerned. However, putting down roots somewhere new takes a lot of effort, and each specific case will play out differently.

You might face difficulties with local authorities, or maybe your own loved ones. You may also have a serious disagreement with your spouse over setting up or acquiring a home, or various financial documents.

Those whose relationship has left something to be desired for some time will have to make a decision over whether to stay or go by the end of the year. Whether that separation is temporary or permanent will not be clear until 2025. Perhaps your children will function as the most important bridge to bring together their warring parents. In any case, it is worth carefully considering a path toward reconciliation.

Many Pisceans will face difficulties involving your home in the second half of 2024. Look at all potential alternatives and do everything you can in order to get through the stormy waters here.

For couples, the first half of the year is fantastic. You might meet people, either while traveling or among people who have come from somewhere far away.

You might also renew your ties to old friends and acquaintances or reconnect with a former flame. Overall, the first half of the year is a wonderful time for romance, which may see you walking down the aisle.

Unfortunately, the second half of the year will be rife with problems. You may grapple with dissatisfaction from your parents, relatives, or an ex-spouse or partner.

But love conquers all, and if it is mutual, all of these obstacles will soon be in your rearview mirror – but this may not happen until 2025.

Health

During the first half of the year, you are healthy, energetic, and leaving lasting impressions on everyone Fate sends your way. After June, and especially from August to November, you can expect emotional turbulence and you might occasionally feel empty, powerless, and unsure of exactly what you need to do.

Build your morale and spirit back up by getting enough sleep, taking a walk in nature, and leaning on those who you love and trust unconditionally.

January

New York Time			London Time		
Calendar Day	Lunar Day	Lunar Day Start Time	Calendar Day	Lunar Day	Lunar Day Start Time
01/01/24	21	10.18 PM	01/01/24	21	10.02 PM
02/01/24	22	11.16 PM	02/01/24	22	11.08 PM
04/01/24	23	12.14 AM	04/01/24	23	12.14 AM
05/01/24	24	1.14 AM	05/01/24	24	1.22 AM
06/01/24	25	2.16 AM	06/01/24	25	2.32 AM
07/01/24	26	3.20 AM	07/01/24	26	3.44 AM
08/01/24	27	4.26 AM	08/01/24	27	4.57 AM
09/01/24	28	5.30 AM	09/01/24	28	6.07 AM
10/01/24	29	6.31 AM	10/01/24	29	7.10 AM
11/01/24	1	6.58 AM	11/01/24	30	8.03 AM
11/01/24	2	7.26 AM	11/01/24	1	11.58 AM
12/01/24	3	8.13 AM	12/01/24	2	8.44 AM
13/01/24	4	8.53 AM	13/01/24	3	9.16 AM
14/01/24	5	9.27 AM	14/01/24	4	9.42 AM
15/01/24	6	9.59 AM	15/01/24	5	10.05 AM
16/01/24	7	10.29 AM	16/01/24	6	10.25 AM
17/01/24	8	10.58 AM	17/01/24	7	10.45 AM
18/01/24	9	11.29 AM	18/01/24	8	11.07 AM
19/01/24	10	12.04 PM	19/01/24	9	11.32 AM
20/01/24	11	12.42 PM	20/01/24	10	12.02 PM
21/01/24	12	1.26 PM	21/01/24	11	12.39 PM
22/01/24	13	2.16 PM	22/01/24	12	1.25 PM
23/01/24	14	3.11 PM	23/01/24	13	2.19 PM
24/01/24	15	4.10 PM	24/01/24	14	3.21 PM
25/01/24	16	5.10 PM	25/01/24	15	4.27 PM
26/01/24	17	6.10 PM	26/01/24	16	5.35 PM
27/01/24	18	7.10 PM	27/01/24	17	6.43 PM
28/01/24	19	8.08 PM	28/01/24	18	7.50 PM
29/01/24	20	9.06 PM	29/01/24	19	8.56 PM
30/01/24	21	10.04 PM	30/01/24	20	10.01 PM
31/01/24	22	11.02 PM	31/01/24	21	11.08 PM

You can find the description of each lunar day in the chapter "A Guide to The Moon Cycle and Lunar Days"

ARIES

The year is starting on a high note. You can be proud of yourself and all of your accomplishments. No matter how you look at it, you're once again ahead of the game!

Work

The second 10 days of the month are the best time for anything work-related. During this time, you will be able to resolve any thorny or unclear issues you had to put on the back burner in December. This may involve business partners from other cities or abroad, or relationships that were once again under pressure from above. However, things are beginning to shift, and of course, that's in your favor. Finally, you will be able to talk to your partners on your terms and they will have no choice but to accept it. Keep in mind, though, that there are many bumps on the road ahead, and you may have won this battle, but not yet the war.

Employees will see they hold noticeably more authority than in their current job, and during the second 10 days of the month, you will have a good opportunity to try your luck somewhere new. In both cases, you will see more income, as well as bonuses and some other pleasant financial surprises.

Any travel planned from January 9-31 is sure to be a success.

Money

Your finances are looking up in January. You will have a regular income, and significantly more of it. Expect to receive the significant sums on January 1, 2, 10, 11, 18-20, 18, and 29, with the largest on January 10-11.

Your expenses are low and necessary, predictable, and reasonable. Most importantly, anything you spend in January goes hand in hand with money coming in.

Love and family

Your personal life looks unpredictable and stormy. You may be consumed with business-related affairs and successes at work, but this will be a roadblock for any communication with your loved ones. On the other hand, you may be short on patience, sensitivity, and tact. Your partner is in a somewhat weakened position now, and he or she may feel dependent on you. Keep this in mind and don't exert any additional pressure.

This goes for whether you are married or not.

The stars hope that you realize that sometimes, a spat is just a spat, but remind you that living a peaceful life is preferable to even a lover's quarrel. The ball is in your court, but you are responsible.

A long-distance trip will bring you closer together and give you some fresh perspective. Perhaps you will do just that in mid- to late January.

Health

This month, your energy is a thing to envy, and you have no fear of any illnesses. However, some Aries will find themselves caring for parents or loved ones who may require special attention.

TAURUS

Your friendship with Jupiter, the planet of good luck, continues on solid footing, which means you are lucky at work, in your personal life, and other relationships. Keep moving forward and remember that the path is determined by he who walks it!

Work

For many Taureans, strengthening your relationships with colleagues in other cities or abroad is the main event this month. In January, you may see a significant breakthrough in resolving several challenging, thorny issues you previously were struggling to overcome.

However, there are still some issues that will require your attention, and during the last 20 days of the month, they will be related to financial and material matters.

During the first 10 days of January, this will be especially noticeable, but later somewhat resolved in the latter part of the month.

Any travel planned for January will be a success, and help you strengthen your position, whether you are an employee or work for yourself.

Members of the military can expect professional opportunities in the very near future.

Money

Things are on an upward swing at work, but money is still a challenge for you, and you can expect to spend a lot of money, especially in the first 10 days of the month, which will be the most ruinous period.

Some will find themselves paying off old debts, others will have to deal with financial disputes involving old friends, like-minded people, or someone highly placed.

You might also find yourself spending money at home, for example, if you go on vacation to somewhere far away or have to pay for your family's needs. Don't worry, however, any gaps in your wallet will be filled in by February.

Love and family

You will find yourself putting out one fire after the next in your personal life. This generally applies to those in romantic relationships, as, in stark contrast to the cold January weather, things are heated, complicated, and incredibly emotional. With qualities like this, avoiding an argument seems harder than ever.

This trend will be most noticeable during the first 10 days of January, when you might run into misunderstandings, jealousy, and other unpleasant feelings. During the second half of the month, things are quieter, and any tensions will resolve themselves.

You might take a trip, which will give you colorful experiences and smooth over any potential conflict, whether you are married or not.

Many will have to overcome household issues and spend the lion's share of their family budget on this.

Health

During this month, especially the first 10 days, you may feel a lot of ups and downs, with periods of high energy unexpectedly followed by fatigue. Take some time for yourself and lead a healthy lifestyle if you can.

During the last 20 days of the month, things will get better, your energy will be more stable, and this will continue into February.

GEMINI

January is a time to address both household issues and things on your mind right now, but don't expect any serious resolutions. The stars urge you to get some rest and follow their advice.

Work

For most of January, things are quiet, boring, and routine, but it would be better to just accept it. Dive into the tasks you have been putting off for a while now. They may not be that interesting, but they're things you have to do. January is the best time to deal with these matters, rather than letting them drag on even further into the future.

When it comes to work, the last 10 days of January are the busiest, though they are also the most difficult. During this time, you can expect problems involving colleagues in other cities or abroad, as well as claims from various auditing authorities.

Alternatively, you may also find secret intrigues and enemies coming out of the shadows. This will be a problem in late January, as well as February, so tread lightly. If you can, hunker down for stormy seas ahead.

Money

Your finances look unpredictable and uneven this month. During times of difficulty, however, you can expect support from your parents, loved ones, and in the end, you will find your way out.

Love and family

In many cases, your personal life will take up much of your energy in January.

Anything related to improving your home will continue on a positive note, and you might even say that this month, you will find a breakthrough in something that has been bothering you for some time.

Your relationship with your family is calm and harmonious, and your loved ones support your endeavors in words and deeds. You might have some difficulties with one of your parents, either you will have to take care of them, or for various reasons, you will find yourself facing conflict with relatives.

Either way, this area of your life will require some special attention, and it is best to be ready in advance.

Health

In January, you are feeling sluggish. Young people are likely to experience lethargy, fatigue, and mood swings. If you are elderly or weakened, an old, chronic disease may flare up, or perhaps you will find yourself grappling with a new diagnosis.

The stars recommend that you engage in some serious self-care- go on vacation, spend some time letting your body recovery, or simply get some sleep.

Slow down on the exercise this month and if you absolutely can't, just replace it with walking.

CANCER

January is a great time to strengthen your relationship with your environment and seek support from the right people. A friend in court is better than a penny in purse.

Work

After the holidays are over, Cancers can expect to focus on work instead, and resolving old problems.

This may include legal issues, or possibly something involving colleagues from other cities or abroad. The first 10 days of the month will be the rockiest. Things will start looking up during the latter part of the month, and you can expect help from a friend or someone in a position of influence, who will support you in both words and deeds, or might act as an intermediary. Thanks to your shared efforts, things will be safely resolved by the end of the month.

Many Cancers will meet someone influential or powerful. Their help will prove to be swift, effective, and timely. If they want to go into business together, the stars recommend you accept the offer, after carefully reviewing all of the documents and any financial risks.

Money

Your bank account is looking stable, but that is it. Your income is modest, but your expenses are reasonable and predictable. Many will have to pay back old debts, and in this regard, the entire month, especially the first 10 days, will be somewhat challenging.

Love and family

January is a great time for strengthening your business relations, as well as making romantic connections. You might Mr. or Ms. Right, and you will not be disappointed later on.

After a long period of turbulence in your personal life, which many Cancers have gone through, the stars will shift from anger to mercy, sending new people and opportunities your way. The best time for this is after January 11.

This is not a bad time for relationships with family and others, especially if there are no financial claims at stake.

Be careful when traveling in January, because things may not turn out as you had hoped.

This is especially true for any travel abroad, where you may run into all kinds of obstacles.

Health

For most of January, you are feeling energetic, and you have no reason to fear falling ill. From the 22nd to 31st, the stars recommend you take it easy and focus on yourself. During this time, you might expect periods of fatigue, lethargy, or colds, and chronic conditions may exacerbate.

LEO

Expect Destiny to shower you with gifts in the new year. However, this only applies to the professional part of your life, where you will achieve what you have long dreamed of.

Work

The entire month of January is a great time for business, especially in the second half. Things will be booming at work, and you will feel ready to move mountains. What's more, you will not have to act alone, because both colleagues and your superiors will be by your side.

Business owners and managers can trust in subordinates, who will prove themselves to be wonderfully responsible and diligent. You may receive attractive proposals that are worth considering and discussing. Time will tell that they hold promise.

Employees will have an opportunity for a promotion, possibly right where they are, or somewhere else with a brighter future.

Your connections with colleagues in other cities or abroad are moving along nicely overall, but the astrologer sees you still have a lot of serious work to do here.

Money

January is a great time for your wallet. You will have money coming in regularly, and that is most noticeable from the idle to the end of the month. Expect to receive the largest amounts on January 2, 10, 11, 19, 20, 28, and 29. Your expenses are low, and all of them are related to household upkeep or your personal life. Your children, loved ones, the recent holidays, that is, things you have both planned for and can't avoid.

Love and family

Things are calm and harmonious in your personal life. Those with families will be delighted by their children's successes at work, and they are on a good streak. You may find yourself supporting your children as they forge their own path, whether morally or financially, but this, as they say, is a sacred duty.

Those in a romantic relationship will enjoy their partners, but don't expect any more than that. Don't expect to take anything to the next level this month. Closer to the end of January, you will reach an understanding that things are going to remain as they are, at least for now. You might have a squabble over something material, or maybe one half of the couple is irritated with the other's behavior. This also applies to those in a rocky marriage.

Health

This month, you are feeling sluggish, especially if you are elderly or weakened by chronic illness. If that sounds like you, be sure to lead a very healthy lifestyle and avoid any overindulgence.

Those who are young and healthy should take care of themselves, their image, and their appearance. This month is a good time for updating your wardrobe, trips to the beauty salon, or giving up any bad habits.

In sum, this is a time for revitalization and renewal.

VIRGO

January is a time to focus on your family and private life. Spend it being a bit of a shut-in and forget about work for a while. Your work will still be there tomorrow, after all.

Work

During the first 20 days of the month, don't expect to see a lot of success at work. The exception is those working in the creative professions – actors, artists, singers, musicians, and anyone who works in the arts. These Virgos will be on the receiving end of accolades from the public, handsome royalties, and other gifts from capricious Fortune. If you work in another field, expect to have a lot of free time until January 20, before putting your nose to the grindstone as the month draws to a close.

For many Virgos, there are changes underway at work – what once looked stable, promising, and financially sound has proven otherwise. This is not a new development, but something that has been brewing for a few years now, and the time has come to turn the page and start over with a clean slate. Expect new plans and a complete overhaul of your path in life this month. That may be related to a move, or perhaps a new business or job. You have a full plate, plans to make, and in general, plenty to live for.

Your ties with colleagues in other cities or abroad are coming along nicely, and you may take a trip, successfully resolve some legal issues, or those related to residence abroad.

The good news is that in January, you will renew some old connections, and that may happen while you are traveling or with people from somewhere faraway.

Money

Financially speaking, you might describe January as uncertain. Your income is low, but your expenses are, too. You can expect Fortune to shine down on you, for example, nothing is stopping you from buying a lottery ticket. Your chances of winning are high.

Love and family

January is a time to immerse yourself in your personal life. During the first few days of the month, married couples can expect some friction on various issues, but things will improve drastically after the 15th.

Those who are divorced or in a marriage on the rocks will end up coming together over concerns over your children, and you might even take a family trip together. If you want to soften your spouse's heart, now is the time.

Unmarried couples will also have a good second half of January. Your relationship will grow warmer, and you might travel together, which will be an opportunity to both enjoy yourselves and iron out any contradictions.

Those who are single might have an interesting encounter and exciting romance. Even if it doesn't lead to marriage, it will certainly brighten your month.

Health

You are feeling energetic this month and have no reason to fear falling ill. The best time to change up your image, go shopping, or undergo any aesthetic surgery would be after January 10.

LIBRA

January is a great time to stop, take a look around, and gather some reinforcements, in all areas of your life, from the political to the personal.

Work

Not much of any significance will happen at work during the first 10 days of January. You might be distracted thinking about your holiday travel or taking care of your loved ones and family members. Business owners and managers with business in other cities or abroad, however, will once again find themselves facing off with partners. But you are used to this by now, and many Libras probably are well-versed in how to handle it.

The rest of the month is a time for major organizational tasks. Business owners and managers of every level will be planning on expanding their business and sphere of influence, as well, and be busy with various matters related to real estate. That may include construction, purchasing production areas, or land, and this time, things will turn out in your favor.

Employees will take a step back for a bit to deal with family and personal matters.

At the same time, Libras who are part of the working world would be wise to pay special attention to their colleagues and subordinates. Things here are not quite as stable as you might like them to be. Keep that in mind.

Money

Your finances are looking stable this month, but a lot hinges on business partners, your spouse, or those close to you.

You may carry out successful real estate transactions, such as a profitable purchase or a windfall from a sale. Alternatively, you may come into a loan, credit, or sponsorship.

Love and family

Expect important and fateful events in your personal life this month. You are actively working on improving your home, and you might reach a real breakthrough here. In any case, many families are now talking about moving.

Spouses are getting along well, but everything comes down to tact and diplomacy. Your better half is flourishing, which is a delight for you, but perhaps also lacking tact.

Your children are looking at some major changes in their lives, and will need your attention, assistance, and of course, money.

Many families are welcoming children, grandchildren, or at least in the careful planning stage.

Those in romantic relationships may decide to live together. Those who recently moved in will be discussing starting a family or other domestic activities.

Health

This month, you are feeling a bit tired. It isn't likely to be anything serious, but you may find yourself feeling sluggish and fatigued with some frequency.

Those who are elderly or weakened would be wise to take preventive measures to avoid any chronic ailments and winter colds.

SCORPIO

The stars are promising an exciting, active, and productive month for you, both at work and in your personal and romantic life.

Work

The first week of January might look somewhat uncertain, perhaps due to the traditional holiday period, when you will see some time off and get to relax.

For the rest of the month, however, you will be busy. You might go on a trip, where you will meet the people you need, or renew your relationships with previous business partners.

People with connections, influence, and money will appear on your horizon, and they might help take your business to the next level.

The astrologist also urges you to be more attentive, especially when it comes to long-term cooperation, construction, or various real estate operations. When discussing any future projects or signing important papers, be sure to carefully study each item, and consult a good lawyer if you have any doubts at all.

Expect to see things pick up if you are an employee, as well. You are climbing the ladder and there is more work to be done. A small raise might also be in order.

Money

You are seeing a lot of ups and downs in your finances this month. Your income is not the issue – that is not changing. Rather, you will be spending significantly more than usual. That may be related to various holiday activities, or possibly addressing your children's and loved ones' needs.

Love and family

Important things are happening in your personal life, as well. Those who are single and have been disappointed by previous entanglements can count on a fateful encounter, and that may happen on a trip or with people from somewhere faraway. This time, things are on a path toward marriage or something lasting and profound.

Those who are already partnered up can strengthen their relationship and a loved one will play a key role in this. Your partner is seeing positive changes at work and is more than willing to share that success with you.

Any trips planned in January will be a success, especially if you plan on going somewhere you have been before.

Your relationship with relatives will become more important. Many Scorpios will be in touch with family members living faraway and may even go visit them.

Health

In January, you are feeling energetic, adventurous, and ready to move mountains. It comes as no surprise, therefore, that you have no reason to fear falling ill.

SAGITTARIUS

Surprisingly, a slow-paced, idle January can turn out to be quite productive for many Sagittarians. You are not afraid of hard work, and in turn, your work is delighted with you!

Work

January is a great time for anything work-related, especially after the 10th. During this time, you will have a lot on your plate, but time to do it all. Employees may receive new job offers, or possibly recognition right where they are.

Business owners will be busy with new projects, while they also finish up old tasks.

Your relationships with colleagues in other cities or abroad are changing a lot these days, and during the last 10 days of January, that will become clear. For now, things are still challenging, and you have a lot of work to do here, but don't give up just yet. During the second half of the year, everything will become clear that your efforts were not in vain. Do not despair if things do not go your way, keep your eye on the prize, especially if your work with colleagues from other cities or abroad is a priority for you.

Money

January is a great time for anything material in nature. Your income will be steady, and significantly higher. You might even say that everything you touch turns to gold.

Expect to receive the largest amounts on January 2, 6, 7, 10, 11, 18-20, and 28-30.

Your expenses are modest and mostly related to your personal life.

Love and family

Your personal life is not so rosy, however. Many Sagittarians will confront issues involving their parents or older family members. That may involve illnesses, or perhaps problems that will require your time and attention.

In some cases, you will deal with challenges involving your housing or real estate, and they are likely to be long-term, though eventually you will resolve them. You have money and plenty of opportunities to smooth things over.

Your relationship with relatives is changing, and not necessarily for the better. You might argue or go your separate ways, and the last 10 days of the month will be very indicative. However, this is only temporary, and everything will change in the next six months, so don't jump to any hasty conclusions, or throw the baby out with the bathwater.

Nothing notable is happening with your romantic relationships, and your main task right now is to hold onto what you already have.

Health

In January, you are feeling sluggish, and may have bouts of lethargy, fatigue, or mood swings. Pay attention to your body and remember you need to eat and sleep. This is especially important for the workaholics, who might deplete all of their reserves this month.

Those who are weakened or elderly would do well to take steps to avoid flare-ups of any old illnesses, as well as winter infections or colds.

CAPRICORN

For most of January, you are confident, calm, and composed, while also remaining active and focused on success. There's nothing new here. Good luck!

Work

Surprisingly, all month long is a good time for you at work, including during the first week, despite just coming back from the holidays. Those who work in a creative profession – actors, artists, musicians – will be especially successful, and can expect a jump in both popularity and earnings to match.

After January 10, things will pick up even more, and it seems that nothing can stop you. This is a great time to meet new people or make new, long-term alliances and share your work with the public in general.

Your relationship with colleagues in other cities or abroad is a bit shaky during the first half of January. You can expect to make progress here after the 15th, and it will be entirely thanks to your efforts. Your partners from afar look rigid, difficult, and disagreeable. However, you should be able to sit down and negotiate during the second half of the month, and this is a positive trend that will continue into February.

Money

Your finances are looking stable overall. Your income is predictable and stable this month, though you shouldn't expect any windfalls. Your expenses will be largely pleasant and related to your personal life. Your children, loved ones, vacation, travel will take up the lion's share of your family budget.

Love and family

Many Capricorns will find that much of their energy will be focused on their home and inner circle this month. Those with a family will be pleased with their children's successes, and you can expect some positive changes here. Many families may welcome babies or grandchildren.

Romantic relationships will be generally stable, though you may see some minor disagreements in the first 10 days of the month. They will not affect the overall positive mood this month and will be quickly resolved after January 15.

If you are planning any travel, choose a place you have been to before, in order to avoid any disappointments or other problems.

Your relationship with relatives is not particularly stable, and here, you will need to focus some more attention. You can't expect any positive initiatives from your family members right now, and the ball is in y our court, so act accordingly. During the second half of the month, something here will work out in your favor.

Health

In January, you are not feeling particularly energetic, especially during the first 10 days of the month. During the rest of the month, you are supported by Mars and Mercury, and then Venus will join you. That means that you will get a surge of energy, after all.

AQUARIUS

You are entering a calm month, largely spent at home. You are sure to do everything you had planned, to the benefit of everyone around you.

Work

For most Aquarians, January is a time to focus on your family and household. The exception is anyone working in construction or real estate and land. If that is you, your business is charging ahead, and you can expect no problems here. Entrepreneurs will continue to expand and perhaps even transform their business.

In early January, many Aquarians will run into disagreements with a friend or someone highly placed. That may involve money or something material, but things will be quickly resolved after the 15th. However, this is a wake-up call. These issues will crop up again, so be careful and don't make any promises you can't keep.

Money

Financially, you can expect a lot of ups and downs this month. During the first half of January, you may find yourself spending more than you make, and that will be mostly due to your personal life. During the second half, things will improve, and you will be back in the black. You might receive a windfall from a profitable real estate transaction, or support from your parents or loved ones. You are likely to come into some favorable credit, or possibly even an inheritance.

Love and family

For many Aquarians, January will be a time to focus on your home and family. You might be working on improving your living space, and you can expect a real breakthrough here, even on challenging household issues.

Your relationship with your family might be turbulent. The cause is a disagreement over your home, or perhaps financial matters. You need to have hope that this will eventually be a thing of the past, since it is naturally easier to settle everyday issues together.

It is difficult to say anything about those in romantic relationships this month, as everything depends on your history together and your intentions for the future. In many cases, however, you can expect to discuss living together or setting up a future home.

Health

In January, you are feeling rather sluggish, and you might have frequent bouts of lethargy, fatigue, and mood swings. The stars recommend doing a little less physical activity and engaging in self-care. Take the time to get a massage, take a walk in nature, or visit a doctor. This is not the time for any radical changes in your appearance, however, and that includes plastic surgery or updating your wardrobe.

PISCES

January is a vibrant, exciting, and positive month for you. You are taking leaps and bounds, and the positive changes will continue.

Work

For Pisceans who are part of the working world, all of January will be a time for success, especially the second half. You will be actively communicating with colleagues from other cities or abroad. This trend will accelerate your development even further.

You might take a trip, which will turn out surprisingly well. In addition to renewing old ties, you can expect to meet new people who will turn out to be reliable partners, and in time, even loyal friends.

January is a good time to present projects, make connections, and seek out support from your superiors.

Employees would do well to pay attention to your managers, and remember that the first 10 days of January will be the most difficult period for this relationship. If you are needed on an urgent project of some sort, you can forget about any holiday vacations, but things will turn out for the best.

One more important piece of advice for Pisceans, regardless of your field – if you are starting any important business, or signing anything, be sure to cross your t's and dot your i's. Remember that life is constantly in flux, and what seems reliable now may not be in the future.

Such is life, and we have to anticipate all of its twists and turns, including those that may be less than favorable to us.

Money

Financially, this month is not bad at all, though you will not come into any large sums of money. Your expenses and income are predictable and reasonable.

Love and family

January is a great month for your personal life, too. Both married and unmarried couples will spend some time traveling together, and things will go swimmingly. In some cases, you might be talking about a move to another city or even abroad, and one way or another, these plans will come to fruition, if not now, in the near future.

Couples will be getting along harmoniously, and many will be thinking about marriage or be headed in that direction. If you are in fact newlyweds already, you can count on positive developments in your life together.

Your relationships with relatives will improve, and you might visit family members who live in another city or abroad.

Health

All month long, you are feeling fairly energetic and have no reason to fear falling ill.

February

New York Time			London Time		
Calendar Day	Lunar Day	Lunar Day Start Time	Calendar Day	Lunar Day	Lunar Day Start Time
02/02/24	23	12.02 AM	02/02/24	22	12.16 AM
03/02/24	24	1.04 AM	03/02/24	23	1.25 AM
04/02/24	25	2.07 AM	04/02/24	24	2.36 AM
05/02/24	26	3.11 AM	05/02/24	25	3.46 AM
06/02/24	27	4.12 AM	06/02/24	26	4.51 AM
07/02/24	28	5.10 AM	07/02/24	27	5.48 AM
08/02/24	29	6.00 AM	08/02/24	28	6.35 AM
09/02/24	30	6.44 AM	09/02/24	29	7.12 AM
09/02/24	1	6.00 PM	09/02/24	1	11.00 PM
10/02/24	2	7.22 AM	10/02/24	2	7.41 AM
11/02/24	3	7.56 AM	11/02/24	3	8.06 AM
12/02/24	4	8.28 AM	12/02/24	4	8.28 AM
13/02/24	5	8.59 AM	13/02/24	5	8.49 AM
14/02/24	6	9.30 AM	14/02/24	6	9.11 AM
15/02/24	7	10.04 AM	15/02/24	7	9.36 AM
16/02/24	8	10.42 AM	16/02/24	8	10.05 AM
17/02/24	9	11.25 AM	17/02/24	9	10.39 AM
18/02/24	10	12.13 PM	18/02/24	10	11.22 AM
19/02/24	11	1.06 PM	19/02/24	11	12.14 PM
20/02/24	12	2.03 PM	20/02/24	12	1.13 PM
21/02/24	13	3.03 PM	21/02/24	13	2.18 PM
22/02/24	14	4.03 PM	22/02/24	14	3.25 PM
23/02/24	15	5.02 PM	23/02/24	15	4.32 PM
24/02/24	16	6.01 PM	24/02/24	16	5.39 PM
25/02/24	17	6.59 PM	25/02/24	17	6.45 PM
26/02/24	18	7.57 PM	26/02/24	18	7.51 PM
27/02/24	19	8.55 PM	27/02/24	19	8.57 PM
28/02/24	20	9.54 PM	28/02/24	20	10.04 PM
29/02/24	21	10.54 PM	29/02/24	21	11.13 PM

You can find the description of each lunar day in the chapter "A Guide to The Moon Cycle and Lunar Days"

ARIES

Your relationships with people are the most important thing this month. Strike a healthy balance – be open and friendly, but don't let anyone exploit you, either.

Work

The stars hardly have any complaints about the way things are going for you at work this month. Business owners and managers will spend a lot of time developing their business and be rewarded in kind.

Employees will be doing well, too – they are gaining more authority and greater influence on their colleagues and can also be sure of their bosses' support. At the same time, many Aries may run into problems that require their utmost attention. It may be a relationship with friends or someone influential. You can expect some contradictions here, which will likely be related to finances or other things of material value.

In the best-case scenario, you might see major investments in expanding your business. Alternatively, you might have to support a friend, pay someone back for services rendered, or settle accounts with people who hold influence and power.

In the worst case, you might find yourself entangled in serious financial disputes, which will have a most negative effect on your relationships. You may even have to part ways with an associate, or at least start making moves in that direction.

Money

Your finances are looking up and down this month. On the one hand, you will not find yourself penniless, but your expenses will be fairly high. And due to certain issues involving those around you, you might be spending a lot on your family, children, or household needs.

Expect the largest sums to come in on February 7 and 8, and your biggest expenses to come on February 9, 10, and 27-29.

Love and family

Your love life is looking turbulent and unpredictable. Mars and Venus are in conjunction in the most unstable sign of the Zodiac – Aquarius – and their conflict with Jupiter will only add fuel to the fire.

Once again, this may depend on notorious financial matters – don't be stingy, and things will work out well. If you can't cover your partner's growing appetite, then conflict is simply inevitable. In either case, the stars recommend you try to keep to a golden mean, and do only what is necessary, useful, and perhaps, pleasant. But if you can see that you are being taken advantage of, find the courage within to say, "No".

This advice applies to lovers, as well as friends, if one of them tends to be a bit of a mooch.

Married couples might argue over resolving household issues, and here, the crux of the issue may be material in nature. However, you will continue to improve your home, and this is where you will focus the lion's share of the family budget.

Health

For most of February, you will be feeling fairly energetic, and you have no reason to fear falling ill. You might feel a little sluggish toward the end of the month, however.

TAURUS

Taureans are embarking on one of the best months of the year for them, but only as far as work is concerned. Your romantic life is once again upside down...

Work

When it comes to work, February is a lucky time for you, and the best will come from the 7th to 19th, when you have the energy to tackle any task.

Business owners and managers might be moving ahead with projects begun earlier, or perhaps discussing new business.

Employees might receive a job offer, and if that is something that has already happened in the recent past, things are finally being set in stone.

Your relationship with colleagues in other cities or abroad is developing nicely, and any trips you take this month will turn out well.

Most Taureans will renew old ties with friends, or perhaps someone highly placed. If you had some loose ends in the recent past, now, things will come full circle.

The stars recommend that you don't repeat earlier mistakes, don't try to beef up your own credentials and have a clear-eyed view of your own limitations. That is the only way to smooth things over, both now and in the future.

Money

Financially, February is a great time for you. You will have a regular income and significantly more of it than usual.

Your expenses are modest, predictable, and reasonable.

You can expect to receive the largest sums on February 1, 9, 10, 17, 18, 27, and 28.

Love and family

Your personal life is a bit of a soap opera. Single people are likely to start a new romance, and that will probably happen at work. You will share a lot of interests and emotions might run high. But you might be lacking in sensitivity, tact, modesty, and humility. The stars recommend you forget about any of the conceit or megalomania that comes courtesy of Jupiter, as it might get in the way of your happiness and harmony.

Those with families, who may have grown less fond of their better half, might also get carried away, but here, it's each man for himself.

The stars warn you that this situation might turn out to be more serious than it initially appeared. So remember, you're in charge and the ball is in your court.

Health

This month, you are feeling full of energy and have no reason to fear falling ill.

GEMINI

February is full of contradictions for you. In some areas, you will be lucky, and in others, not at all. But there's not much you can do about it, that's just life.

Work

Calm, quiet January is giving way to a restless, hectic February.

Managers and business owners might run into various sources of resistance to their initiatives. That will probably involve connections in other cities or abroad, which, for various reasons, might cause you trouble. Obstacles will spring up with no warning, and where you least expect them. So examine all the options, so the stars don't catch you off guard.

Some Geminis can expect to deal with serious legal issues, and you will not manage to overcome them until March.

At the same time, you will continue with your projects aimed at expanding your business, and that, at least, is on the upward swing. You can expect serious progress as you navigate this difficult task.

Employees might have to deal with intrigue on their team, so it's better to keep your mouth shut and listen. Be as unobtrusive as possible.

Overall, any challenges you find in February are things you can overcome.

Money

Financially, this is a relatively neutral month for you. You have a lot of expenses, but if things get really difficult, your parents or a loved one can lend you a hand.

Love and family

You will continue to make progress as you improve your home this month, and that is a task that will require all hands on deck.

Couples might find themselves quarreling. Mars and Venus are in conflict with Jupiter, which, toward the end of the month, promises stormy relationships. One reason for this is sharing secrets, various grudges, and jealousy. Everyone has skeletons in their closet, so keep that in mind and be fair. If something has gone awry, as a rule, your partner isn't the only one at fault, and it takes two to tango. Keep your nerves in check, keep an eye on your partner's mood – if you do, your relationship will once again bloom with the vibrant colors of friendship, love, and trust. This also applies for married couples in a rut.

If the object of your affection lives somewhere far from home, you will need to overcome obstacles of all kinds, in addition to your emotions. But you need to hold onto hope that in the end, everything will be resolved.

Health

This month, you are not feeling as energetic as usual, and the stars recommend that if you are weakened or elderly, you keep a close eye on how you are feeling.

Young and healthy Geminis should be careful driving and be meticulous when planning any travel, whether near or far.

CANCER

After a successful January, you will start to see that your luck and energy are beginning to wane. February will require both restraint and discretion in all areas of your life, from the romantic to the diplomatic.

Work

Cancers who are part of the working world would do well to concentrate on the projects that are already in motion and not start anything big right now.

Your main problem this month might be a relationship with someone around you, especially when it comes to finance. You might have a disagreement with friends or someone who provided you with some kind of service recently, and probably over debt, money, or some other tangible asset. It's entirely possible these claims are justified, and you will have to pay what you owe.

Your relationship with colleagues in other cities or abroad is moving along nicely, and you might take a trip or start organizing one.

Employees will have an opportunity to take some time off and head somewhere far away, or maybe just to your family's cabin. Take advantage of a chance like this, because life doesn't revolve around work, and you can take some time away from the office. What's more, nothing major is happening right now, anyway.

Money

Your bank account is less than stable right now.

You will be spending constantly, as many Cancers are repaying their debts, settling credit, or perhaps facing unexpected home expenses. Get ready for February ahead of time, so that you aren't caught off guard.

You may have less income than usual, and things will only improve after March, so keep an eye on your budget and try to cut out any unnecessary spending.

Love and family

Your romantic and family relationships are looking rather stormy. Misunderstandings and arguments might set the backdrop for the entire month, perhaps over unresolved financial issues, or possibly clashing worldviews or even differing value systems. Can you get through it? Yes! The stars predict that if your love is strong, you will have the strength to overcome any obstacle.

If this is a recent romance, be careful, though. February will reveal your partner's true colors. That is, you will have a moment of truth, and it's always better to know for sure.

Any trips planned this month will go well, though you will find yourself spending a lot of money.

Health

In February, you are not feeling very energetic, and you might have bouts of fatigue, sluggishness, or even depression.

If you are elderly or weakened in any way, chronic conditions are likely to return, and it's worth heading them off right away. The stars suggest taking care of your body and avoiding any colds, infections or other dangerous situations.

LEO

In February, you will have to deal with other people's opinions, and they may run into direct conflict with your own. There's nothing insurmountable, however, and they're likely two sides to the same coin, and you can easily reach some consensus.

Work

Things are looking great for you at work in February. You have a lot of work, your projects are moving ahead the way you want them to, and things are looking up.

Managers will be able to count on their subordinates, who will climb mountains and bring new trends to your projects.

Employees will enjoy the approval of their managers and support from colleagues.

What's more, all month long, you might not be able to carry out everything you've been planning and dreaming about.

Business owners and managers will face trouble with partners, who may have a different opinion on business development. You can expect arguments over this all month long, and the root cause is probably money or some other tangible asset. It's not to the point of splitting up your business just yet but prepare for some conflict.

An ambitious employee may present competition, and this will only drive him or her even more. You will come out as the winner, here.

Money

Financially, February is a great time for you. Your income is stable, and your expenses are both predictable and modest. Expect the largest sums to come in on February 7, 8, 15, 16, 24, and 25.

Love and family

The main events this month will take place in your personal life, and you can expect some major events.

Your relationship with your spouse or long-term partner looks stormy and full of emotions. You might be dealing with complaints from your partner, and it is up to you to decide whether they are justified or not.

This is especially difficult for those who are currently straddling two options and can't decide who they want to be with and what they want to do. If that is your case, the turbulence in your relationship may go off the charts.

Those in stable relationships may find themselves arguing, but here, things will be much simpler. Your spouse might be facing financial challenges or issues at work, or perhaps an unexpected health issue. Either way, however, expect a month full of anxieties.

The stars believe that you will have the energy to deal with everything that comes your way, as long as you keep a cool head and avoid making a scene. Be methodical as you solve your problems, and everything will turn out just fine. That advice applies both at home and at work.

Health

You will have enough energy most of this month and you have no reason to fear falling ill. Expect a drop in energy during the last 10 days of February, and during this time, the stars suggest you take it easy and spend most of your time on self-care.

VIRGO

This month, many Virgos will run into obstacles, and might be feeling less than confident. Rely on your mind and sound logic – in this case, the stars will provide an answer to many of your problems.

Work

For most of the month, you will be running on fumes as you run around dealing with difficult tasks at work, but at the last minute, all of your efforts might go to waste.

Both business owners and managers will deal with disagreements with their colleagues from other cities or abroad, who might suddenly impose conditions that are far from what you had earlier agreed on.

You might also face inspections or have old legal problems unexpectedly come back into your life.

In the face of any difficulties, you can count on support from previous business partners, or perhaps someone close to you. They might act as an intermediary or provide moral and material support.

Through your joint efforts, some of these issues will be resolved by March, and the others will disappear somewhat later.

Students might face challenges in February, especially if their studies have something to do with another country.

February is also a good time to both renew old ties and make new connections.

Money

Financially speaking, February is looking somewhat bumpy. While you won't find yourself penniless, you are spending a lot of money. That may be due to business or perhaps your personal life.

Love and family

Your personal life is more stable than things at work. Those who recently endured a breakup will be pleased to discover that any cracks in the relationship can be mended with a little hard work. In many cases, your children will be of assistance, as taking care of them builds a bridge between former spouses.

Though the situation is not ideal, there is still a chance of reconciliation or at least healthy communication, but it will require restraint, humility, understanding, and forgiveness.

Couples who get along will be pleased to see that their children are on a successful streak.

Be especially careful traveling in February, including with your documents and laws in foreign countries.

Health

Those who manage to find harmony at home and at work are likely to run into health issues this month, especially if they are elderly or weakened and therefore especially vulnerable to pressure from the heavens. If that is you, be sure to take protective measures when it comes to any chronic illnesses and take care of yourself.

Those who are young and healthy would be wise to be careful when traveling or behind the wheel. All month long, the likelihood of traffic accidents is very high, with the worst between February 17 and 27.

LIBRA

This month, your fantasies might be a bit beyond your limitations. Balancing what you want and what is possible is your main task this month.

Work

Many Libras will spend most of their energy on their personal lives this month. Only the most incurable workaholics, managers, or responsible workers will be busy with both work and their home life.

You will continue to work on expanding your business, and that will naturally require a lot of resources. You might need to demonstrate your achievements to colleagues or a wider circle of people, and in order to not lose face, it's wise to prepare for that ahead of time.

In all areas this month, you can certainly count on your subordinates and colleagues, who will prove themselves to be both serious and responsible.

Despite all the difficulties, especially those that are financial in nature, time will tell that all of your efforts were not in vain. A series of important decisions you made recently will significantly strengthen your position and stability in the future.

Money

Financially, February is one of the most difficult months of the year for you. You will be spending money constantly, perhaps due to business, or maybe your personal life and your family's and children's needs.

But you won't get out of this quagmire alone. You can expect help from a business partner or perhaps a loved one will help with your expenses or provide you with a loan on beneficial terms.

All signs point to Luck still being on your side, and you will not have to deal with anything extreme.

Love and family

The lion's share of February's events will take place in your personal life. Issues related to real estate will be resolved in your favor, though that will require some spending on your part.

Couples who get along will be fully immersed in their children's affairs, which will take up the bulk of the family's budget.

Romantic relationships are looking very colorful and emotional but will also bring some conflict. Your ruler, Venus, is in conjunction with Mars, and that is a combination that always casts an exciting, sexy mood. No life is perfect, and now is no exception. Couples, whether married or not, might argue over money. As long as you're not stingy, things should work out.

Many Libras will be frequent guests at parties and easily attract colorful, interesting characters. This is great for singletons but might bring trouble for those already partnered up.

Remember that any romance you start right now might be short-lived, and so it's better to hold onto what you have.

Health

All month long, you are energetic and have no reason to fear falling ill.

SCORPIO

This month, your minimum responsibility is to maintain an emotional balance in the face of any situation you may face. Your inner peace is the key to stability this month, both at work and at home.

Work

Many Scorpios will be more focused on their personal life this month. Therefore, the stars recommend that you take a few days off to calmly focus on your family.

If that is not possible, the stars suggest that you tread lightly with any business partners. Conflicts are likely all month long, and it may be over a real estate dispute. It is hard to predict exactly what will happen but expect the unexpected.

Your relationships with colleagues from other cities or abroad are coming along nicely and things are looking promising.

Money

Financially, February is a neutral month for you. You will have an income, as usual, but don't expect any windfalls. Your expenses are modest, and most of them are related to your personal life.

Love and family

Your personal and family life is the focus during this cold, winter month. However, things are looking less than tranquil. Many Scorpios will be busy with home repairs, building a summer home, or dealing with other household tasks.

Spouses may have differing views on how their home should look, or perhaps regarding their family relationship in general. Arguments might be the backdrop of the entire month, though you will be able to sit down and have a calm chat. The astrologist cannot predict how things will turn out, however. Your partner is stubborn, and that can easily agitate you.

If things seem to spiral out of control, your children or perhaps an older relative might serve as a mediator. Thanks to their efforts, things might have quieted down by March.

Unmarried couples might run into arguments with their parents, who might be less than thrilled with the way things stand. By March, you will be done with this obstacle course, and it should be smooth sailing.

This applies to all problems this month, whether work-related or within your family.

Health

In February, you will not be feeling particularly energetic, but you are also not vulnerable to any serious illnesses, so long as you make sure to get enough sleep or let yourself be overcome with emotions.

The best investment you can make this month is a vacation, perhaps a plane ticket somewhere warm, or even the neighboring town. Spend a few days away from work and come back feeling fresh and renewed.

SAGITTARIUS

Your sign's inherent ingenuity and wit will be a bright spot this month. But don't overdo it! Otherwise, your humor and words might lead to serious conflict.

Work

You are still busy with work, and things are going well for you here. As you progress, you might start to bring in the income to go with it.

You can expect to conclude projects started earlier and open the door to new opportunities.

In other cases, luck is certainly not on your side, especially when it comes to your relationship with colleagues in other cities or abroad. Here, you can expect issues with contacts, setbacks in any planned business trips, or disagreements over red tape and documents.

Alternatively, you might run into issues with colleagues and subordinates, which you will not overcome until March.

All month long, you might have problems involving connections, electrical appliances, machines, or any type of technology.

Students would do well to focus on their studies, as any negligence is sure to be noticed and you will pay a heavy price later on.

Money

Financially, you will not have any trouble in February. Your income will be regular, but you will have to give blood, sweat, and tears in order to get it.

Expect the largest sums on February 2, 3, 7, 8, 15, 16, 24, and 25.

Your expenses are low, and all of them are both predictable and reasonable.

Love and family

Your personal life might be more important than work this month. Those who are single might have an interesting encounter, and perhaps even a turbulent, thrilling romance. Only time will tell how long it lasts, but as long as it makes life a little more exciting right now, that's already a good thing.

Those in a stable family relationship will support one another as you navigate choppy waters this month.

You will see a lot more of your relatives this month, though maybe not the way you would have liked. You might experience disagreements, conflicts, or complaints about one another.

In order to shed light on things, you will need to look to the past, to the history of your relationship with your loved ones. The root of the problem lies in something that caused you difficulties before.

Health

All month long, you are feeling a lot of ups and downs. You might feel liveliness, followed by bouts of fatigue and exhaustion. The stars recommend that if you are tired, you rest, and remember that work isn't going anywhere.

CAPRICORN

A decisive approach to anything will always bring fantastic results. That's the case right now – everything you want, you are sure to get!

Work

Congratulations to you – February is a great time for you, workwise. Mercury, Venus, and Mars are in your sign, bringing you energy, speed, and original ideas. With all these qualities, there's nothing standing in your way.

In addition to the favorable streak at work, you will also get a great opportunity to show your work to a wider audience. Even if it comes at some expense to you, it's worth taking advantage of this!

Your relationship with colleagues in other cities or abroad is settling down and you might have constructive negotiations, take a trip, or discuss future projects and how to further develop what you've already started.

The stars are still particularly favorable to those working in the creative fields and will bring them both popularity and greater income.

Money

Despite the upward trend at work, things are not so rosy when it comes to your bank account. It's not that you aren't earning anything, but that your expenses are rather high. You will be bleeding money, and the astrologist predicts that it will mostly be due to your personal and family life.

Expect to receive the largest sums on February 1, 9, 10, 17, 18, 27, and 28.

Love and family

Your romantic relationship will be as interesting as ever this month, and as turbulent as ever, too. This is especially the case during the second half of the month, when everyone's true nature will come to light.

You may clash over how you want to live your life, or differing value systems. In more difficult, primitive cases, you may disagree over money and unpleasant calculations, like who owes whom, and each partner's financial obligations.

It is difficult to give any advice here, but the stars still recommend talking to your partner, if his or her desires are not too demanding. You tend to be materialistic, but it's not a time to be stingy if you want things to get better.

Those with a stable family will address issues involving their children, and help them with words, deeds, and money. This month, your children will be the source of most of your spending.

Your relationship with relatives is calming down. This month, your efforts will reign in a certain peace.

Health

This month, you are feeling energetic. The only thing you have to worry about is the surge of emotions, which is not something you are used to.

AQUARIUS

Slowly but surely, your former energy, wit, and restlessness are returning to you. Use it for peaceful means, and you won't have to wait long to see results!

Work

At work, you are still immersed in administrative, mundane tasks. They may occupy both business owners and managers of any level.

Your business is expanding well, and various real estate transactions are on the agenda. Though things will run smoothly during the first half of the month, during the second half, expect conflict and stress. You will have to re-do some things, some people will argue with you, and you may even have to resolve some unexpected problems.

During the second half of the month, employees would be wise to keep an eye on those around them and avoid any criticism of colleagues or managers. Emotions may be running high, and you might find yourself saying or doing something you will come to regret. This is true for any Aquarians, regardless of what field they work in.

Money

Financially, February is a great time for you. You can expect money to come in from various sources, whether official or not.

If you need any help, your business partners, parents, or loved ones will come to your aid. You might profit from various real estate transactions or favorable credit. You might even come into an inheritance.

Love and family

Many Aquarians will be focused on their home and family this month. You will be working on improving your home, and things will be progressing in your favor. During the second half of the month, things will become more challenging. Spouses will disagree over various issues – perhaps differing views over home repairs or financial difficulties.

You might also face problems involving your parents or older family members.

If you are divorcing, you will argue over dividing up your home, and there is a high probability of unexpected problems during the second half of the month.

Romantic relationships might sour a bit this month, in the face of household, organizational, or financial issues. However, Mars and Venus are conjoined in your sign, which means you can expect emotions to run high, which can bring its own set of problems.

In any case, try to make sure that the turbulence during the second half of February doesn't tarnish your relationship with relatives and loved ones.

Health

This month, your energy levels are fairly high, and you have no reason to fear falling ill. Remember, however, that the days before your birthday are always difficult, and try to take it easy.

PISCES

Keep your head down and you'll go much further. This month, that advice seems tailor-made to you. Follow it, and you will manage to avoid most problems, both at work and at home.

Work

Those who are part of the working world would do well to move quietly and methodically because trouble can come from all sides.

Business owners and managers will deal with colleagues from other cities or abroad behaving erratically and may have to swallow their pride a bit to overcome this.

You may come across undesired information, intrigue from your competitors or rivals, as well as covert enemies.

Employees may run into the same challenges. The stars recommend that you take a look at everything you've done ahead of time to find any weak points and fix them if you find any. This advice is especially relevant for those who may be the subject of any audits or inspections.

All Pisceans would be wise to remember that you will be under a microscope this month, and both your achievements and shortcomings will be on display. Act accordingly.

As you put out the fires, you can expect an old friend or someone highly placed is highly likely. However, many other issues will also fall into place on their own, and by March, you will be home free.

Money

Financially, February is not the best time for you. You will be spending constantly, and your income will be a bit lower than usual. Keep an eye on your expenses and do away with anything unnecessary.

Love and family

Those who are more focused on their personal life will also face challenges this month.

Those who have moved somewhere far away will have to deal with thorny legal issues related to the laws of a foreign country.

You may have to tackle mountains of red tape or delays in any planned travel.

Your relationship with relatives will suffer a bit, too. You might come across unpleasant secrets, either your own or a family member's. Those who are dating someone may find their relationship marred by intrigue.

Expect setbacks everywhere this month, don't allow yourself to be provoked, and be methodical as you address them and forge your path. Remember that by the time your birthday rolls around, most of them should be resolved.

Health

Those who manage to avoid trouble at work and at home might run into health-related problems. Right now, you are vulnerable to colds and viruses, so take care of yourself and be sure to lead a healthy lifestyle.

You may also experience the return of old, chronic conditions, so if you are elderly or weakened, it is worth taking extra steps to protect yourself. The stars also recommend being careful when driving and meticulously plan any travel. There is a high likelihood of accidents on the road.

March

New York Time			London Time		
Calendar Day	Lunar Day	Lunar Day Start Time	Calendar Day	Lunar Day	Lunar Day Start Time
01/03/24	22	11.56 PM	02/03/24	22	12.22 AM
03/03/24	23	12.57 AM	03/03/24	23	1.30 AM
04/03/24	24	1.58 AM	04/03/24	24	2.36 AM
05/03/24	25	2.55 AM	05/03/24	25	3.35 AM
06/03/24	26	3.48 AM	06/03/24	26	4.25 AM
07/03/24	27	4.34 AM	07/03/24	27	5.05 AM
08/03/24	28	5.14 AM	08/03/24	28	5.38 AM
09/03/24	29	5.50 AM	09/03/24	29	6.05 AM
10/03/24	1	4.02 AM	10/03/24	30	6.28 AM
10/03/24	2	6.23 AM	10/03/24	1	9.02 AM
11/03/24	3	6.55 AM	11/03/24	2	6.50 AM
12/03/24	4	7.27 AM	12/03/24	3	7.12 AM
13/03/24	5	8.01 AM	13/03/24	4	7.36 AM
14/03/24	6	8.38 AM	14/03/24	5	8.04 AM
15/03/24	7	9.21 AM	15/03/24	6	8.37 AM
16/03/24	8	10.08 AM	16/03/24	7	9.19 AM
17/03/24	9	11.01 AM	17/03/24	8	10.08 AM
18/03/24	10	11.57 AM	18/03/24	9	11.06 AM
19/03/24	11	12.56 PM	19/03/24	10	12.09 PM
20/03/24	12	1.56 PM	20/03/24	11	1.16 PM
21/03/24	13	2.55 PM	21/03/24	12	2.23 PM
22/03/24	14	3.54 PM	22/03/24	13	3.30 PM
23/03/24	15	4.52 PM	23/03/24	14	4.36 PM
24/03/24	16	5.50 PM	24/03/24	15	5.42 PM
25/03/24	17	6.48 PM	25/03/24	16	6.48 PM
26/03/24	18	7.47 PM	26/03/24	17	7.55 PM
27/03/24	19	8.47 PM	27/03/24	18	9.03 PM
28/03/24	20	9.48 PM	28/03/24	19	10.12 PM
29/03/24	21	10.50 PM	29/03/24	20	11.21 PM
30/03/24	22	11.50 PM	31/03/24	21	12.27 AM

You can find the description of each lunar day in the chapter "A Guide to The Moon Cycle and Lunar Days"

ARIES

After the obstacle course that was February, things are finally settling down again. This gives you an opportunity to both deal with the present and plan the future.

Work

You can divide March into three distinct periods at work. During the first 10 days, you will be finishing up loose ends from February.

That includes financial issues, as well as your relationship with friends and those who are highly placed in society. You need to hold onto hope that the very worst is resolved, and you will be able to move forward.

During the second 10 days, things will be much calmer, and you are likely to still be working on expanding your business and finding the resources you need to make that happen.

This is a good time for relaxing or dealing with personal matters, if you are an employee. Your work won't go anywhere if you spend a few days away from the office doing what you have always wanted to do.

For the last 10 days of March, things will be busy and exciting. The eclipse on March 25 will force you to focus on your relationship with business partners as well as other important people. New contacts and encounters are likely, and one of them may be fateful.

Money

Your finances are looking sustainable in March. You will be receiving a regular income, both from official and unofficial sources. You might find support from business partners or a loved one, too. There are always expenses but expect to spend the most on March 9 and 10.

Love and family

Your personal, and especially, your family life, is looking quieter this month. Couples who get along will overcome difficulties related to improving their home, and this time, an injection of funds from a loved one is looking very likely.

Those in romantic relationships will begin a new chapter, which will be calmer and more stable. However, there is a lot of uncertainty, and it is unclear where your feelings will lead you. In the last 10 days of the month, it will become clear that there is potential for positive change, here.

After March 20 and all of April is a good time for those who have yet to find their better half. Any encounters you have this month will lead to a lot of deep emotions and totally change your life.

Health

In March, you are less energetic than usual, and that will be especially noticeable during the New Moon, from March 9-11.

Take care of yourself and avoid any colds or infections. Stay away from anything dangerous, too. You might book a massage or a trip to the spa, or perhaps some minor cosmetic procedures. You deserve it.

TAURUS

In March, you will have an excellent opportunity to continue what you have started and strengthen your position, too. But don't exaggerate your capabilities, and remember, "A great man is always willing to be little".

Work

At work, things are looking up this month. Your projects are moving ahead, and you will have new allies and assistants on hand. You might also receive support from friends or someone highly placed.

Luck is on your side, but there is one thing that might undo all of your recent achievements, and it is none other than your pride and ambition. Jupiter and Uranus are together in your sign, and that influence might be generally positive, but it can also lead you to act a bit recklessly.

If that sounds like you, avoid any conflicts with your managers or any other superiors. Know when to listen to others' opinions, even if they are not in line with your own, and remember you are not the center of the universe. If you manage to avoid this temptation, everything will be yours.

Money

Financially, March is a stable time for you. You will have a regular income, and be earning more than usual.

Your expenses this month are a bit higher than usual, but the astrologist predicts that most of them are pleasant in nature. You will be spending on gifts for loved ones, travel, and shopping.

Things are stable and you have no reason to fear any financial ruin.

Love and family

Things are not as easy or smooth as you would like in your personal life. Feelings are fickle, and can vanish at any moment, without any rhyme or reason.

March is a good time to sit down and work out what you really want – and what you don't. This is especially true for couples who recently began a relationship. After a stormy start, take the time to reflect on what is happening. This is a natural process, and you can certainly get through it.

Those who are in stable, family relationships might delight their loved ones, for example, by taking a trip together or finding the time for a romantic, candlelit dinner. Or you may simply buy your better half what he or she has been dreaming of, you will find the money for it.

Health

For most of March, you are feeling energetic and have no reason to fear falling ill. During the last 10 days of the month, things might get more difficult. The lunar eclipse on March 25 will bring fatigue, and it may make itself felt for some time. Those who are elderly or weakened by chronic disease should be especially careful during this time.

Those suffering from cardiovascular diseases or problems with their nervous system are under particular pressure from the heavens. They would do well to take it easy from March 24 to 31 and take care of themselves.

GEMINI

Life is moving at a faster pace these days, and there are more rocks in your way, both underwater and on the surface. You are strong, however, and you will be able to roll with the punches.

Work

March is a busy time for you, and overall, you will be successful. Work is moving ahead, whether you are a business owner or an employee. You might be negotiating new projects or perhaps a prestigious new job. The results won't be immediate, and may even take a few months, but things will play out in your favor.

Your friends or someone highly placed may play an important role in all of this. Their support will significantly strengthen your position in everything you do. Moreover, while March isn't without its challenges, things are fairly calm.

Many Geminis will face problems involving colleagues from other cities or abroad, and the most difficult days will be those of the New Moon from March 9 to 11. During this time, expect the unexpected, including legal troubles. Keep your finger on the pulse of things, and if you can, take steps ahead of time.

Money

Financially, March is a great time for you. You will have money coming in regularly, and somewhat more of it, too. Expect the largest sums on March 1, 2, 9, 10, 18, 19, and 27-29.

Your expenses are low and most of them will take place during the last 10 days of the month.

Love and family

You will see what you began in the recent past continuing in March.

Those who are busy improving their home will see real progress in this tedious task.

Many families are planning for the arrival of a baby or grandchild, and the last 10 days of March will be the most telling.

March, and especially the last 10 days of the month, is a great time for new encounters, as well as for strengthening earlier romantic ties, and if your relationship has cooled recently, it is worth taking advantage of this.

If you are planning any travel, try to aim for the second half of the month, as from March 5 to 13, you might run into obstacles that seem to emerge right out of the blue! If you decide to take the risk, anyway, carefully read the laws of other countries and keep an eye on the company you keep.

If you are planning on traveling in your own car, avoid any breakdowns and be very attentive.

Health

In March, your energy is high, but be careful when traveling and driving.

CANCER

After a murky, troubling February, March looks more positive and more interesting, as well. Life is going back to normal, so go for it!

Work

You can divide March into three distinct periods. The first 10 days is a good time to work on your relationship with colleagues in other cities or abroad, or even take a trip. During this time, you might meet new business partners or someone influential who might open new doors.

After March 10, you will be fairly busy, but financial matters will become a sore spot. You may need to settle old debts, or alternatively, fulfill obligations you took on earlier. You might clash with someone over material issues, which is especially likely if you have differing viewpoints on money or other tangible assets.

For the last 10 days of the month, things will be much more positive. You will be able to settle any delicate issues and things will start moving along quickly.

Money

Financially, March is not a great time for you. You won't end up penniless, but you will be bleeding money this month.

Many Cancers will have to settle old debts or close out credits, or otherwise handle matters related to earlier obligations.

Expect to spend the most from March 7 to 10, but you can expect a healthy sum to come in during the last 10 days of the month.

Love and family

Those who are more focused on personal matters will also run into money trouble this month. That may be due to expenses related to travel, which is highly likely during the first 10 days of March. Alternatively, it may be due to a conflict with friends or a group of people who may demand you settle old debts.

Financial issues may mar things for couples, whether they are married or not, but here, things may also depend on your real feelings and both parties' intentions. If you aren't stingy, you will manage to avoid the very worst.

Many Cancers will be running into old friends, and your relationship with them will develop very nicely.

That is especially the case for friends living in different cities or countries, as well as relatives.

Health

In March, you are feeling noticeably more energetic, and have no reason to fear falling ill.

LEO

In March, teamwork will be key. Even if you don't see eye to eye, it is worth listening to others' points of view and reaching a consensus. That goes for both work and your personal life. Do you want to be right, or do you want to be happy?

Work

Your relationship with business partners and hierarchies are your main problem this month.

Business owners and managers can expect serious disagreements with colleagues over the way things are going, business development, and most importantly – financial investments. Conflict here might be the backdrop of the entire month, and things will come to a head during the New Moon from March 9-11. However, despite the disagreements, you will find an acceptable compromise that allows you to get at least some, if not all, of what you want.

Employees might run into intrigue from competitors and disagreements with management. There's nothing you can't overcome, and a little later, things might work out in your favor. Those who have tried to throw a wrench into the works will not get what they want, and victory will be on your side.

Money

The most important thing this month is money matters. In addition to difficult negotiations with business partners over joint business investments, you might also be addressing issues related to credit or settling old debts. That may be related to work or your personal life.

Love and family

If your interests are more focused on your personal life, here, you can also expect conflicts to arise. Divorcing couples might argue over how to divide up joint property, and if you have a shared business, that will only add fuel to the fire.

For all of March, you will be hashing things out. There will be no winners, at least, for now. The astrologist predicts that you will reach a mutual understanding, if not this month, some time later. However, you may be taking some steps in this direction right now.

Those in a stable relationship might be grappling with their partner's problems. That may be work-related, a health issue, or household problems. Here, everything depends on how things stood previously, your current intentions, and your plans for the future.

Those in a romantic relationship might once again clash with their parents, and over various financial matters. Alternatively, you will have to admit to yourself that your better half and you may have differing worldviews, opinions, and values, and you will have to accept this and move on.

Health

If you manage to escape any strife at work or at home, you might instead face health issues. March is never the best time for you, so remember that and take care.

VIRGO

In March, you will become a part of a complex game, which may consume your entire surroundings. That goes for both work and your love life.

Work

For many Virgos, your professional interests still lie with developing your relationship with colleagues in other cities or abroad.

During the first 10 days of the month, you might go on a travel or meet with colleagues and strengthen old ties or make new ones. However, despite the friendly atmosphere, not everything will run so smoothly. During the New Moon, from March 9 to 11, you might again hit obstacles, which might look different. They may involve dealing with laws in other countries, or possibly handling legal matters.

It's not worth trying to go it alone. An old business partner might serve as an intermediary and you can expect to grow much closer in March.

Business owners and managers would be wise to keep an eye on their subordinates. Their zeal might help, but it might also hurt. Employees should be careful with the way they communicate with colleagues and avoid any intrigue. It's just not worth it.

Money

Financially, March is a neutral time for you. Your income is moderate, but your expenses are modest, too. In difficult cases, you might lean on a business partner, spouse, or loved one for help.

Love and family

As usual, nothing is quiet in your personal life, either. For a year now, Saturn, a harsh and unforgiving planet, has been in the sector of the sky responsible for marriage and long-term connections. This is why so many people have been reconsidering their relationships, and in some cases, separating. However, Jupiter is now in contact with Saturn, which significantly improves things. You might reconnect with an old flame, and even (in the most acute cases), receive help from him or her. Things are unlikely to last long, but for now, take advantage of what is in front of you.

If you are planning any trips, try to avoid traveling during the New Moon from March 9-12.

Long-term couples will support one another in overcoming any obstacle during this tumultuous spring month.

Health

You are not as energetic as usual this month, and to varying degrees, that will impact all Virgos. If you are young and healthy, think about relaxing, and finding the time to do it. If you are elderly or weakened by chronic illnesses, take it easy, and if you need, see a good doctor for help. Drivers and travelers should be especially careful during the New Moon from March 9-11.

LIBRA

Despite the obstacles that pop up every now and then, you are confident as you strive toward your goals. It's worth it, and you deserve it.

Work

March is a busy time for you at work, and it's paying off.

Business owners and managers at every level are still busy expanding their business, and this time, you will receive a welcome bonus of financial support from a business partner or stakeholder. That will allow you to charge ahead more quickly as you resolve the largest tasks ahead. Your colleagues and subordinates are people you can trust, and they will become the backbone of this month's activities.

Employees will receive additional responsibilities, and income to go with it. Your relationships with colleagues and managers are even, positive, and comfortable.

Though the first 20 days of March might feel like you are working nonstop, after the 20th, you will have some important meetings. That is especially the case during the Full Moon, which will take place during the eclipse from March 25 to 26. All meetings during this period might turn out to have a positive influence on your plans and business.

Money

March is not a bad time at all for your wallet. You will be earning money regularly, and somewhat more than usual, too. This might not be from your own income, but perhaps thanks to support from business partners, favorable credit, or profits from other unofficial sources.

Those who are not part of the working world might receive support from loved ones. Your expenses are not small, either, though most of them are related to your personal life, children, or the demands of your loved ones.

Love and family

You might expect some turbulence in your personal life. Love and romantic relationships are particularly under attack from the heavens. You might face complaints or capriciousness from your better half, who may be behaving inappropriately, erratically, and generally make you question how reliable your relationship is, and whether there is a future. Expect complaints over money.

Those who have been married for a while will not be faring much better. You might disagree over how to set up your home, especially how to pay for it.

Your relationship with children is uneasy, as well. That may be because you are forced to solve their problems, or perhaps you will have to finance their education or development.

Mid-March will be the most challenging time for all relationships, especially from the 9th to the 11th. Things will improve significantly after the Full Moon and eclipse on March 25.

This is a time for clarity, understanding, and openness, which will be the key to smoothing over many thorny issues.

Single people should remember that any encounters during the last 10 days of the month might be life-changing.

Health

You are feeling sluggish in March, so take care of yourself and don't go overboard. This is a great time to quit bad habits, have a massage, visit a cosmetologist, or do something else for your health.

You might spend a few days away from work and instead have some time with loved ones or just yourself.

A loved one may fall ill, and will require your care and attention.

SCORPIO

For you, March is a time to seek both inner and outer harmony. Of course, this is a tall order, but for you, nothing is impossible!

Work

The tidal wave of events this month will take you by storm. Despite your jam-packed schedule, however, you will somehow manage to keep up with it all. You are bound with energy, and attention from people whose opinions matter to you will significantly improve things for you, including your self-esteem.

The first 20 days of the month are a good time to develop old connections and meet new people, but the last 10 days will have you putting your nose to the grindstone as you resolve the most difficult tasks that will require even more diligence and knowledge.

March is a promising time for those who work in creative fields – actors, artists, journalists, and musicians. Your popularity will grow, as will your income.

Moreover, March is also a good time for those in other professions. You will be coming up with creative ideas, thinking outside the box, and showing your achievements to colleagues and a wider audience in general.

The right people will appreciate and support your creative solutions.

Money

Financially, March is not particularly noteworthy. Your income is stable, your expenses are low, and all of them are personal or pleasant in nature. You will be spending money on relaxation, your children, and your loved one – that will require some money, but there's no way around it. And the best way to spend your money is on your loved ones, and, naturally, yourself.

Love and family

Many Scorpios will be more focused on their home and family or romantic relationships this month.

Those who are immersed in day-to-day matters might occasionally have as spat, but in the end, you will find a compromise. Your children will require your attention and some action on your part to resolve their problems, and this concerns even couples on the rocks.

Your relationship with your romantic partner will settle down, and many couples will start taking steps toward marriage.

Friction with your parents is highly likely from March 9 to 12, but things should be smoothed over by the end of the month.

Most Scorpios will see a lot of changes in their social circles. The stars recommend that you attend more parties than usual and take care to always look your best. You are in the limelight and making a great impression on everyone worth talking to!

Those who don't have a steady partner can count on luck this month. Those who aren't single may find themselves tempted. The choice is yours.

Be sensitive to your loved ones, and you will be pleased with their response.

Health

You are feeling energetic in March and have no reason to fear falling ill. You might feel a bit tired from all of the hustle and bustle during the last 10 days of the month, and especially during the Full Moon and eclipse from March 24-26. During this time, take care of yourself and practice moderation.

SAGITTARIUS

In March, you are restless, hyperactive, and capable of dodging any obstacle. And as always, there are plenty of them.

Work

You recently made some important decisions, and they are now bearing their fruit. Work is moving forward, though not as quickly as you had hoped and planned. The stars advise not to rush things, and methodically overcome any difficulties that pop up along the way.

Once again, you may find yourself grappling with issues involving colleagues in other cities or abroad, or perhaps you are overcoming complexities at work.

Business owners and managers would be wise to keep an eye on their subordinates, as someone may have their own agenda or be afflicted with delusions of grandeur.

Employees should be careful with colleagues and learn to listen more and speak less. Do your job carefully and ignore any rumors, gossip, and intrigue.

The most difficult period this month will be during the New Moon, from March 9 to 11. The last week, during the Full Moon from March 24-26, which falls during the eclipse, will be the best time. For you, this eclipse is a positive thing, and a time for meetings and making important connections.

Money

March is a stable time for your finances, but no more. Your income is modest and predictable, and your expenses are low, mostly related to your personal or family life.

Love and family

Many Sagittarians might be focused on home and family this month. You might have guests over more frequently, or perhaps a relative will come visit you. Your relationship with family members will totally change, and you will find them more difficult.

This is not something new, but in February and March you might find yourself running into endless problems here. In the best case, you might find yourself neither at war nor peace, and in the worst, you will clash and argue.

However, the astrologer reminds you that this only applies to relatives with whom you have had longstanding issues. Harmonious family ties will remain as such.

Spouses who get along will be busy with spring cleaning, and maybe some minor repairs. During the last 10 days of March, you will be busy with your children's affairs, but taking care of them is usually a joy.

Unmarried couples will find that the last 10 days of the month will be the most interesting, when your relationship will become more romantic and exciting. Spring is in the air, and there are more opportunities to meet someone new. Those who have not yet found a partner might take advantage of that.

The Full Moon and eclipse on March 25 will leave a powerful mark on the romantic sector of your sky, so spend time among other people and make sure to always look your best.

Health

In March, you are feeling tired and might have frequent bouts of fatigue and exhaustion, especially during the New Moon from March 9-11.

These are difficult days, so take it easy and be careful behind the wheel! In addition to falling ill, there is a high risk of accidents on the road or simply as you live your life.

CAPRICORN

Right now, your sign is free from the influence of any oppressive planets, so you can return to your former confidence and composure, as well as your creativity. Keep it up!

Work

March is the perfect time for expanding your sphere of influence and showing your achievements to a wider audience.

You are spending more time talking to contacts in other cities and abroad, and you may take a successful trip. Alternatively, your partners from far away might come to your neck of the woods, and any conversations you have will be positive and constructive.

Those who are busy expanding their business might be busy putting on the finishing touches, which will complete the overall favorable path you are on.

Many business owners will be thinking of expanding to another city or abroad, and if that already happened recently, you might be hoping to strengthen your position.

Things at work are smooth and quiet for employees. You will have an opportunity to take a short trip and spend more time with your loved ones and family.

Money

Despite the overall favorable tone of this month at work, you may run into some money trouble. Your income isn't going to drop, but rather, your money is going to be burning a hole in your pocket.

The astrologist predicts that most of this will be because of your children and loved ones. You might also have what people like to call "entertainment expenses".

Love and family

Many Capricorns will be more focused on matters with their family and romantic relationships this month.

Couples who get along will be busy with their children and invest a significant sum into their education and development. If they really need your help, then give it to them! If your children are really being unnecessarily demanding, it is worth carefully analyzing the situation.

Remember that there is a huge gap between these two positions, and act accordingly.

Many families are still likely to welcome new babies or grandchildren.

Romantic relationships are developing with varying levels of success. Capricorns tend to be overly pragmatic, if not outright stingy. However, it is better to leave that quality behind, right now. This month will bring a lot of expenses, and they will be related to a loved one. Accept it in order to avoid further trouble. What could be better than spoiling someone you love, and yourself?

During the last 10 days of the month, you might be drawn to changing your interior decorating, or sprucing up your house or cabin. This will finally happen in April.

Health

In March, you are active, attractive, and healthy. This is the month when you have no reason to fear falling ill.

AQUARIUS

March is a time to strengthen your position on all fronts – moral, financial, and emotional. This is not an easy task, but you are a tough cookie. So do what you can, and what will be will be!

Work

The important decisions you made recently are now bearing their fruit.

You will have to put in some elbow grease, but it will be well worth it. Business owners and managers will be busy expanding their business and might start to consolidate their success with tangible results. You will find the money you need to continue what you have started, and that will allow you to look boldly toward the future and do what is required.

During the last 10 days of March, you will be speaking more frequently to colleagues in other cities or abroad, and you might take a trip or begin preparing one.

Despite this overall positive tone in March, you are still likely to run into problems. That may be at work, related to rebuilding your business.

Those who are busy with construction or repairs should be especially attentive and come from a position of flexibility and diplomacy rather than force. However, if you are confident, then do what you see fit.

March 9-11 is the time you can expect the most conflicts this month, and that applies to all Capricorns, regardless of what field they may work in.

Money

Financially, March is not a bad time for you at all. You will have a regular income, and significantly more of it. In addition to your usual revenue, you might profit from various real estate transactions.

Love and family

If your interests are more focused on your personal life, here, things may look differently this month.

Many families are still busy with various real estate transactions. Some are working on major repairs, and others are moving somewhere far away, while others have decided to buy a home, apartment, or cabin.

In March, you might be immersed in setting up your home, though there may be many obstacles in your way. Spouses might clash over this, and from March 9 to 11, expect a serious argument.

Alternatively, you might run into issues involving your parents or elderly family members.

During the last 10 days of the month, you will spend more time talking to relatives. You might take a trip or meet with family members who live in another city or abroad.

Many Aquarians will take a trip during the last 10 days of March, and it will be a great success.

Health

During the first 20 days of March, you will not be feeling as energetic as usual, though you are unlikely to fall seriously ill as long as you take care of yourself and protect your body from colds and infections.

During the last 10 days of March, things will be much more dynamic, and you will feel more alive and be thinking more clearly once again.

PISCES

Your task is to leave the past behind and begin a new chapter with a clean slate. The process has already begun, and there is no stopping it. The changes may be physical or mental.

Work

Many Pisceans are still focused on somewhere far away when it comes to work. If this brought a lot of issues in February, now, things are looking up. Though things are not fully resolved yet, most of them will be this month. You will not be able to count on any help here, however. Things will work out if you take the reins.

This may involve the laws of another country, or perhaps legal troubles, or, alternatively, intrigue involving colleagues from afar.

The most difficult period is during the New Moon from March 9 to 11. After that, things will start to fall into place, and you can count on success by May.

Students might also face a series of trials, but they will manage to overcome it all.

Money

March is not exactly stable for your wallet. You might be spending constantly, and that will be most noticeable during the last 10 days of the month. Be especially careful with money and other things of material value during the Full Moon and eclipse on March 25 and 26, when there is a high likelihood of expenses or heavy financial loss.

Love and family

Processes begun earlier are also continuing in your personal life.

Those planning a move to another city or abroad might once again face challenges but be enthusiastic as they overcome them. There is still a long road ahead, but by the end, things will work out as you had planned.

Couples would be wise to be attentive and not give into rumors or intrigue. Maybe this happened in the recent past, and now, things are playing out. Your relationship may be somewhat tarnished when you learn something about one another you would have preferred to keep in the dark.

Things will become clearer in time, however, and everything will fall into place. Most likely, that will be solely thanks to your efforts.

Your relationship with relatives will also become clearer, calmer, and your influence may be decisive.

Health

In March, you are feeling significantly more energetic, but the stars urge you to be careful when traveling or driving. The darkest days are from March 9-11.

April

New York Time			London Time		
Calendar Day	Lunar Day	Lunar Day Start Time	Calendar Day	Lunar Day	Lunar Day Start Time
01/04/24	23	12.48 AM	01/04/24	22	2.27 AM
02/04/24	24	1.40 AM	02/04/24	23	3.19 AM
03/04/24	25	2.27 AM	03/04/24	24	4.02 AM
04/04/24	26	3.08 AM	04/04/24	25	4.36 AM
05/04/24	27	3.44 AM	05/04/24	26	5.04 AM
06/04/24	28	4.18 AM	06/04/24	27	5.28 AM
07/04/24	29	4.49 AM	07/04/24	28	5.50 AM
08/04/24	30	5.21 AM	08/04/24	29	6.12 AM
08/04/24	1	2.23 PM	08/04/24	1	7.23 PM
09/04/24	2	6.54 AM	09/04/24	2	6.35 AM
10/04/24	3	7.31 AM	10/04/24	3	7.01 AM
11/04/24	4	8.12 AM	11/04/24	4	7.32 AM
12/04/24	5	8.58 AM	12/04/24	5	8.11 AM
13/04/24	6	9.50 AM	13/04/24	6	8.58 AM
14/04/24	7	10.47 AM	14/04/24	7	9.55 AM
15/04/24	8	11.47 AM	15/04/24	8	10.58 AM
16/04/24	9	12.47 PM	16/04/24	9	12.04 PM
17/04/24	10	1.47 PM	17/04/24	10	1.12 PM
18/04/24	11	2.46 PM	18/04/24	11	2.19 PM
19/04/24	12	3.45 PM	19/04/24	12	3.26 PM
20/04/24	13	4.43 PM	20/04/24	13	4.32 PM
21/04/24	14	5.41 PM	21/04/24	14	5.38 PM
22/04/24	15	6.40 PM	22/04/24	15	6.45 PM
23/04/24	16	7.40 PM	23/04/24	16	7.53 PM
24/04/24	17	8.41 PM	24/04/24	17	9.02 PM
25/04/24	18	9.43 PM	25/04/24	18	10.12 PM
26/04/24	19	10.45 PM	26/04/24	19	11.20 PM
27/04/24	20	11.43 PM	28/04/24	20	12.22 AM
29/04/24	21	12.37 AM	29/04/24	21	1.17 AM
30/04/24	22	1.25 AM	30/04/24	22	2.02 AM

You can find the description of each lunar day in the chapter "A Guide to The Moon Cycle and Lunar Days"

ARIES

This month, you might run into setbacks, but with enough effort, you will be able to not only overcome them, but create a winning streak for yourself that will last for the rest of 2024. Your steadfast motto is: "Charge forward"!

Work

April is a promising enough time for you at work. The only drawback is that all the events you planned will go somewhat more slowly than you had initially anticipated. You may have to put on some finishing touches, add some bells and whistles, or carry out some preparatory activities, and all of that takes time.

However, closer to the end of the month, you will reach your desired goal, and will be dealing with other, less important tasks.

Expanding your business will turn out favorably, and the lion's share of this endeavor is probably already done. Activities related to construction, repairs, and other matters are also moving toward the finish line.

You will be developing your contacts, especially with business partners in other cities or abroad.

Employees might be negotiating a new job or a new direction right where they are. You might also put out feelers for a bonus or higher salary.

Money

Financially, April is not a bad time for you. The best period is after April 20, when you may come into additional sums of money and can expect favorable negotiations about a salary increase.

Love and family

Your personal life looks like smooth sailing. Any recent arguments with your partner are a thing of the past, now, and it is time to work together to finish some difficult activities involving home improvements.

From April 2 to 25, Mercury will be in retrograde, and this is a bad time for any major purchases. If you absolutely cannot wait, try to do that at least after April 25 or in May.

Couples' relationships will also become more stable; however, nothing is perfect. You may have had disagreements in March, and you might still be feeling a bit of a grudge now.

It might be time to consider what you really need, or how you can avoid trouble. While Mercury is in retrograde, you might take the time to reflect deeply on what has happened, without empty platitudes or making a fuss.

Health

In April, you are healthy, energetic, though a bit anxious and tense. The stars recommend that you remember that your nerves are at the root of all illnesses and resolve problems as they come.

TAURUS

You are embarking on a month that is unlikely to be your best. Avoid any major activities, and instead sit down to deeply analyze what has happened. Slow and steady wins the race.

Work

For anything work-related, April is unlikely to be particularly productive. Things are likely to be hanging in the air, and you might run into minor, but annoying obstacles that will significantly slow things down for you everywhere.

Business owners and managers will have to deal with complicated red tape, as well as various reports required by auditing or investigation bodies.

A silver lining this month may be support from old friends or someone influential whose services you have turned to before.

April is not a bad time for any preparatory activities or thinking about what you have already completed and your plans for the future. The astrologist predicts there will be a lot of them.

Employees would be wise to display modesty, responsibility, and tact. April is not a time to approach your superiors, and it is even less appropriate for confrontation with them. Right now, patience is the key.

What's more, April might bring an opportunity to relax and get away from work, and it is worth taking full advantage of this. The world won't stop turning if you are out of the office for two or three days.

If an old friend unexpectedly offers you a new job, it is worth carefully examining all the pros and cons. It is better to wait until later in May to make a decision.

Money

April is a stable time for your bank account, but no more. You will not see any windfall, but there is hope for the future. You might have some profits from unofficial sources or help from loved ones.

Your expenses are low, so you will remain in the black this month.

Love and family

There are no changes in your personal life this month.

Spouses will be handling minor, day-to-day issues and calling on the wisdom of eternal love. Your better half may have a major impact on all household matters this month. In mid-April, you will see some old friends, and perhaps someone will come to visit you.

Unmarried couples' relationships will be put to the test, but that is an internal dilemma, and not something others will see. Slowly but surely, you will come to a conclusion, and by May, you will be able to talk about it with your partner. The astrologist predicts that all is well.

Health

In April, you are significantly less lively than usual, and even the young and healthy might feel fatigued and sapped of energy.

Elderly and weakened Taureans suffering from chronic illnesses might suffer a relapse, so take preventive measures in advance and, if you can, see your primary doctor. Be sure to find the time to relax whenever possible.

GEMINI

The future is looking up, but for now, you might not see it. In a few months, your life will look very different, but for now, deal with problems from the past and get ready for the achievements to come.

Work

This month, your ruler, Mercury, will be in retrograde from April 2 to 25, which means that things will slow down a bit. You might have to spend most of your time in negotiations, discussing things you have already completed, and how they can be perfected.

You will not run into any conflicts, and your biggest issue is that things will not be resolved as quickly as you might have hoped. Perhaps a friend or someone influential will decide to take a wait-and-see approach or simply need more time in order to make a change.

Business owners and managers who are busy expanding their business will have to complete this job, as well as to make changes and updates.

Employees will also see changes in their organization, perhaps there will be new leadership or even new goals to achieve. Things are hectic, but the results are undeniably positive.

Many Geminis will be engaged in negotiations for a new job, and that will be successful. You can expect to see results closer to June.

Those who work in construction, or anything related to land and real estate will be pleased with how things go this month. Your influence is growing and so is your income.

Money

April is not a bad time for your wallet. You will have money coming in regularly, and not only from work. You might have additional profits from real estate or support from loved ones, or even sponsorship or favorable credit. Your expenses are certainly not disappearing, but they are modest, and by the end of the month, your accounts will still be in the black.

Love and family

This month promises a lot of contacts with others. You might see old friends or people you have not visited in a long time.

Strengthening old ties is the main theme of this month, but be skeptical of any new encounters, who may not turn out to be as you expected.

This is because of the influence of Mercury in retrograde' new people who appear during this time usually disappear from our lives, leaving nothing more than a less-than-pleasant memory, whether we met them in a personal or professional context.

Your relationship with your partner might change a bit and become cooler and more rational. This is not a problem, times like this happen and are useful to you.

You will be very close to finishing improvements on your home, and soon you will be able to leave these troublesome tasks behind.

Health

In April, you are feeling energetic and have no reason to fear falling ill. You may feel a bit sluggish during the last 10 days of the month, so try to spend some time in nature and get enough sleep.

CANCER

You may have won the battle, but that doesn't mean the war is over. In April, you will once again have to reexamine your goals and make some necessary changes.

Work

April is a busy month for you, but also a time for anxiety and general fussiness. You might be involved in negotiations with colleagues from other cities or abroad, who will drag things out, but closer to May, you will come to a positive result. You may also even take a productive trip during this time.

Business owners and managers might finish up previous projects and make changes to whatever is standing in your way. Your friends or someone influential may play an important role this month. This time, their influence will be positive.

Any problems from earlier months have already been resolved, and things are looking calmer, now.

Employees might spend a lot of time discussing their responsibilities or a new title with management, and by late April or perhaps the first half of May, you will get your way.

Money

Financially, this month is not a bad time for you. You will have money coming in regularly, and somewhat more than usual.

Expect to receive the largest sums on April 8, 9, 16-18, 26, and 27.

Your expenses are low, and most will take place during the last 10 days of the month.

Love and family

Your personal life will be on the back burner this month, as you will be so focused on work during the first 20 days of April. For this reason, your relationship with your partner or spouse might cool a bit. In order to avoid trouble here, try to take the time to explain to your better half why you are so busy, and you will be pleased with their response.

Things will change a bit during the last 10 days of April. Here, you will have an opportunity to spend more time with friends and loved ones and to attend more events and generally be more present in your own life.

You might see people from your past such as old friends, and perhaps even an old flame. This encounter will be both pleasant and useful to you.

However, if you meet anyone new while Mercury is in retrograde from April 2-25, this encounter may prove superficial and unreliable, so don't place too much stock in them.

Health

In April, your body is at its very peak and any illnesses will pass you by.

LEO

You are making steady progress, but there are still a lot of obstacles in your path. You will have to grapple with some of them right now.

Work

Leos who are part of the working world will have to develop their ties with colleagues in other cities or abroad this month, and that will be your main task. Though the work itself will not be particularly difficult, your relationship with partners might be problematic. Someone may have a hidden agenda, or someone may inexplicably hit the brakes. Alternatively, you may need to come back to the same issues over and over again, after you thought they were resolved. However, the final phase of this process is looking positive, and that's what counts.

Any trips planned from April 2-25 might not turn out the way you expected, so be sure to plan everything carefully and thoroughly.

Business owners and managers might be laying the groundwork for new business all month long, while employees may be getting ready for a new job.

Money

Your finances may take center stage this month, and you may find yourself in negotiations trying to resolve these issues.

That may be due to work or perhaps your personal life. You may need to reach an agreement, and by May, the thorniest issues will already be fixed.

Love and family

Pluto, the planet of transformation and harsh pressure has been in the sector of the sky responsible for any partnered relationships for some time now, and that has the greatest impact on your personal life.

Pluto brings separation and divorce, as well as general changes to your relationship with others. Are you ready? If so, there's no problem here, but if not, you will not be in control of the situation.

Separated or divorcing couples might spend a long time discussing financial matters, and you may have to give in on something.

Couples who get along might work together to address various issues related to real estate or even a move. Closer to the end of the month, everything you had planned will come to fruition.

Health

In April, you are feeling a lot of ups and downs with the spring weather – sometimes you are bouncing off the walls, and others, you can barely drag yourself out of bed. Keep an eye on your body and take care not to overdo it.

Take some vitamins, move around in the mornings, and most importantly, get enough sleep, in order to stabilize your energy supply and avoid any illnesses.

VIRGO

The New Moon and eclipse on April 8 will force you to stop, take a look around, and batten down the hatches.

Work

In addition to the harsh influence of the eclipse, your ruler, Mercury, will be in retrograde from April 2-25, meaning that any Virgos who are part of the working world can expect to face a series of challenges. During this time, it is not worth getting into any major business, starting new projects, or trying to make too much progress. It is, however, a great time to cross your t's and dot your i's or address any cumbersome administrative issues.

Your relationship with business partners from afar is moving along with varying success. You might have difficult negotiations over financial and material issues. You will not resolve this quickly, but by May, things will be looking rosier on both sides.

If you are planning on travel or on opening a business in another city or abroad, this month may bring a variety of administrative troubles and you will have to overcome them on your own.

April is a tough time for most employees. Your colleagues and managers will notice both your qualities and your shortcomings, so be very attentive and don't lose sight of the details.

Carefully plan any business trips in April, and if you can, put them off until May.

Money

April is also a hard time for your wallet. You have few expenses, but they are probably related to either business or your personal problems.

You can expect tense negotiations with business partners over financial assistance or investments. Many will be thinking about taking out credit and filling out forms with this aim.

Love and family

Those who are more focused on their personal lives might have to grapple with challenging household issues. Those who are moving somewhere far away will be busy dealing with their home, or perhaps buying a new residence or making repairs right where they are.

Divorcing or separated couples might decide how to divide up their finances, and you can expect a real breakthrough here. Many couples may be seriously wondering if their relationship is really over for good, or if there is some way to reconcile. Here, the ball is in your partner's court, and all you can do is listen to your own intuition. Right now, it speaks the truth.

A major trend this month will be renewing your ties to old friends, acquaintances, or a former flame. Anyone new you meet between April 2 and 25 is probably not as reliable or trustworthy as he or she appears at first glance.

Health

All month long, you might feel a bit under the weather. Avoid any physical stress right now and be sure to relax instead.

Those who are weakened, or elderly should be especially attentive and take preventive measures ahead of time.

You might see a resurfacing of old illnesses or accidents this month. The likelihood is very high.

LIBRA

Attentiveness and patience are highly valuable qualities, and this month, you are sure to need them. Hold your horses – this isn't the Kentucky Derby.

Work

April is a very difficult month for you. Business owners and managers of every level are still busy with expansion and your team will be working on just that. Right now, you can be sure to count on your subordinates – most of them are responsible and reliable. There are a few outliers, but right now, they are not dragging down the rest of the team.

Not everything will go according to plan for you this month. That especially concerns those around you and certain business partners. They might behave inconsistently or drag out decisions and nothing will be resolved until May. That may involve money or financial support, or perhaps something of material value. Despite the holdup, however, things will work out in the end. Since these matters are crucially important, use April to carefully study everything that has happened hitherto and to conduct a thorough audit.

Money

Financially, this month might be a time for laying the groundwork. You will see major events happen either in late April or in May, and the sum will be unexpectedly high. Most likely this is due to bonuses or awards, or perhaps financial support from your business partners or favorable terms of credit.

Those who are not part of the working world might receive support from parents or a spouse, and the amount is growing.

Love and family

Your personal life is not smooth sailing, this month. Your partner might not agree with your decisions, especially over household matters. However, the ball is in his or her court right now, and perhaps you are in the wrong.

Try to listen to your better half and help out, because things will probably turn out like that. What's more, he or she might be ready to take on a lot more and provide you with moral and material support.

You will see big changes with your children, and they may grow distant or even alienated. That may be due to an argument, or perhaps one is simply moving away.

Health

You are less energetic this month, so take care of yourself and don't overdo it. If you don't feel important, take a few days off and just relax. Your health comes first, and the rest will follow.

SCORPIO

Remember this month that slow and steady wins the race. Haste makes waste. This month, you might experience some losses and need extra time even for simple tasks.

Work

April is a time for burdensome, fastidious tasks, when you have to put out various fires that fate sends your way. You might have to come back to the same issues time and again or make corrections on work you already started. The stars predict that it will all turn out brilliantly, and in time, those around you will understand. Right now, however, is the time to focus on the details and don't let anything slip through the cracks.

Managers would be wise to keep an eye on subordinates, and, if you can, keep your finger on the pulse of things.

Employees will work in a team, and be sure to carefully follow the instructions, especially when it comes to red tape and financial documents.

In late April, you will see new business partners on your horizon, or perhaps someone from the past. The stars recommend you remain vigilant for any invitations they offer, which may be financially very attractive.

Money

Financially, April is neutral. You have a stable and predictable income, and your expenses are modest, and mostly related to your personal life.

Expect the largest sums on April 1, 8, 9, 16-18, 26, and 27.

Love and family

The eclipse this month will take place in the sector of the sky responsible for work and tiresome everyday tasks. During the first half of the month, you may not have time for much of a personal life.

During the second half, however, those with families will be immersed in their children's affairs, and they may have to help adult children or care for younger family members.

Your relationship with family members is stable, without any major ups or downs.

Single people might meet someone new, and the last 10 days of April and all of May is when this is most likely to happen. In addition to new encounters, you might also run into someone from your past, and your relationship may be much more interesting and improved this time around.

Health

In April, you are feeling sluggish, especially if you are elderly or weakened. You should be more careful during the New Moon and eclipse from April 7-9. Those who are young and healthy should lead a healthy lifestyle and take good care of themselves.

SAGITTARIUS

This month, you are bounding with energy, but it is important you channel it correctly, especially since you will be fighting on all fronts – at work, at home, and in your personal life.

Work

You are still on a challenging streak at work. Business owners and managers of every level will have events related to expanding their business and setting up their offices or other production facilities. This time, things may not move as quickly as you would like, but it is not worth getting upset over. Let things play out as they play out.

Your main task this month is to carefully read and check everything, and don't forget the details. Everything that you have planned, you are doing, even if it is slightly later than you expected.

Closer to the end of the month, you might receive new, attractive offers, which are worth looking into. Make the adjustments you need, and then accept.

Employees will be dealing with a lot of personal and family issues this month, and it might be hard to concentrate on work. Many Sagittarians will have a chance to spend a few days away from work and visiting with their children or loved ones.

In late April and into May, many will have a unique opportunity to find a new outlet for their talents, which is worth carefully taking into consideration and maybe even accepting.

Money

Your finances may be unstable this month. On one hand, you won't end up penniless, but on the other, you can expect some losses. That may be due to work, or possibly your personal life and your family's or children's needs.

Love and family

Your personal life will be no less significant than work in April. Many Sagittarians will be improving their home, and by late April, you will be pleased with the results. The solar eclipse on April 8 will force parents to focus more on their children.

The stars recommend that you keep an eye on your younger children, and help out your adult children, who may really need it right now.

Expect an interesting period if you are in a romantic relationship.

The turbulent spring weather sets the stage for a lot of changes, and remember that the distance between love and hate is a very short one...

Try to exercise self-control and keep an eye on your partner. If you do, you will be surprised by the reaction.

Health

All month long, you are energetic, active, and the picture of health. The stars recommend that you avoid any rumors and pay more attention to your appearance.

Remember that first impression matter and you certainly have no problem with smarts!

CAPRICORN

You might see your greatest victories this month in your personal life, and the stars promise you dazzling success. At work, remember to keep your head down and you will go far.

Work

Capricorns who are part of the working world will be busy with administrative tasks. You might be working with your team, or perhaps going through changes at the management level.

Your relationship with colleagues from other cities or abroad is coming along nicely, and many will wish to find an opportunity to expand their business or open an office somewhere far from home. You might be negotiating on this front throughout April, and you might also deal with administrative issues related to this troublesome task.

It is not worth rushing things. From April 2-25, Mercury will be in retrograde, and during this time, you should carefully study things, but don't expect any breakthroughs.

Employees might be busy with their personal matters, so they would be wise to take a few days off to be with family.

If you are unable to do that, the stars recommend paying close attention to your obligations and be sure to cross your t's and dot your i's. You are unlikely to see any major achievements, but the devil is in the details, and your future depends on them.

Money

Financially, April is a neutral time for you. You will not see any windfalls, but you also won't run into trouble.

Your income is modest, and your expenses are predictable and reasonable. The astrologist predicts that most of them will be related to your personal life, family, and children.

Love and family

Things will be busier in your personal life this month. Many Capricorns will once again be dealing with complex matters related to real estate. The eclipse will bring just that, when it happens on April 8. You might plan on traveling to another city or even abroad during this time of change.

Alternatively, you might be busy with your children's needs, or those of younger family members.

Parents will be focused nearly entirely on their children, who will bring them joy. In many families, you may be expecting new babies or grandchildren.

Divorcing couples or those whose marriage is in serious trouble might be haggling over real estate or their future. This time, things will fall into place, and you will find a peaceful path forward.

Couples might be talking about moving in together or their life together.

Single people might count on an unexpected encounter toward the end of the month, and an exciting romance.

Health

In April, you are not feeling as energetic as usual, and you might not feel quite yourself for a few days. The stars recommend not rushing around and taking the time to relax. Don't refuse any help if you need it.

AQUARIUS

What happens this month will have far-reaching consequences, so don't take any unnecessary risks and behave accordingly. Remember, haste makes waste.

Work

The solar eclipse on April 8 will force many Aquarians to focus their valuable attention on connections in other cities or abroad. Those who are busy expanding their business somewhere far away might be busy negotiating with partners, and this may take longer than you'd like.

Alternatively, don't try to force things. Right now, with things slowed down, it is a good time to carefully discuss and plan your future projects. The results depend on it.

Many will be busy dealing with red tape, documents, and other bothersome paperwork.

Expanding your business is moving along favorably, and you will find both the resources and the strength to make it happen.

Be careful during any travel planned for April and be sure to pay attention to the details. Employees might be combining work with family matters, and the stars predict that everything will work out at both ends.

Money

April is not a bad time for your bank account, and you will have a regular income, but significantly more of it. In addition to your usual sources of money, you might also profit from various real estate transactions. Expect to receive the largest sums on April 1, 2, 5-7, 14, 15, 24, and 25.

Your expenses are very low, and your income more than compensates.

Love and family

Your personal life is no less active. Those who are planning on moving to a new home might be almost done with construction, repairs, and other matters.

Those who are moving somewhere far away will have to deal with paperwork, documents, and also the laws of another country.

Closer to the end of the month and into May, you might see major changes related to your home. Keep your eyes peeled here, because new opportunities might solve old problems.

Your relationship with your spouse or partner is stable now, and you will be getting along as you set up a new home.

If you are planning on traveling together, choose a place you have been to before. Mercury will be in retrograde from April 2-25, so any new acquaintances or places might only lead to disappointment.

However, during this period, it is worth rekindling your ties with people you have not seen for a long time, or calling your relatives, parents, or old friends.

Health

In April, you are feeling energetic enough and naturally, the stars might recommend you avoid getting worked up. Remember that if you keep quiet, you will go much further.

PISCES

A bird in hand is worth two in the bush. Everything will work out, as long as you give your desires a reality check!

Work

On April 8, there will be a solar eclipse in the financial sector of your sky, which means that any issues related to material things might come to a head.

Business owners and managers will have to scrupulously calculate what they can spend right now, and what can be put off for later.

Your relationship with colleagues in other cities or abroad is developing in your favor, thanks to your generous personal efforts here.

Those who are planning on opening business in another city or abroad might reach a breakthrough in late April or May.

During this time, employees might receive an unexpected offer related to a move.

Discuss all financial matters when striking new deals or looking at job offers and be sure to read the fine print.

Remember that no matter how things look right now, they can always change in the future.

Things can stabilize now, and with the right amount of effort, things will fall into place.

Money

April is not a bad time for your bank account, as your income will be regular and somewhat greater than before. Expect to receive the largest amounts on April 1, 2, 7-9, 16-18, 26, and 27.

Accountants, brokers, and bankers, or anyone else who works with other people's finances, would be wise to look closely at documents as the risk of errors is high right now. Mercury will be in retrograde in the financial sector of your sky, and there will be a solar eclipse at the same time. All of this promises to place a great strain on anything related to money, so be careful!

Love and family

Your relationship with your family is stable, and spouses who get along will be dealing with household matters and some financial disagreements may pop up, but overall, this month is looking harmonious. Remember, the truth is born out of debate.

Those planning a move to another city or abroad will be closer to achieving their dreams. The biggest tasks are already done, and what is left will be completed by late April or May.

Those dreaming of moving somewhere new, including abroad, will also reach their goals.

Pisceans planning any major purchases should deal with their finances first, especially if the idea is to buy a car or home. Avoid finalizing any purchases this month, especially while Mercury is in retrograde from April 2 to 25, but you can certainly get your ducks in a row.

In late April and early May, you might meet someone new, who will bring some color to your life if you are single and have been disappointed by love in the past.

Health

In April, you are not feeling as vigorous as usual, but you have the support of the planets, especially Mars, which is a powerful source of energy, so you won't fall seriously ill, as long as you live a healthy lifestyle and take care of yourself.

May

New York Time			London Time		
Calendar Day	Lunar Day	Lunar Day Start Time	Calendar Day	Lunar Day	Lunar Day Start Time
01/05/24	23	2.07 AM	01/05/24	23	2.38 AM
02/05/24	24	2.43 AM	02/05/24	24	3.07 AM
03/05/24	25	3.16 AM	03/05/24	25	3.31 AM
04/05/24	26	3.47 AM	04/05/24	26	3.53 AM
05/05/24	27	4.18 AM	05/05/24	27	4.14 AM
06/05/24	28	4.49 AM	06/05/24	28	4.35 AM
07/05/24	29	5.23 AM	07/05/24	29	4.59 AM
07/05/24	1	11.24 PM	08/05/24	1	4.24 AM
08/05/24	2	6.02 AM	08/05/24	2	5.27 AM
09/05/24	3	6.46 AM	09/05/24	3	6.02 AM
10/05/24	4	7.36 AM	10/05/24	4	6.46 AM
11/05/24	5	8.33 AM	11/05/24	5	7.39 AM
12/05/24	6	9.33 AM	12/05/24	6	8.41 AM
13/05/24	7	10.34 AM	13/05/24	7	9.48 AM
14/05/24	8	11.36 AM	14/05/24	8	10.57 AM
15/05/24	9	12.36 PM	15/05/24	9	12.06 PM
16/05/24	10	1.35 PM	16/05/24	10	1.13 PM
17/05/24	11	2.33 PM	17/05/24	11	2.19 PM
18/05/24	12	3.31 PM	18/05/24	12	3.25 PM
19/05/24	13	4.29 PM	19/05/24	13	4.32 PM
20/05/24	14	5.29 PM	20/05/24	14	5.39 PM
21/05/24	15	6.31 PM	21/05/24	15	6.49 PM
22/05/24	16	7.33 PM	22/05/24	16	7.59 PM
23/05/24	17	8.36 PM	23/05/24	17	9.09 PM
24/05/24	18	9.37 PM	24/05/24	18	10.15 PM
25/05/24	19	10.33 PM	25/05/24	19	11.13 PM
26/05/24	20	11.24 PM	27/05/24	20	12.02 AM
28/05/24	21	12.07 AM	28/05/24	21	12.40 AM
29/05/24	22	12.45 AM	29/05/24	22	1.11 AM
30/05/24	23	1.19 AM	30/05/24	23	1.36 AM
31/05/24	24	1.50 AM	31/05/24	24	1.58 AM

You can find the description of each lunar day in the chapter "A Guide to The Moon Cycle and Lunar Days"

ARIES

You know that money can't buy happiness, but it can certainly take care of your problems for you. That might be your motto in May. But remember, money is here to serve you, and not the other way around.

Work

For anything work-related, May is an incredibly lucky month for you. Business owners and managers may be completing important tasks related to expanding their business and thinking about new opportunities, which will make themselves known in late May. You may be developing ties with colleagues in other cities or abroad or opening a business somewhere far from home. With all of this going on, you may receive help from new acquaintances, whose positions will turn out to be stronger than yours.

Employees will have a rare chance for a promotion or perhaps a whole new job.

Either way, you will have a chance to earn significantly more money, and to make your job far more exciting and interesting in the process.

You may receive offers related to a trip or even a move.

Money

Financially speaking, May might just be one of the best months of 2024 for you.

Many Aries are on a golden streak of both cash income and other material riches. In addition to your usual income, you might count on awards, bonuses, or even an unexpected win at the lottery.

You may also see profits from various real estate transactions or credit on favorable terms.

Business owners can count on profits from various transactions as well as support from business partners, whether moral or financial in nature.

Those who are not part of the working world will receive help from loved ones.

Your expenses are low this month, and all of them are more than covered by your income.

Love and family

May is a great time for your personal life, too. Many Aries might be busy with repairs, if not moving to a new home or apartment. Finally, some will manage to make a big decision about purchasing real estate in another city or abroad.

Your relationship with your family members is harmonious, and full of love and affection.

Everything is going well with your romantic partners, as well. You may decide to live together or take steps to make that happen.

Near the end of the month, you will start talking more to your relatives, and you might receive some as visitors. Alternatively, you might go to see them.

Those who want to study in another city or abroad can be sure to see success in this arena.

In any case, whether personal or work-related, this is a time to rely on old friends, especially those whose capabilities far exceed your own.

Luck is on your side, so keep charging ahead!

Health

You are feeling energetic in May, but you might have a tendency to gain weight. If that sounds like you, then watch what you eat and keep an eye on how many calories you consume.

TAURUS

Jupiter, which is the planet of good fortune, has now safely completed its journey through your sign. There is no shred of doubt that your life has changed over the last year, and for the better. But what lies ahead is certainly not a downgrade. So don't rest on your laurels just yet, and instead keep putting in the hard work.

Work

In May, you will be beginning a new chapter in your professional life, which will be more focused on money and material matters, especially if you are a business owner or manager, as Jupiter is transiting through the financial sector of your sky. That means that the time has come to expand your business, and you can be sure that you will find the money to make it happen.

Negotiations here are possible during the second half of the month, and closer to the end of May or perhaps in June, the results will reveal themselves to be positive.

Employees can count on some new responsibilities right where they are with the higher salary to match, or perhaps a job offer somewhere more promising. Work overall is stable and looking up!

A difficult relationship with management or perhaps government agencies will significantly improve, and you will really notice that in late May.

Money

For most Taureans, May is a stable time for your finances, with a clear upward trend. Expect to receive the largest sums on May 28 and 29. Your expenses are modest and certainly covered by your income.

Love and family

This time, your personal life isn't looking so bad. Couples who get along will be discussing plans for the future, and that may include home improvements or even purchasing a new place to live. For now, they're just in the planning stages, but over the next year or year and a half, your intentions will become a reality.

In May, many couples might fully make a decision, and it will probably be one of unity. That means marriage, living together, or getting a new place to live… By the end of the month, that will be a reality.

For those who are having trouble deciding exactly WHO they will choose, the stars advise you to move cautiously and keep in mind that sooner or later, all secrets come to light.

Health

All month long, you are feeling energetic enough and have no reason to fear falling ill.

May is a great time for changing up your image, or any other self-care. Whether overhauling your wardrobe or cosmetic procedures, including plastic surgery, now is the time!

If you have the chance and desire, leverage the stars' influence this month, and don't waste any time!

GEMINI

This month, Jupiter, the planet of good fortune, is entering your sign. That will happen on May 25, and in the meantime, you will be busy tying up loose ends, in order to start your next chapter with a clean slate!

Work

Business owners and managers will be completing major tasks related to expanding their business.

Your springboard to the future is ready, and great achievements and important work lie ahead. In late May or early June, you will meet new business partners from other cities or abroad. They may be VIPs, and your cooperation with them will bring favors your way.

In order for this to come to fruition, however, you will have to say goodbye to your old ways of doing things and overhaul the way you work, if not your entire life. That will not be something that happens overnight, but you may be taking your first steps in that direction right now.

That means that the future is now, and it is finally time to turn your back on all the chatter and roller coaster of the last few years.

Employees can expect new opportunities as well, most likely in the form of a new job. A move is not off the table. These important shifts are taking shape right now and will come to life sometime later.

Money

Financially, May is not a bad time for your wallet at all. In addition to your usual sources of income, you might also profit from other sources. For example, some will receive help from parents, loved ones, or profits from a real estate transaction. You might even receive an inheritance.

Love and family

Your personal life is no less exciting. Most Geminis will be completing important steps to improve their homes. In May, you will finally put an end to these bothersome household tasks.

Spouses are unusually friendly to one another, and thanks to this, everything will be resolved quickly, without any trouble or setbacks.

In late May or early June, you might take a successful trip, which will be a chance to get a change of scenery and relax a little.

Single people will have a great chance to meet someone new and interesting, and that may happen in late May or early June.

For the rest of the year, expect a cornucopia of other opportunities to set up your life just the way you like.

Health

During the first 20 days of May, you are not feeling particularly energetic, and may even feel exhausted and irritable with the mountain of household tasks you have had to complete. During the last 10 days, however, things will start to change for the better, and by June, you will be back to yourself.

CANCER

You will remember most of May as an exciting, successful time. However, nothing is permanent, and this will be clear by the end of the month. Cinderella is leaving the ball and will have to take care of herself for a while.

Work

During the first 20 days of May, you will run into friends, business partners, and influential people. You might have intensive communication with colleagues in other cities or abroad, or even take a successful trip.

What's more, any further progress will require you to establish a firm foundation, which will keep you busy for the rest of the year.

Business owners and managers will be thinking about expanding their business and completing various tasks related to this meticulous endeavor. That will take place during different periods from 2024-2025, but by late May or early June, you are starting to transition to a new reality. It is not easy, but right now, you have no other choice.

Many Cancers will have to deal with unpleasant matters, as well. For example, past legal troubles may rear their ugly heads again. That will happen a little later, but it's worth bracing yourself for the inevitable now.

Money

Financially, May is full of ups and downs. You are spending almost as much as you earn, but there is reason to hope that by June, you will be back in the black.

Love and family

The best time for your personal life is the first 20 days of May. This is a great time for many Cancers to be busy with a variety of people, all of whom you love to be around.

You might get back in touch with old friends or someone from another city or abroad, or perhaps even take a successful trip.

During this period, single people and those who have been let down by past relationships might have an interesting encounter, which will bring some joy to their lives.

Even if your romance isn't for the long term (here, everything depends on your personal horoscope), it will give you life experience and happy memories.

Parents are pleased with their children, who are on a positive streak.

Though the first part of the month is a busy time full of activities, during the last 10 days, things will start to change. You will want to spend more time alone, or with loved ones, or perhaps setting up a home. The latter is a thing for the future, but you may be in the planning stages right now.

Health

For most of May, you are healthy, full of energy, and a social butterfly. After May 20, however, that will start to drop off.

Be very attentive to yourself if you are elderly or weakened, as you are embarking on a rather unfavorable time, when you may run into old illnesses or unexpected new ones, and this will last for the rest of the year.

LEO

This month, you will learn just how far you have traveled, and how many obstacles you have overcome. It's only up from here on out!

Work

May is one of the best months of 2024 for you at work. Things are moving, and you have new projects and new opportunities on your hands. What's more, by the end of the month, or early June, you can expect new business partners with power and influence. That will strengthen your position, however, by the middle of the year, you can expect disagreements over material matters, and it is worth keeping that in mind right now.

Your relationship with colleagues in other cities or abroad is developing in your favor, and here, things are going as planned.

Employees will once again have a nice opportunity to improve their position right where they are, or perhaps take their skills somewhere new. Either way, it is worth discussing your salary, bonuses, and anything related to material matters. Have these conversations with an eye toward the future, which may not be as rosy as it appears from here.

Money

Financially, expect good tidings in May. Money will be coming in regularly, and you will be earning noticeably more of it, too. In addition to your usual income, you might have additional sources of money, such as bonuses, dividends, and prepayments for future projects.

Expect to receive the largest amounts on May 7-9, 16-18, 26, 27, 30, and 31.

Your expenses are low, and your income is certainly enough to cover them.

Love and family

Not everything looks so positive in your personal life. Gloomy Pluto, which has been in the sector of the sky responsible for long-term relationships for some time now, is forcing many to reconsider their relationship with their partners.

Pluto drives changes to relationships, transformation, and purifying everything that fails to meet its demands.

Keep that in mind and be mindful of any turbulence, which may have been a reality in your personal life for some time now.

This month, support from Jupiter means you will be able to make great progress in strengthening your relationships, including in terms of love and honesty.

Support your loved ones, if they are going through tough times, and you will be pleasantly surprised by their response.

Single people may have a fateful meeting in late May or early June. This will probably take place while you are with old friends or at a new job.

Health

In May, you are bounding with energy, and have one task: use it for peaceful purposes.

VIRGO

The time for ideas and long-term planning has concluded, and now, it's time for you to roll up your sleeves and get to work!

Work

You have embarked on a very important phase at work. Those who lost ground in the past are gradually recovering, and here, you can get back in the saddle.

Those who are planning a move or to open a business in another city or abroad seem to have achieved what they wanted. Ahead, expect a lot of work, a new professional cycle, which will bring you utmost success for the next three to four years.

In one way or another, all Virgos will be impacted by these new trends. You will be able to start a new business or job if you stay right where you are, as well, or perhaps you will go back to school for something new. The stars support and value all of these steps.

Initially, you will be able to count on old friends and former business partners. But it is worth remembering that that is only temporary. Later on, things will change, and not necessarily for the better. For various reasons, by the fall or winter of 2024, your relationship will have soured with people who might be lending a helping hand right now, and you will have to part ways. Remember and act accordingly.

Money

Your finances are improving, slowly but surely. This is especially noticeable during the last 10 days of May and in June.

Expect to receive the largest sums on May 9, 10, 18-20, and 28-30.

Love and family

Your personal life looks less tranquil. Harsh Saturn is firmly entrenched in the sector of the sky responsible for marriage and all long-term relationships, and that does not bode well for most Virgos.

For now, you can still count on support from your better half, even if you have recently fought.

Divorcing spouses might have to communicate for various reasons, and that will be surprisingly peaceful. In some cases, that will be very beneficial to both parties. You may have your children or a shared business to thank for that, or perhaps there are simply some burning embers of feelings left.

If that is the case, you might try to start over with a clean slate.

But remember, that later on, this situation will unexpectedly repeat itself, and things will not turn out quite the way you had hoped.

In addition to encounters with an old flame, the stars promise new acquaintances, who might develop into a passionate romance. You have plenty of choices right now, and that's a good thing.

Health

In May, you are healthy, energetic, a social butterfly, attractive, and making lasting impressions with everyone Fate throws your way.

LIBRA

In May, an important phase in your life will come to an end and you will begin a new chapter in its place. This time, things will be freer, more exciting, and happier. The stars are lighting the way, and with their help, it won't be hard to follow it.

Work

In May, you will finally be able to complete all of the organizational and administrative tasks you have been so busy with for so long.

Business owners and managers will have to evaluate work that was done related to expanding your business and make some plans for the future.

Many will be focused on something in another city or abroad, and this is where you will be channeling your efforts. From May 25 and throughout June, things will be very interesting here, as the situation involving business partners from somewhere far away will change for the better. Obstacles that stood in your way when you wanted to cooperate in the past will start to gradually fade away, and very soon, the path forward will be relatively clear. Why "relatively"? Despite the significant improvements here, there is still some residual difficulty in the way, and you will have to deal with it a few more times.

Business owners and managers will have to conduct yet another purge of their subordinates, and this will occupy them for nearly the entire year.

Employees might be thinking about a new job, which is sure to appear on the horizon, though a little later than this month.

Money

Financially, May is not bad at all, though maybe not because of any money you earned yourself. Rather, you might be reaping the benefit of a successful real estate transaction, support from business partners, or favorable terms of credit.

Those who are not part of the working world can count on support from loved ones who are currently experiencing a positive streak.

Love and family

There are major things underway in your personal life. Many Libras will be completing construction, major repairs, or talking about moving somewhere new. In many cases, that may involve another city or even abroad.

As May draws to a close, and into June, you are likely to take a trip, which will be a great success.

Your relationship with your children is changing, and this time, for the better. That will become more noticeable during the last 10 days of the month and continue into the future.

Single people, the last 10 days of May and all of June also hold a lot in store. You have a good chance of meeting just the person you need, they may even change your life!

That might happen on a trip or among people from somewhere far away.

Health

You are not as energetic as usual for most of May, and you might experience fatigue and exhaustion, which comes as no surprise given how much you've been running around and the amount of work you've been doing. But by the last 10 days of the month, Jupiter is on your side, which promises that things will move quickly, and you are sure to be delighted.

SCORPIO

May is an unusual month for you. You are seeing major changes at home, at work, and in your surroundings. As they say, it's all for the best.

Work

The most important thing this month is your relationship with business partners. The ability to listen, understand, and even give in a little from time to time is the key to success, both now and in the future. You might be surrounded by all different kinds of people – both new acquaintances and partners from the past.

Business owners and managers will be planning on expanding their business, and that will likely entail major purchases and various real estate transactions. This month, you may count on both moral and financial support from business partners.

Employees may be thinking about a new job, but things will not happen so quickly. More likely, you might be thinking about taking some time away from your current job, either due to family business or simply a long leave of absence.

Alternatively, you might find work under the wing of an old friend, where things are also undergoing changes.

Money

May is looking very turbulent for your wallet. You won't end up bankrupt, but you will be spending a lot due to business partners, parents, or perhaps a loved one.

You might have some profits from successful real estate transactions, or perhaps receive some very favorable terms of credit or an inheritance.

Love and family

Your personal life may be more important to you than work in May. Those with families will be addressing issues related to your home and taking steps in that direction. A loved one may play a major role here, and you would be wise to follow his or her lead.

Some Scorpios will be thinking about a new addition to the family, and this year, those plans will come to life.

Those who are single or have been let down by love in the past are in for an exciting and unusual time.

You are very likely to have a fateful encounter in May, and there is a chance that it will lead to deep feelings and even marriage.

Your relationship with an old flame is not entirely over, but in the next three to four months, it will gradually fade away.

Your relationship with older children is noticeably improved, and you might see each other frequently and make your peace, if you recently had an argument or went your separate ways.

Health

This month, you have no reason to fear for your health, but in the last 10 days of the month, you might feel tired from all of the hustle and bustle.

If that is your case, spend a few days away focused on yourself.

SAGITTARIUS

You never know what you're capable of until you try – keep this in mind all month long. You will be rewarded with attention, respect, and honor.

Work

You have a lot on your plate at work this month.

Business owners and managers at every level will be concluding projects started previously and assessing those that lie just around the corner.

Business owners can be sure to count on their subordinates – right now, you have a great team, and thanks to their help, you can move mountains. You might also gain new, valuable team members.

Employees can count on increased authority, a promotion right where they are, or a new job offer.

While the first 20 days of the month are a time of making leaps and bounds at work, the last 10 days look very different. During this time, expect to be busy with communications, meeting new people in your surroundings, and also showing off your achievements to a wider audience.

During this time, you will be talking more to colleagues in other cities or abroad, and that is something you can expect to continue into the future. This is a fateful trend that will change not only your job, but your entire life. Be sure to keep an eye on the future, and trust in the stars and fate.

Money

Financially, this is a great month for you. You might be receiving profits from previous projects, as well as frequent payments for new jobs. Employees can count on a bonus for a job well done, in addition to their usual paycheck. Expect to receive the largest amounts on May 3, 4, 7, 8, 16, 17, 26, and 27.

Your expenses are low, and your income is sure to cover them all.

Love and family

The last 10 days of May are the most exciting for your personal life. During this time, you will spend time meeting old acquaintances and new people. Generally speaking, this is the beginning of a fun, new chapter in your life, which will continue for the rest of the year.

Single people and those who have been disappointed by previous entanglements can expect a fateful encounter, and there is a high likelihood of it leading to a happy marriage. The right time begins now! So take care of yourself and always be in top form.

At the end of the month, you may go on a trip or at least be planning one.

Your relationship with relatives is significantly improved, and you might see relatives who live in other cities or abroad.

Health

In May, you are not feeling particularly energetic, and that may be due to working too much, which is never easy on the body. Try to spend some time away from work, which will bring you both strength and mental clarity.

CAPRICORN

The coming month is a great time to take a cue from Eat, Pray Love.
That is, take a break from it all, and relax, rather than working.
After all, there's more to life than work!

Work

Incurable workaholics might take advantage of May, as it is a great time to show your colleagues or a wider public all of your accomplishments, as well as for meeting new acquaintances.

That is how the first 20 days of May will play out. But during the last 10 days, things might change, and it will become very clear that there is a time for work and a time for play. Of course, this is a familiar condition for you, and it is sure that you will be more than happy to return to work as usual.

You have a whole year ahead of you to move mountains.

Those who recently left a job for various reasons might return in late May or June.

May is a great time for those who work in the creative fields – actors, writers, journalists, musicians, and artists. Your popularity will grow significantly, along with your income to match.

Your ties to business partners in other cities or abroad will be moving along in your favor, and you might go on a trip or plan for one.

Money

May is a time for major spending for you, though all of it will be pleasant in nature – you might end up buying things for yourself, loved ones, or giving yourself what you never had before. You won't end up in the red, however, and the last 10 days of May are especially telling here.

During the first half of the month, you might be in for unexpected but very pleasant surprises – gifts, bonuses, or even a winning lottery ticket. The lottery, of course, depends on your individual fate, but it's worth a shot!

Love and family

May, especially the first 20 days of the month, is an ideal time for your personal life. Couples who get along will be pleased with their children's success, as they will be experiencing a rare winning streak. In many families, you may welcome children or grandchildren.

Your relationship with relatives is noticeably improved, and you may have your children to thank for playing an important role here.

What's more, May is an extremely romantic time! Love is the greatest joy in life, and it will simply be permeating the spring air. That means this is a great time for meeting new people, romantic intrigue, and stormy, passionate romance. However, those who are already coupled up should tread carefully. You may experience unbearable temptation, so it is worth thinking not only of the rush of the moment, but future consequences, as well.

Health

In May, you are healthy, energetic, a social butterfly, and very attractive. With these qualities in tow, there is no reason to fear any illness.

AQUARIUS

Your task is to shore up your position, and it seems that you are well on your way to doing just that. Another, freer, more inspired life awaits.

Work

During the first 20 days of May, business owners and managers at every level will be successfully tying up loose ends with meticulous tasks related to expanding your business. You may be dealing with real estate, construction, repairs at production sites, or perhaps acquiring land. Things are coming to a close, and most likely, the lion's share of the work is already done.

Those who work in construction can expect particular success – business is booming and bringing in the corresponding income.

Employees might take on a more active role in overhauling their organization, something they recently began. Alternatively, you might take some time away from work and focus on your household issues, where major changes are also underway.

During the last 10 days of May, things will change abruptly. Here, powerful Jupiter, the planet of success, is changing signs, and thus your entire ambiance. A more interesting time is beginning, and you will be able to show your colleagues and a wider public what you can really do.

Money

Financially, May is a stable time for you. You will have your usual income coming in, along with earnings from various real estate transactions.

You might also receive favorable credit or help from a sponsor. Don't rule out support from parents or a loved one.

In some cases, you may even come into an inheritance.

Love and family

There are changes afoot at home, too. Here, you are dealing with construction, repairs, and other home-improvement matters.

The worst is over, and now, you can sit down and tie up the loose ends.

Your relationship with your family is calm and harmonious, and couples who recently went through a rough patch are once again able to enjoy their relationship, thanks to their hard work.

During the last 10 days of the month, you might be busy with your children. Here, they are beginning a winning streak, and you will have to provide them with the necessary support.

In late May and all of June, those who have long been waiting for a partner are in for a ride. This endeavor will now become easier than it has been recently, a trend that will last all year!

Health

In May, your health is strong, though you may tend to gain weight, so keep an eye on your diet and watch what you eat. During the last 10 days of the month, you would be wise to take some time off, you deserve it!

PISCES

May will go down in history as an exciting, busy, positive time for you. Things are moving and changing, which is great!

Work

The main trend this month is still developing your ties to other cities and abroad. You recently completed a lot of work in this direction, and now, you can reap the rewards.

Everything you planned on doing, you will do, and expect to explore new spaces in the near future.

Closer to the end of the month, those planning on a move or opening a business in another city or abroad will be able to consider what kind of real estate they need in order to make that happen. This year, you will be sure to find what you need.

Employees will start to want something of their own, perhaps opening a family business, and you can count on help from a relative.

Many Pisceans will meet new people, who might be helpful in the future. Reconnecting with old friends might lead to cooperation with former business partners.

Any business trips planned this month will be a smashing success.

Money

Your finances are looking stable, and you will have a regular income, and not only from work. You may also receive support from business partners or loved ones.

Love and family

There are plenty of changes happening in your home life, as well. Those planning a move to another city or abroad this month will see their wishes come true. All of your preparations are complete, you've overcome all the hurdles, and nothing can get in your way, now. By the last 10 days of May, many Pisceans will be busy with household matters, for example, looking for a new place to live, or if you have already done that, making home improvements.

Single people will have an excellent opportunity for a fateful meeting, which may happen while you are traveling or among people from far away.

Health

All month, you are feeling healthy, energetic, and ready to move mountains. You may not even have to – the mountains might just come to you, first.

June

New York Time			London Time		
Calendar Day	Lunar Day	Lunar Day Start Time	Calendar Day	Lunar Day	Lunar Day Start Time
01/06/24	25	2.19 AM	01/06/24	25	2.19 AM
02/06/24	26	2.49 AM	02/06/24	26	2.39 AM
03/06/24	27	3.21 AM	03/06/24	27	3.01 AM
04/06/24	28	3.56 AM	04/06/24	28	3.26 AM
05/06/24	29	4.37 AM	05/06/24	29	3.57 AM
06/06/24	30	5.24 AM	06/06/24	30	4.36 AM
06/06/24	1	8.40 AM	06/06/24	1	1.40 PM
07/06/24	2	6.18 AM	07/06/24	2	5.25 AM
08/06/24	3	7.17 AM	08/06/24	3	6.24 AM
09/06/24	4	8.19 AM	09/06/24	4	7.30 AM
10/06/24	5	9.22 AM	10/06/24	5	8.39 AM
11/06/24	6	10.23 AM	11/06/24	6	9.49 AM
12/06/24	7	11.23 AM	12/06/24	7	10.58 AM
13/06/24	8	12.22 PM	13/06/24	8	12.05 PM
14/06/24	9	1.20 PM	14/06/24	9	1.11 PM
15/06/24	10	2.18 PM	15/06/24	10	2.17 PM
16/06/24	11	3.17 PM	16/06/24	11	3.24 PM
17/06/24	12	4.17 PM	17/06/24	12	4.32 PM
18/06/24	13	5.19 PM	18/06/24	13	5.42 PM
19/06/24	14	6.22 PM	19/06/24	14	6.53 PM
20/06/24	15	7.25 PM	20/06/24	15	8.01 PM
21/06/24	16	8.24 PM	21/06/24	16	9.04 PM
22/06/24	17	9.18 PM	22/06/24	17	9.57 PM
23/06/24	18	10.06 PM	23/06/24	18	10.40 PM
24/06/24	19	10.46 PM	24/06/24	19	11.14 PM
25/06/24	20	11.22 PM	25/06/24	20	11.42 PM
26/06/24	21	11.53 PM	27/06/24	21	12.05 AM
28/06/24	22	12.23 AM	28/06/24	22	12.25 AM
29/06/24	23	12.52 AM	29/06/24	23	12.45 AM
30/06/24	24	1.23 AM	30/06/24	24	1.06 AM

You can find the description of each lunar day in the chapter "A Guide to The Moon Cycle and Lunar Days"

ARIES

June is a great time to show off all your achievements to the world. Don't let the chance pass you by!

Work

From a business perspective, June is a time for smashing success. This is especially the case during the first 10 days, when you are bursting with energy and ready to complete any task.

During this time, you will be spending more time talking to colleagues in other cities or abroad, and you might take a trip that will turn out in your favor. During this time, you may also see influential and powerful people appear around you, and their help may be just what you need to climb mountains.

From June 9-18, things are not quite as lucky, and you may have to grapple with some annoying headwinds at work, which you will manage to overcome successfully during the last 10 days of the month. In order to smooth things over, the stars recommend that you keep a close eye on any documents and carefully follow foreign countries' laws.

Business owners and managers of every level may catch the attention of government auditing agencies. Alternatively, you might have to handle difficulties stemming once again from colleagues who live far away. The stars recommend that you look into all potential options and select the most appropriate one. Knowledge is power.

During the last 10 days of June, things will be calmer, and many Aries will be busy with administrative or organizational tasks.

Money

Financially, things are less rosy for you in June, compared to last month. You are earning less but spending a little more. Expect to spend the most on June 10, 11, and 18-19.

After raking in so much money in May, it might be time to invest some of that money, perhaps in work, or your personal life.

Love and family

Those focused on their personal lives will also be focused on places further afield, and perhaps you will take a trip or even move. Of course, moving to another city or abroad is not something that happens overnight, but you have the entire year ahead of you to make that happen.

You will be spending more time with relatives who live far away, perhaps you will travel to see them or one of them will come and stay with you.

Those who have spent a long time looking for their better half will be embarking on a romantic time. You will have an excellent opportunity to meet someone interesting, and that will probably happen while traveling or among people from far away. This trend will continue all year, but June, especially the first 10 days of the month, is the best time of all.

During the last 10 days of June, Aries will be busy with their home and family, which will continue into July.

Any trips for fun would be best for the first or last 10 days of the month, as June 9-18 will be difficult and somewhat risky.

Health

In June, you are feeling energetic and have no reason to fear falling ill. From June 9-18, however, be careful when traveling or driving..

There is a likelihood of conflict or accidents during that time.

TAURUS

This month, a series of activities will play out, just the way you need them to. Recently, you made the right choice, and now you are reaping the rewards, especially at work and at the bank.

Work

June is not a bad time at all for anything work-related. Business owners and managers at every level will have an opportunity to make their achievements shine, especially during the first 10 days of the month. You may even receive new, large-scale, and lucrative offers.

Despite all the success, the stars recommend that you keep an eye on things, because during the second 10 days of June, there is trouble looming on the horizon – and you may be the culprit, here. Your recent success has gone to your head, and this is a straight path to conflict with influential, powerful people. The stars recommend that you don't exaggerate your abilities and remember that in any situation, modesty is better than pride.

You won't have to wait for the backlash, which will be overwhelming.

You will overcome all of this during the last 10 days of the month, but some residue will remain.

This goes for managers and business owners, as well as employees, who will likely face real issues with the higher-ups from June 9-19.

After June 20, you will be spending more time talking to colleagues in other cities or abroad, and you might either take a trip or begin planning one.

Money

June is a great time for your finances, especially the first 10 days of the month. During this time, you might come into a large sum of money, which will seriously strengthen your financial position.

During the second 10 days, you can expect both conflict and even devastation. Many Taureans will be forced to part with their money, either due to work or debts, as well as responsibilities you recently took on.

Love and family

During the first 20 days of June, you will be busy with work and other stress, and your personal life might go on the back burner, for lack of time and energy.

The last 10 days of the month will be more interesting from a family and romantic perspective, when you will have the free time to yourself and your loved ones. You might take a trip during this period, meet up with old friends and relatives, or people you have not seen in a long time.

Those in romantic relationships will strengthen their bonds, and single people will have an opportunity to meet someone new.

June 9-18 is a hard time for everyone. Many Taureans will experience problems involving their parents or elder family members.

Aggressive Mars will be entering your sign, and its confrontational aspect will make you unyielding, rigid, and ambitious. Remember that, and if you don't want to argue with your loved ones, keep a lid on it.

Health

In June, you are feeling energetic, but from June 9-19, there is a high likelihood of accidents and injury. Remember that and take care of yourself.

GEMINI

Your time has come! Jupiter is in your sign, which means that you will have many chances to make changes in your life – for the better, of course. So keep moving forward!

Work

Many Geminis will be talking to colleagues in other cities or abroad during the first 10 days of June and receive an interesting offer. In some cases, that may totally overhaul your business, or even your life. What's more, everything will happen smoothly, with minimal effort. You will have to change your way of doing things and turn away from anything holding you back.

You will have to deal with this from June 9-19. Business owners will face conflict involving business partners or government agencies, and employees will disagree with management.

Things will start to shift again during the last 10 days of June, when you will have an opportunity to solve your problems. This may actually take place sometime later, so tie up loose ends and don't leave anything for later.

You are beginning a new cycle in your professional and personal life, and its active phase will last at least three years. You are sure to run into changes, but keep in mind that everything happening is for the best, and the stars provide you with unwavering support.

Money

Financially, the best time in June is after June 20. During this time, you will receive income from work completed earlier, and maybe even some dividends. Expect to receive the largest amounts on June 17-19, and 26-28.

Love and family

You are opening a new door in your personal life. Venus, Jupiter, and Mercury will be in your sign for most of the month, which promises serious improvements in your relationship, whether you are dating or married.

After a lot of chatter, single people and those who have been let down by previous entanglements might feel calmer and more confident. Someone will have a fateful meeting this month, while for others it will happen later in 2024 or early in 2025.

From June 9-19, many Geminis will face trouble involving parents or an elder family member.

You may have to help your relatives with both words and deeds.

Health

In June, you are right where you need to be, but from June 9-20, you should be careful when driving and traveling. There is a high likelihood of conflict and accidents.

CANCER

In June, you would be wise to keep your ambitions in check and remember that the more vigorously you strive to reach your goals, the harder you will make things for yourself. Slow and steady wins the race.

Work

Jupiter is shifting signs, which means abrupt changes in your situation. You will have less people around you, but more problems. Things will be quiet during the first 10 days of the month, but from June 9-19, expect a lot of challenges your way. Many Cancers will be dealing with past legal problems, or perhaps old debts or obligations will rear their ugly heads once again. You may even receive an unexpected visit from an auditing agency, so business owners and managers at every level need to be ready.

Employees would be wise to remember that their shortcomings and flaws will be more noticeable right now, and act accordingly.

You may deal with intrigue among colleagues and competition or come into undesirable information. Be very cautious and quiet during this difficult period.

Those with ties abroad will also face unpredictable situations. Slowly but surely, you will run into headwinds and even breakdowns starting around June 10, and don't expect any relief until after the 20th.

The last 10 days of the month will be calmer, and one way or another, your problems will start to resolve themselves, but that's no reason to let your guard down. Later on, things may repeat themselves, and the second time around will probably be more difficult.

Money

Your wallet will take a beating in June. You will be spending constantly and expect to spend the most during the second 10 days of the month. Overall, you are beginning a long period in which you will have to keep an eye on your money, as for various reasons, you may suddenly find yourself with much less of it.

Love and family

Your personal life is in a lull, right now. Your relationship with your spouse or better half might grow much cooler, or for various reasons, start to fade away.

In that case, the second 10 days of the month are the hardest. You may have a disagreement over various issues involving money, or alternatively, you may have clashing world views and values systems.

During the last 10 days of June, things will once again become peaceful, and you will be able to restore harmony to your lives. However, all year long, Jupiter is in the sector of the sky that is unfavorable to you, which means that your problems in June may repeat themselves from time to time.

Health

Those who manage to escape any professional or personal strife might instead face health issues.

Those who have old, chronic diseases might experience a relapse. The hardest time here is June 9-20, when, in addition to illnesses, you might also face a high chance of accidents and injury. It is not worth traveling during this time, either near or far, and the stars recommend being careful behind the wheel.

L E O

June looks a little like an obstacle course. But you don't have to get used to it, for some time now, you've been charging ahead!

Work

The first 10 days of June stand to be a highly successful time for you. This would be a good time to start not only your most important tasks, but also your most important meetings. You might meet new people and business partners who will offer wide-ranging and beneficial cooperation. However, when discussing this new job or project, pay very close attention to the financial side of things, in order to avoid trouble down the road. Questions such as who owes whom, and who needs to do what might crop up in the near future, and it's better to nip them in the bud. Agree on the terms before you launch.

During the second 10 days of the month, things will be much more difficult. During this time, you might disagree with past business partners, and the reason will probably be over money or debt obligations.

Things will calm down after June 20, which will be peaceful, or at least neutral. This is not a bad time for making compromises, but it is worth looking into all the details.

Employees who are starting a new job would be wise to remember that whether or not they get a raise does not yet mean they have won the battle. Your new responsibilities will not be easy. Show those around you how confident you are and learn as you go.

Money

Your finances are looking unstable and unremarkable in June. Many Leos will have to settle debts or fulfill financial obligations, and that may be related to either work or your personal life. The most difficult time here is the second 10 days of the month.

Love and family

Your personal life will see a continuation of the processes you began in the recent past.

Separated and divorced couples might once again discuss how to divide up their property. Your ex's claims are serious, and your task here is to find a compromise you can both live with. That will happen during the last 10 days of the month, but later on, you will have to deal with this issue again.

Alternatively, your partner will run into various challenges, and you will have to lend a helping hand – both morally and financially.

Your children's issues will also require a lot of resources and effort on your part, but this is a sacred duty. Who, if not you?

Couples who have been together for a while might spend some time apart, perhaps because you are extremely busy, due to financial issues, or things have simply cooled off. There's not much you can do, just be patient and this too shall pass.

Those who are still single might expect a fateful meeting, which is very likely during the first 10 days of June.

Health

For much of June, you will be healthy, energetic, and extremely attractive to anyone Fate sends your way. However, during the second 10 days of June, which are the most difficult, you face a high likelihood of injury and accident, so be very careful.

During the last part of the month, you might be tired from work and so many meetings, so the stars recommend you think about taking some time off, which is highly likely in late June or July.

VIRGO

For you, June is one of the busiest times of the year. You have made the right choice, and there is a long road ahead, but you're only just beginning.

Work

The best time for anything work-related is the first 10 days of June. During this time, you will come up with brilliant ideas, and a real chance to bring them to life, too.

For many business owners and managers of every level, your priorities are still your relationship with colleagues in other cities or abroad. You can expect some impressive professional achievements here, which will breathe new life into your business.

Not everything will turn out as you might have hoped, and this will become clear during the second 10 days of the month. During this time, you might run into serious disagreements with business partners over your business development, or perhaps financial issues.

Some of these problems will involve colleagues from far away. Things will improve during the last 10 days of June, when an old friend or someone highly placed in society might bring a peace offering. Thanks to them, your opponents will simmer down, or at least be open to a compromise.

Employees might receive a new job with great opportunities for the future, and you might even start this month.

Money

Financially, this is not a bad time for you at all. You will have money coming in regularly, and significantly more than usual. Most of your expenses will take place during the last part of the month, and they might even be pleasant.

Love and family

During the first 20 days of the month, you will be immersed in work, and your personal life might be on the back burner.

However, those who are totally focused on family or romantic relationships would be wise to keep their eyes open during the second 10 days of June.

During this time, you may experience serious troubles with your loved one, who might ignore your needs, offend you, and appear unaware of everything you are willing to do for him or her. That goes for whether you divorced long ago, are in the middle of divorcing, or your current relationship simply leaves a lot to be desired.

Couples who get along will overcome a series of difficulties together, and thanks to your wisdom and undying love, your partner will be able to get through this rough period.

During all of the potential clashes this month, seek support from a circle of friends. Only they can influence your better half. The best time for this is during the last 10 days of June.

Health

This month, you are full of energy, but during the second 10 days of June, be careful when traveling and driving, especially from June 10-13.

LIBRA

You are embarking on a new future, and it is very promising. Yes, it is what you always dreamed of, but you can also clearly see the shortcomings. But you're a tough cookie, and you can take a lot!

Work

Your main task this month is developing your relationship with colleagues in other cities or abroad. Business owners and managers will be busy with cooperation involving partners from far away, and perhaps you will be opening a business far from home. The best time for this is the first 10 days of June, which is also the best time to plan travel, meetings, or sign any documents. During the second 10 days of the month, things are looking less favorable, and many Libras will have to deal with a series of setbacks, including subordinates who fail to complete their tasks, production issues, or problems related to slowdowns on any cooperation.

However, during the last 10 days of June, things will fall into place, and you will be back on the right track.

Employees will be thinking about a new job, and in the last 10 days of June or perhaps in July, you might get your wish. That may involve frequent travel or a move.

Money

The best time for anything related to money is after June 20. During this time, you can count on large sums of money coming in, a positive trend that will continue throughout July.

You can expect large expenses during the second 10 days of the month, most likely related to your children or loved ones.

In some cases, you might once again have to spend money on your home and continuing repairs, or real estate related to work.

Love and family

Many Libras will be looking at a move to another city or even abroad this month, or perhaps just a new home right where you live now. Your spouse or a loved one might play a major role in this development.

During the second 10 days of June, many families will deal with problems involving their children, and this will require some major expenses. The stars recommend that from June 9-19, you get involved in your older children's affairs, and keep a closer eye on your younger children.

This is also a difficult time for most couples. The root of the problem may be financial in nature, or perhaps differing lifestyles and value systems. Things may come to a head when you least expect it, in the blink of an eye, and in a fit of rate, so hold your tongue and try to control yourself.

Health

During this time, you are feeling energetic and have no reason to fear falling ill. From June 9-19, however, be careful when traveling and driving.

SCORPIO

You are embarking on one of the most difficult months of the year, so it is best not to rush things. The key to stability both at work and in your relationships is to strike an inner balance.

Work

The stars' influence will be most felt when it comes to relaxation and your personal affairs this month.

But if you have to work anyway, the best thing you can do in June is focus on administrative tasks, get your office in order, or spruce up other production spaces.

Business owners and managers will be thinking about expanding their business and taking the first steps in that direction. You will be busy with various real estate transactions or acquiring the best land, which will help grow your business more successfully.

Employees might be thinking about leaving their job to work for a quieter company, perhaps a family business, and opportunities will arise during the last 10 days of the month. From June 20-30 is the best time to start talking to your contacts in other cities or abroad, and you might take a successful trip.

Money

Financially, the second 10 days of June will be a mess for you. During this time, many Scorpios will lose a large sum of money, and most likely, that will be due to your personal life, family demands, or most likely, your children.

Nonetheless, you will not end up in the red, and during the first 10 days, you might actually come into a decent profit from a real estate transaction. You can expect support from your parents, a loved one, or favorable terms of credit, as well.

Love and family

Most Scorpios will be much more focused on home and family this month. You might be busy with repairs, changing up the interior, or even drawing up plans related to a move.

Stormy skies loom ahead during the second 10 days of June. From the 8th to 11, you might unexpectedly experience arguments, which will have longstanding consequences.

The stars recommend that couples, whether they are married or not, tread lightly and avoid pushing your loved one's buttons.

During this time, you may experience trouble involving your children, and that will involve spending a large amount of money. This situation does not look like it will be short-lived, so be attentive to your younger children, and help your older ones however they need it.

Health

In June, you are feeling sluggish, and the most difficult time will be in the middle of the month. During this time, take care of yourself and take any precaution you can.

During the last 10 days of the month, things will be much more favorable. Your energy will be back, and the exhaustion will fade away.

SAGITTARIUS

After a long period of hard work, the time has come for you to stop and take a look around. After all, there's more to life than work!

Work

June is a great time to broaden your horizons and meet new people, as well as show what you can do to a broader audience.

Your relationship with partners from other cities or abroad is developing favorably, and you might receive an interesting offer from colleagues who live far away, or perhaps take a successful trip.

The best time for any type of activity is the first 10 days of the month. Pay special attention during this time, as it might be the springboard for achievements all year long, and into the first half of 2025.

The second 10 days of June do not look so bright. From June 9-19, you might have disagreements with former business partners, probably over real estate issues. Additionally, you might argue with colleagues from far away.

During this time, managers would be wise to keep an eye on subordinates, as they might not show as much helpful initiative as you'd like.

Employees should carefully watch colleagues and avoid any office intrigue.

During the last 10 days of the month, things will be much calmer, and things will start to fall into place, mostly in your favor.

There are still some loose ends related to real estate, which might re-emerge later on, so pay special attention to these issues.

Money

Financially, this is what we might call a neutral month. Your earnings are what they usually are, and you are avoiding serious spending. Expect to receive the largest sums on June 4, 5, 12, 13, 22, 23, 27, and 28. Most of your expenses will take place around the Full Moon, from June 22-23.

Love and family

Your ruler, powerful Jupiter, has crossed into the sector of the sky responsible for love and lasting bonds, and it is supported by fateful Pluto. This changes your relationship with those around you, but the results may vary.

You may meet new people, who might totally change your life. That is good for single people, but for those who already have a partner, you would be wise to tread carefully here. The new arrival may sour your long-term relationship, and you will come out ahead in the end. The choice is yours, but the burden is, too...

Spouses who get along will be pleased with each other's success, as they advance at work.

During the second 10 days of the month, couples on the rocks might be busy resolving issues related to real estate, which will only lead to more conflict.

During this time, couples who get along will work together to overcome various issues related to their home.

Any trips planned in June will be a great success, especially if they happen during the first or third 10 days of the month. During the second 10 days, expect conflict, as well as injuries and setbacks. Be careful.

Health

This month, you are not feeling particularly energetic, and the stars recommend that you take utmost care of your body. Watch what you eat, don't overdo things, and get enough sleep. Closer to the end of the month, you will have time to relax, and it is worth using this opportunity to head to a warm, sunny beach or perhaps a vacation home.

During the second 10 days of the month, be careful driving and traveling.

CAPRICORN

Jupiter's shifting means one thing for you – less freedom, more work. Rather than focusing on leisure this month, remember that it takes a lot of work to get to where you want to be.

Work

June is a busy time, full of work and various tasks for you. Expect some real achievements during the first 10 days of the month, when business owners and managers will receive offers for new projects, and employees might be invited to accept a new job or additional responsibilities right where they are.

This will be incredibly beneficial to you and will likely strengthen your financial and material position.

Your relationship with colleagues in other cities and abroad is still important, but during the second 10 days of June, you can expect a series of difficulties here. You might argue over who owes whom and how much. During the last 10 days of the month, however, things will relax a little. It is not worth letting your guard down, however – some time later, these problems will come up again. In all things work-related, your friends or perhaps a business partner will act as an intermediary, and with their help, you will be able to navigate the thorniest issues.

Money

Financially, the best time for you is the first 10 days of June, when many Capricorns will be able to count on a large sum of money or other material benefits.

Expect significant expenses during the second 10 days of the month, and the stars predict that they will be related to your romantic affairs or family.

During the last part of June, things are looking neutral, though you can count on large sums on June 15, 16, and 24-25.

Love and family

Your personal life might be less busy than work during the first 20 days of June, however, those who can't imagine life without love or family will also have to deal with a series of challenges this month.

During the second 10 days of June, expect sudden arguments with your spouse or partner. The reason will vary – whether it is over money or clashing world views.

During this time, spouses will face problems involving their children, and this will lead to some serious spending on your part. You might have to provide support once again for the younger members of your family, whether moral or material.

Disagreements with your relatives may also become a theme during this time, and you will argue over old responsibilities, which are both moral and financial in nature. During the last 10 days of the month, however, things will settle down, but it is likely that these issues will pop up again sometime later on.

Health

In June, you are not feeling particularly energetic, and this is a good time for quitting bad habits and otherwise taking care of yourself.

Create a clear plan and find the time to relax or visit a spa. Inner balance is not only the key to success this month, but in the future as well, both at work and in your relationships.

AQUARIUS

You've finished an important project or at least the most difficult part of it, and that means a lot. A weight has been lifted off your shoulders, and after all the bothersome day-to-day tasks, you're beginning a new, more exciting, and creative phase.

Work

During the first 20 days of June, many Aquarians might find themselves far more focused on their personal lives than work.

However, the incurable workaholics might be doing a lot for their business. First of all, they will have an important opportunity to show what they can do to colleagues or a wider audience, and secondly, they will meet a lot of new people.

Employees might be busy with something new, where more depends on their creativity and talent. Maybe that's a new job, or perhaps a promotion.

Business owners will be completing major projects related to expanding their business, organizational tasks, and construction. Things will be much more pleasant going forward, but you will be doing work that is just as important, or perhaps polishing what you already completed.

For many, the best time for anything work-related is before June 10 or after June 20. During the second 10 days of the month, you can expect to face various problems. Perhaps fantasy will exceed your financial realities, and you will have to search for additional resources in order to bring your ideas to life.

Another problem may be your unwillingness to make peace with the shortcomings of a previous job, and you will have to be the one to make the corrections. Going forward, you might say that most of these troubles will be resolved during the last 10 days of June, which looks peaceful, busy, and productive.

Money

Financially, the best time for you is the last 10 days of June. During this time, you will have regular earnings, which will significantly reduce the stress that has haunted you during the second 10 days of the month.

Most Aquarians will have significant expenses related to their personal life and family's or children's needs.

Love and family

Things are booming in your personal life in June. Many Aquarians will find themselves frequent guests at parties and birthdays.

During this flurry of events, you might meet someone interesting and somehow change up your life. The romantic period at the beginning of the month will last all year long. This is a good thing if you are single, but it may bring a whole host of problems if you are already partnered up.

Few people can lead a double life, and you are not one of them. So remember, a bird in hand is better than two in the bush, and act accordingly. That is especially the case for Aquarian men, as Aquarian women tend to be faithful, calm, and reliable.

During the second 10 days of the month, expect many problems with your children, which will entail a lot of spending on your part.

Disagreements with your spouse over how to set up your home may be another source of conflict during the second 10 days of June. The argument might take an unexpected direction and sour your relationship for some time.

Therefore, remain diplomatic and don't give into any of your partner's aggression.

Health

For most of June, you are feeling energetic and only during the last 10 days will you start to feel any fatigue or tiredness.

Be careful and take care of yourself during the Full Moon on June 22-23. These will be the most difficult days of the month.

PISCES

It is time to make a decision, set down some roots, and build your life differently. Daydreaming is a luxury you just don't have right now, so take out your planner and write down your dreams, without forgetting how you're going to make them happen.

Work

This month, things are changing for you. If you are planning on a move or opening your business in another city or abroad, you might be looking at real estate or production spaces. That is a difficult, bothersome task, but the road is paved by those who walk it. The same goes for those busy rebuilding their business in their native land.

The best time for any administrative or organizational tasks is the first or last 10 days of June. During this period, you may be very busy getting your business in shape.

During the second 10 days of June, it is not worth rushing anything. Expect some disagreements with business partners in other cities or abroad, or alternatively, difficulties with foreign laws. During the last part of the month, some of this will be partially resolved, and what's left will be settled during different periods of 2024.

Money

Your finances are looking neutral, and you will get what you deserve. No more, no less.

Love and family

Those who are focused on their family lives rather than work can also expect changes. This is only natural, as you've been preparing them all year long, and now it is time to start putting things into motion. Those who are moving somewhere far away will be busy looking for a new home, and that already happened recently, then you can expect to be busy with repairs or other household tasks. You have the rest of the year ahead of you, and time is on your side.

Those remaining in their home country might be considering a new, more comfortable place to live.

Things will be great during the first and last 10 days of the month, but from June 11-20, there is trouble on the horizon.

Spouses might disagree over how they are setting up or purchasing their home, but during the last days of the month, you will manage to come to an agreement. Your children might act as intermediaries here, and their influence on family life will be unusually positive.

Health

You have enough energy this month and have no reason to fear falling ill. However, many Pisceans will tend to gain weight, so eat a healthy diet and try to move around more, perhaps consider signing up for a gym membership.

July

New York Time			London Time		
Calendar Day	Lunar Day	Lunar Day Start Time	Calendar Day	Lunar Day	Lunar Day Start Time
01/07/24	25	1.56 AM	01/07/24	25	1.30 AM
02/07/24	26	2.34 AM	02/07/24	26	1.58 AM
03/07/24	27	3.17 AM	03/07/24	27	2.32 AM
04/07/24	28	4.07 AM	04/07/24	28	3.16 AM
05/07/24	29	5.03 AM	05/07/24	29	4.10 AM
05/07/24	1	6.59 PM	05/07/24	1	11.59 PM
06/07/24	2	6.04 AM	06/07/24	2	5.13 AM
07/07/24	3	7.07 AM	07/07/24	3	6.21 AM
08/07/24	4	8.10 AM	08/07/24	4	7.32 AM
09/07/24	5	9.11 AM	09/07/24	5	8.42 AM
10/07/24	6	10.11 AM	10/07/24	6	9.50 AM
11/07/24	7	11.09 AM	11/07/24	7	10.57 AM
12/07/24	8	12.07 PM	12/07/24	8	12.03 PM
13/07/24	9	1.05 PM	13/07/24	9	1.09 PM
14/07/24	10	2.04 PM	14/07/24	10	2.16 PM
15/07/24	11	3.04 PM	15/07/24	11	3.24 PM
16/07/24	12	4.06 PM	16/07/24	12	4.34 PM
17/07/24	13	5.09 PM	17/07/24	13	5.43 PM
18/07/24	14	6.10 PM	18/07/24	14	6.48 PM
19/07/24	15	7.07 PM	19/07/24	15	7.46 PM
20/07/24	16	7.58 PM	20/07/24	16	8.35 PM
21/07/24	17	8.42 PM	21/07/24	17	9.13 PM
22/07/24	18	9.21 PM	22/07/24	18	9.44 PM
23/07/24	19	9.55 PM	23/07/24	19	10.09 PM
24/07/24	20	10.26 PM	24/07/24	20	10.31 PM
25/07/24	21	10.56 PM	25/07/24	21	10.52 PM
26/07/24	22	11.26 PM	26/07/24	22	11.12 PM
27/07/24	23	11.58 PM	27/07/24	23	11.35 PM
29/07/24	24	12.34 AM	29/07/24	24	12.01 AM
30/07/24	25	1.15 AM	30/07/24	25	12.33 AM
31/07/24	26	2.03 AM	31/07/24	26	1.14 AM

You can find the description of each lunar day in the chapter "A Guide to The Moon Cycle and Lunar Days"

ARIES

This warm summer month puts you in a softer, nicer mood. Things are on the right track, and "My home is my castle" is your motto this month.

Work

Despite the stars' influence is more geared toward relaxation or family matters this month, the incurable workaholics among us might still make a lot of progress with their business development.

Business owners and managers will find a good opportunity to perfect their current production space, offices, and anything else involving real estate. Fortunately, you will find the money to make it happen.

Employees might take some time off and spend most of the time working on their homes. If you are stuck at work, your mind will be far away.

Your relationship with colleagues in other cities or abroad is still important, and during the last 10 days of the month, many Aries will go on a trip. There's nothing that says you can't combine business with pleasure- relaxing in good company while also discussing your current business affairs.

Money

July is a stable time for your finances. You will have regular earnings, and in addition to your usual income, you might also count on support from partners, as well as profits from successful real estate transactions.

You will likely receive financial support from your parents, spouse, or loved one.

Most of your expenses will take place during the last 10 days of July, and they will likely be related to your family's and children's needs.

Love and family

For most Aries, July will be a time to focus on your personal and family life. Expect a lot of pleasant developments here. You will be getting your home in order, and your entire family will take part in the meticulous tasks involved. Your relationship with your family is unusually calm, warm, and harmonious. It seems that your family has rallied around each other, and you will feel your loved ones' support in literally everything you have to do.

During the last 10 days of July or the first half of August, you will probably take a trip, which, like everything else this month, will be a great success.

Health

In July, you are feeling a little less energetic than usual, which might translate into a sense of laziness, or a desire for calm and relaxation. Remember that the office will not fall apart if you step away for a few days and give your body what it needs.

TAURUS

July opens up a lot of opportunities, whether relaxing in places you have been before, success at work, or perhaps a new job. It's up to you, but you're in charge!

Work

Your main task this month will be developing your connection with colleagues in other cities or abroad. You may begin doing just that if you are a business owner or manager.

This time, things will go the way you need them to, without arguments, setbacks, or other issues.

In whatever you do this month, you will be able to count on help from old friends or people who are highly placed in society, and your relationship with them will noticeably improve.

Employees will go on a business trip, where they will have a chance to shine. The stars still recommend keeping your ambition in check, however, and keeping management at arm's length. At the very least, be diplomatic and don't let your head get too big.

The best time for anything work-related is the first 20 days of July. During the last 10 days, things will be less dynamic, and you might take advantage of this to take some vacation time or focus on your home and family.

Money

Financially, July is not a bad time for you at all. Jupiter, the planet of success, is spending a long time in the financial sector of your sky, which means that money is one thing you don't have to worry about anymore. All of your expenses are low, and you have enough income to cover them, meaning that you can be bold and confident as you look toward the future.

Love and family

Those who are focused on their personal lives this month can also count on travel and seeing relatives, as well as old acquaintances.

After a recent disagreement, your relationship with your partner will improve again, and the astrologist predicts that both sides will easily reconcile with one another.

Many Taureans will see their relatives play an important role in both their professional and personal lives. They will be on a positive streak and more than happy to share that with you.

Your relationship with your parents is difficult, and you can expect disagreements with them all month long, especially after July 20. It is difficult to pinpoint the reason why, but there is reason for concern.

During the last 10 days of the month, you will be busy with your family and household duties, or perhaps a well-deserved vacation – the choice is yours. Generally speaking, you are having a great summer.

Health

In July, you are healthy, energetic, and seeing success on all fronts, both at home and at work.

GEMINI

You are in for a surprising month, with no trouble on the horizon. Yes, sometimes that just happens, and those who work in creative fields or finance can expect particular success.

Work

The first 20 days of July are the best time for anything involving work. You will be able to stand out, both for your patience and concentration, as well as for your willingness to think outside of the box. That is a great combination, which is sure to lead to real success at work.

A difficult relationship with management or perhaps a government institution will normalize one way or another, and this time, things will run smoothly, without any setbacks or trouble.

Business owners will receive handsome profits from previously completed work and begin working on a new project.

Employees can count on a raise or well-deserved dividends.

During the last 10 days of the month, you will be speaking more frequently to colleagues in other cities or abroad, and you might take a trip or start preparing for one.

Overall, things are going well for you here, but you might sometimes need to put in more effort in order to bring your ideas to life.

Money

July is a great time for your wallet. You will have regular earnings, both from your normal income, as well as from unofficial sources.

Expect to receive the largest sums on July 5, 6, 15, 16, 24, and 25.

Your expenses are low and mostly take place during the last 10 days of the month.

Love and family

The first 20 days of July will not be easy, and most Geminis will find themselves utterly focused on work and money. The last 10 days are a better time for anything romantic, as is all of August. During this time, those with families might take some time off of work, so your growing income will make things as comfortable as possible.

You might also visit relatives who live in other cities or abroad, or also people who you have not seen for a long time.

Jupiter is in your sign, and its friendly aspect with Venus is good for those who have not yet found a partner. You have a high chance of doing just that, so be sure to spend a lot of time interacting with others and always look your best.

Couples who have been together for a while might deepen their relationship and think about marriage. You can expect to make some pleasant decisions this month.

Health

In July, you are feeling great and have no reason to fear falling ill. Your vibrant energy may overwhelm those around you!

CANCER

This month is better than the last. You might not get everything you want on the first try, but be patient, and things will work out.

Work

The biggest trend this month is that you will be able to smooth over your relationship with colleagues in other cities or abroad. This will be thanks to your own efforts, as your business partners will not be trying too hard here. Many issues will be resolved in your favor now, but the problems will repeat themselves a little later.

Alternatively, you may have to grapple with legal issues from the past, but here, both old friends and new acquaintances will come to your aid. Keep in mind, however, that your legal issues are long and arduous, and highly unlikely to be resolved overnight. Each tiny step forward is vital through, and the road belongs to those who walk it.

Employees will also see improvements, though this process will take shape somewhat later. Another positive side of this month is that you will spend more time talking to old and new friends. You will need their support, both now and later on, so keep well-wishers around you, as it will make things much easier.

Money

Financially, the best time for you is during the second half of July. During this period, you will receive support from powerful Venus, which means that money will be coming in, and you can expect the largest sums on July 7, 8, 17, 19, 26, and 27.

Of course there are always expenses, but by the end of the month, you will still be in the black.

Love and family

Your personal life is also noticeably better these days. You are receiving support from Mercury, Venus, and the Sun, which will allow you to smooth over last month's disagreements, and you are sure to enjoy the sympathy of those around you.

Many Cancers will go on a trip and bring loved ones with them. The second half of the month is a good time to improve your home or successful shopping trips.

Those planning on buying a new home might make that happen during the last 10 days of the month.

Health

This month, you are feeling much better, but that's no reason to put yourself to the test with excess. You have the whole year ahead of you, and watching your health is going to be much more important than usual, especially if you are elderly or weakened. If that is you, lead a healthy lifestyle and regularly take preventive measures when it comes to chronic illnesses.

LEO

This month you are in a stable, serious mood. These are great qualities, and the key to success, both at work and at home.

Work

July is a time for major transformations at work, especially with anything administrative in nature. Business owners and managers might grow their opportunities, and in many cases, that will involve repairs, redevelopment, and other tasks involving production spaces.

Your problems from last month are partially resolved, now, and that probably includes your relationship with friends, business partners, and people in positions of power. Right now, things are quieter, but it's not worth letting your guard down. Later on, you will address these issues again, most likely as disagreements over money or clashing views over your business development.

Employees might spend some time away from work, you may take some vacation days to focus on your loved ones and yourself.

But you will spend most of the month at work, as both management and employees will have their hands tied with the various changes underway.

Money

This month, your bank account is looking stable, and you might receive support from business partners, or in the form of subsidies and credit. Those who are not part of the working world can count on help from loved ones.

Love and family

Many Leos will be more focused on their personal lives this month. Spouses who get along might work together to resolve various household tasks, and closer to the end of the month, they will be resolved in your favor.

Those who recently separated or are in the middle of a divorce can expect some turbulence and strong emotions. Despite all of the clashes and fighting, some strange thoughts might sneak up on you. You may find yourself wondering if you can turn things back, or if separation is really necessary. The stars predict that anything is possible, and it never hurts to try, especially if you have children together.

Right now, Saturn's energy has you leaning toward reconciliation. However, only you can decide. Make a list of all the pros and cons, and act accordingly.

Health

In July, you are not feeling particularly energetic, and that might be noticeable during the New Moon, on July 5-6, or the Full Moon on July 19-21.

Keep an eye on your body, and don't overdo things with food or drink.

Right now, both the quality and quantity of your food is a key factor in how you feel.

July is a great time to relax, so find a week or two and take some time for yourself.

VIRGO

The big decisions you previously made are starting to bear out. This month, you will see that happen at work, with your finances, and your personal relationships.

Work

In July, your troubles from last month will have been resolved, and a difficult relationship with business partners will now bring you to a positive dialogue. In that case, your friends or someone highly placed may act as an intermediary. Keep in mind as well that a lean compromise is better than a fat lawsuit – that goes for both you and your adversaries. However, any harmony you achieve here might be delicate, and any arguments might repeat themselves in the near future. So do everything in your power and prepare stable ground for your upcoming clashes.

Your relationship with colleagues from other cities or abroad is now actively developing. In addition to former partners, you will also be dealing with new acquaintances, who will give you the support you need, when you need it.

Any trips planned for July will turn out successfully and help promote your projects at a new level of development and prosperity.

Employees will be able to strengthen their position, as well. If you recently began a new job, right now, the time has come to make your voice heard on your team. If you are looking for a new place for your talents, you might talk to old connections, who will be able to help you get what you want.

Money

Your financial position is looking stable, overall. Your expenses are in line with your income, and closer to the end of the month, you will still be in the black.

Love and family

Your personal life isn't easy, but it's on an extremely exciting and positive streak right now. Severe Saturn is firmly in the sector of the sky responsible for love, long-term relationships, and marriages, which has many Virgos separating or pulling away from their partners. But Saturn is now turning to another, lighter side, which will give many an opportunity to reconsider and possibly reconcile. The anger and rage will fade away, and for the first time in many months, you will be able to really feel things and reevaluate.

You might benefit from support from your friends or your shared children, and events that bring you together during this wonderful summer month.

Single people might spend time with new friends, and the warm connections and atmosphere might lead to something more. There are many opportunities this month, and it's up to you to take advantage of them.

Health

During the first 20 days of July, you are feeling fairly energetic and have no reason to fear falling ill. Your charm, sparkling sense of humor, and clear mind will grow even stronger. During the last 10 days of the month, you might feel a bit of fatigue from all of the activities this month.

July is a time for relaxation, and the stars urge you to take advantage of that.

LIBRA

July is a wonderful month that will live up to your boldest expectations. Strive for your highest goals, and you will achieve them all.

Work

July is a month for large-scale major events and accomplishments. You might even say that you haven't had a month like this in a long time. Managers and business owners will be at the negotiating table discussing everything they need. You will have a good start on new projects and from the very beginning, things will be on your side.

Your relationship with colleagues in other cities and abroad is coming along well this month. Recent problems over various issues have settled down a bit, and some friends or someone highly placed might take part in negotiations. Alternatively, your logic, diplomacy, patience, and ability to work over long distances will play an important role here.

With these qualities and the support of the stars, you will make great strides when it comes to business and your career. This applies to both business owners and employees.

Finally, it is important to keep in mind that if you want a new job, there's no better time than now. For anything work-related, all of July is a great time, especially the first 20 days of the month.

Money

Your success at work is being reflected in your bank account. Your material status will improve, and expect to receive the largest sums on July 5, 6, 15, 16, 24, and 25.

Most of your expenses will take place after July 20, and the astrologist predicts that they may be pleasant and personal in nature.

Love and family

July is a busy time at work, which means that many Libras will not have love and romance on their mind.

In order to avoid problems, explain to your loved ones just how busy you are, and they will be sure to understand and lend you their support.

The last 10 days of July look much calmer.

During this time, many Libras will be frequent guests at parties, birthdays, and other celebrations, and will happily share joyous experiences with their loved ones. You might take a trip, which is sure to be a huge success.

Your relationship with your children is difficult, and this will require a delicate hand and a lot of attention on your part. It is impossible to determine exactly what will happen in each individual case, but there will be reason for concern.

Health

This month, you are healthy, energetic, attractive, and you are leaving a lasting impression on everyone Fate sends your way.

SCORPIO

This month, you are overcome with a desire for movement and change. That's no surprise – sitting still and doing the same thing over and over again is not your style!

Work

Despite all of the administrative tasks that you still have to deal with, you are now busy with traveling and active communication with colleagues from other cities and abroad. The great news is that right now, you can be sure to receive support from leaders and power structures, and other powers that be. Your ability to negotiate and get along with others is especially important right now. All of that means that July is a time of great success and promise.

There's another plus here – July is a great time for reconnecting with old friends and making new acquaintances.

It is possible that all of this will happen on a trip or among people from somewhere far away.

If you want a new job or new responsibilities, you will be busy with negotiations and laying the groundwork to make a move later on.

Money

Financially, July is a neutral month. Your income is modest, though your expenses are also low. The astrologist predicts that in some cases, you will be investing in business, or possibly your personal life.

Love and family

July is a great time for your personal life, too. Your relationship with your partner or spouse is much better these days, and you might even describe things as idyllic.

Your relationship with your children is also much better. If you recently had a serious argument, now might be the time to reconcile.

Children and parents who have been separated by time and distance will have a happy reunion. You might take a trip, which will be a great success.

If you want to and are able to take time off to relax, the best destination is somewhere you have been before, in order to avoid being disappointed or other problems.

Health

This month, you are feeling significantly better, and any illnesses from last month will be an unhappy memory.

SAGITTARIUS

In July, you will have to divide your attention between work and personal issues, but you will manage it all! Don't get used to it!

Work

July is an ideal time to resolve a series of administrative and financial matters. On one hand, you will have the energy to overcome any challenges, and on the other, you will have the patience and diplomatic skills to avoid any errors. Thirdly, the stars promise you their golden light will remove any obstacles you might have run into in the recent past.

Business owners and managers will be revising their space and might be busy with minor repairs. Your business is growing, and that expansion requires another approach, as well as additional agreements.

Employees will focus on family matters, but that doesn't mean that you can't also hold your own at work. In other words, you're everywhere, all at once!

Most of your administrative and organizational tasks will take place during the first 20 days of July. During the last 10 days of the month, you will notice that the mood has shifted. You will be spending more time talking to colleagues in other cities and abroad, and you might take a trip or plan one.

Money

July isn't a bad time for your finances. In addition to your usual earnings, you might see profits from successful real estate transactions, or perhaps other sources, as well.

If you want to take out credit, there's no better time than now. Those who are not part of the working world might receive help from parents or a loved one. In any case, your income will be far higher than your expenses, which is already a good thing.

Love and family

Many Sagittarians will be fully focused on their personal lives this month. You are busy with various real estate transactions – repairs, selling an old home, and buying a new one. All of this will go surprisingly well, without any setbacks or trouble.

Your relationship with your spouse is noticeably improved after some tension in June, as the peace you so desired has arrived on your doorstep.

The stars always recommend keeping harmony in your relationships, as things may change in the future, and problems will come back again.

That goes for those who have been facing various conflicts with their parents.

Your relationship with your relatives is both better and worse. Here, things are looking unstable, but gradually, they are trending toward a resolution, and that is worth supporting. You haven't achieved total unity just yet, but you are getting there.

Couples will be dealing with various administrative matters, and perhaps you are discussing moving in together.

During the last 10 days of the month you will make plans related to a vacation and travel in the near future.

Health

In July, your restless spirit is stronger than your body, so try to relax more and remember that health comes first.

CAPRICORN

This month, there's no harm in dreaming, quite the contrary. Your wishes will come true, without too much effort on your part.

Work

July is a great time to improve your relationships with people and build new ties, as well. Difficult relationships with colleagues in other cities or abroad are slowly looking up. This stresses you out, but a business partner or other well-wisher might act as an intermediary.

Of course, a lot of this depends on you. Be open to communication and remember that right now, you are a team player, and together, you and your partners can cover a lot of ground.

July is a great time for anyone who works in the creative fields – actors, artists, singers, journalists. Even if your job has nothing to do with those professions, nothing is stopping you from giving your own creative touch to everything you do.

The best time for anything work-related is the first 20 days of July. During the last 10 days of the month, you will feel sluggish and maybe for that reason, a lot of Capricorns will take time away from work.

Money

Financially, July is an average month for you. Your income is modest, your expenses are in control, and most of them will take place after July 20. You are likely to spend on vacation, your children, and household needs. However, this fall, you will be able to build your balance back up again, and in the end, you are not going to end up penniless, quite the opposite.

Love and family

For many Capricorns, July will bring a lot of feelings of romance. It seems that summer is affecting you more than spring did, and your partner will return to a romantic mood. Your relationship with your spouse or partner is looking rather idyllic these days, something you can't say very often.

Your children will make you happy, but they will need your financial support once again. The last 10 days of July are particularly telling here, when your children will need large sums of money.

Your relationship with relatives is looking somewhat better, and perhaps your spouse or a loved one will play a key role here. However, things are looking far from perfect here, and later on, you will see old problems rear their heads once again.

Health

During the first 20 days of July, you are looking healthy, energetic, and ready to move mountains.

During the last 10 days of the month, however, you are feeling significantly weaker, and the stars urge you to consider forgetting about work for a while.

AQUARIUS

July brings the promise of great success. You will be giving your utmost focus to bringing in results and there are no obstacles standing in your way. So roll up your sleeves and don't waste any time!

Work

July is a time for smashing success at work. Business owners and managers might be preparing a new project and can rely on support from well-wishing subordinates. Employees will be working at maximum capacity, but the stars predict that this will pay off massively in the end. You will be able to significantly improve your relationship with your managers and colleagues, which will go hand in hand with a salary raise.

However, despite the favorable streak and heavy workload, life is never perfect.

This time, the thorn in your side will be a relationship with business partners, and the underlying issue will likely be real estate, land, or other valuable property. Perhaps this comes as no surprise, as it is not your first time on this merry-go-round, and you know exactly what to expect.

However, things are looking like a shadow of your earlier troubles, and you will be able to smooth them over quickly.

Money

Financially, July is a great time for you. You will be receiving a regular income, and significantly more. You might also earn profits from earlier projects, a salary raise or payment for old debts.

Your expenses are low, and you have more than enough income to cover them.

Love and family

Your personal life looks less stable than things at work. After July 20, many Aquarians, many married couples will argue over setting up their home or other household matters. You might disagree with parents or elder family members.

Your children will be a source of joy, and they will be experiencing a positive streak at work, which will mitigate any conflict between spouses.

Couples who are divorcing or separated might also argue over how to divide their shared property, especially real estate, but they will be able to find a solution rather quickly.

Unmarried couples may feel their relationship cool off a bit, but this is no reason to be upset, as it is a natural process. Remember that in love, the less you ask for, the more you receive, and act accordingly.

Health

This month, you are not feeling as vigorous as usual, but July is a great time to take up yoga and spiritual practices or visit the beauty salon – just avoid any plastic surgery or other major cosmetic procedures. Avoid overdoing any physical activities and bad habits and be sure to drink in moderation.

PISCES

You are embarking on one of the best months of your year! Everything is heating up this summer, and you have every right to enjoy the moment. Luck is on your side.

Work

The stars' influence this month is more geared toward leisure and your personal life, but the incurable workaholics among us might also manage to achieve a lot at work. After all, this is a surprisingly good time to reconnect with old acquaintances and meet new people.

Your relationship with colleagues in other cities or abroad is moving along favorably, and you might take a trip or attend meetings, which will be as useful as they are pleasant.

Those dreaming of opening a business in another city or abroad will be considering spaces in July, and if that already happened in the recent past, you will be putting those plans into action. You have the whole year ahead of you for that to happen.

Employees might be spending a lot of this month on vacation or with their family, but after July 20 their minds will be back to focusing on work.

During the last 10 days of the month, things will be less festive and more work-oriented, after all. There will also be more trouble on the horizon. Once again, you might have to deal with problems stemming from colleagues somewhere far away, and they might be legal in nature.

Be careful, as this trend is set to continue into August.

Money

Financially, the best time for you is after July 15. During the first two weeks of the month, you will spend yourself into ruin – though at least all of your expenses are pleasant in nature – vacation, children, parties, and other fun events will all make your wallet much lighter, but without them, life would be dull and boring.

You can count on some money on July 17, 18, 26, and 27. You can also expect gifts and pleasant surprises from loved ones.

Love and family

In July, many Pisceans will be focused on their personal life more than anything. Those with families might spend a lot of time with children, partner, and on various household tasks.

Those who are moving somewhere far away might be happy to set up their new home. Recent tension between spouses or partners is slowly fading away, and right now, things look close to idyllic.

Your relationship with your parents is looking somewhat better, and you will be able to resolve any problems that have been a source of stress for you and your family.

The stars will be shining brightly, and couples can expect a real honeymoon period.

The first 20 days of July are the best time for meeting new people and matters of the heart. After July 20, things will be more pragmatic and there will be less romance in the air.

Health

In July, you are feeling rather energetic, but the stars urge you to be careful after the 15th, as there is a high likelihood of accidents. Be especially careful driving or traveling.

August

New York Time				London Time		
Calendar Day	Lunar Day	Lunar Day Start Time		Calendar Day	Lunar Day	Lunar Day Start Time
01/08/24	27	2.56 AM		01/08/24	27	2.03 AM
02/08/24	28	3.54 AM		02/08/24	28	3.02 AM
03/08/24	29	4.56 AM		03/08/24	29	4.08 AM
04/08/24	30	5.58 AM		04/08/24	30	5.17 AM
04/08/24	1	7.14 AM		04/08/24	1	12.14 PM
05/08/24	2	7.00 AM		05/08/24	2	6.27 AM
06/08/24	3	8.00 AM		06/08/24	3	7.36 AM
07/08/24	4	8.59 AM		07/08/24	4	8.43 AM
08/08/24	5	9.57 AM		08/08/24	5	9.50 AM
09/08/24	6	10.55 AM		09/08/24	6	10.55 AM
10/08/24	7	11.53 AM		10/08/24	7	12.02 PM
11/08/24	8	12.52 PM		11/08/24	8	1.09 PM
12/08/24	9	1.52 PM		12/08/24	9	2.17 PM
13/08/24	10	2.54 PM		13/08/24	10	3.25 PM
14/08/24	11	3.54 PM		14/08/24	11	4.31 PM
15/08/24	12	4.52 PM		15/08/24	12	5.32 PM
16/08/24	13	5.46 PM		16/08/24	13	6.24 PM
17/08/24	14	6.33 PM		17/08/24	14	7.07 PM
18/08/24	15	7.15 PM		18/08/24	15	7.42 PM
19/08/24	16	7.51 PM		19/08/24	16	8.10 PM
20/08/24	17	8.24 PM		20/08/24	17	8.33 PM
21/08/24	18	8.56 PM		21/08/24	18	8.55 PM
22/08/24	19	9.27 PM		22/08/24	19	9.17 PM
23/08/24	20	9.59 PM		23/08/24	20	9.39 PM
24/08/24	21	10.35 PM		24/08/24	21	10.05 PM
25/08/24	22	11.15 PM		25/08/24	22	10.35 PM
27/08/24	23	12.00 AM		26/08/24	23	11.13 PM
28/08/24	24	12.52 AM		28/08/24	24	12.00 AM
29/08/24	25	1.48 AM		29/08/24	25	12.56 AM
30/08/24	26	2.48 AM		30/08/24	26	1.59 AM
31/08/24	27	3.50 AM		31/08/24	27	3.07 AM

You can find the description of each lunar day in the chapter "A Guide to The Moon Cycle and Lunar Days"

ARIES

You may associate August with summer celebrations, but that is not the case this year. But man plans, and God laughs in our face...

Work

For Aries who are part of the working world, your main problem this month will be a worsening relationship with business partners in other cities or abroad. Here, the second half of the month will speak volumes, when you encounter a series of setbacks on your path toward cooperation. This is not a new situation, and you will manage to overcome it. Even though the problems are complex, it is worth being prepared in advance.

Business owners and managers will have to get ready for audits, which are highly likely during the second half of August and September. It is worth keeping an eye on your subordinates, who may not be as reliable as you might have hoped, and circumstances require.

Employees would be wise to be meticulous as they carry out their responsibilities and avoid getting involved in workplace gossip.

Aries should also keep in mind that during the second half of August, they might see undesirable information come to light, so remain cautious. You may have secret foes lurking in the shadows!

All of the trends you see in August will continue into September.

Money

August is a time of massive spending, for a variety of reasons. Maybe it is on vacation, problems involving your children, or resolving work-related issues.

You will have less money this month, so watch your budget and avoid unnecessary expenses.

Love and family

During the first half of the month, most Aries are busy arranging vacations somewhere far from home. If that sounds like you, remember that the second half of the month is not a good time for that. You may run into various challenges, so if you are going somewhere far away, plan things for mid-July or early August, when things will be calmer, and you can actually enjoy your family.

Couples' relationship will cool down a bit, and after August 15, expect secrets – either yours or your partner's – to come to light. He who lives in glass houses shall not throw stones, as they say.

Many will also face challenges involving relatives. You might have a serious argument, or perhaps have to resolve close relatives' problems by helping out with either words or money.

Health

In August, you are feeling rather energetic and have no reason to fear falling ill.

During the second half of the month, however, be careful when traveling or driving. All signs point to this being a rather dark period in August.

TAURUS

In August, you will have to grapple with a mountain of administrative and financial matters, both at work and in your personal life. It's hard to stay quiet about what's bothering us.

Work

You are embarking on a difficult, conflict-filled, and turbulent month.

That is especially the case after August 15, when you will face an onslaught of full-blown problems, which will probably be related to money or material issues.

You may also face complaints from old friends, or a new acquaintance who happens to be a VIP. In either case, things look harsh, and you will not be able to rush anything if you hope to resolve it. You may already know what the problem is so that you can prepare ahead of time.

Many Taureans will have to deal with difficult administrative issues, as well. That may include production space repairs, construction, or something similar. It is worth knowing that you will not succeed the first time here, and that later on, you will have to reconsider much of what you do manage to accomplish this month.

Mercury will be in retrograde from August 5 to 28, and this is a time when you need to be extra cautious. Remember that haste makes waste, so keep a cool head and keep your eyes peeled at work.

Money

August will have you in the poor house. You will be bleeding money, perhaps because of work or business. In the worst situations, you will need to put up money at every turn.

Love and family

Many Taureans will be more focused on their personal life this month.

You might be putting a new home together, or else focused on repairs and other, similar activities. If you are planning any major purchases, avoid pulling the trigger while Mercury is in retrograde, from August 5-28. Anything you acquire during this time might turn out to be full of flaws or perhaps the process will simply cease to be useful in time.

In many families, you will deal with problems involving your children.

In the best cases, you will have to support their initiatives, both morally and materially. In the worst-case scenario, you might have a serious quarrel. The most difficult time for this is the second half of August.

August is a time of emotional turbulence, as well, so buckle up if you are in a relationship. Your respective dissatisfaction will boil over during the last 10 days of the month, and you can expect a blowout fight. That may have negative consequences, so keep that in mind.

Mars and Venus will be in severe conflict, and you will be feeling it. Expect some emotional ups and downs, which will exaggerate many issues and prevent you from resolving them. Be calm, controlled, and cautious – that is the panacea for a harsh time like this. Remember that and think hard before doing or saying anything.

Health

This month, you are not feeling particularly energetic, which might be reflected in frequent bouts of fatigue and exhaustion. The star recommend that you spend some time relaxing. You will have an opportunity to do just that in August. Use it and remember that your health comes first.

GEMINI

Mars and Jupiter are in your sign, which means that you are bursting with energy. Use this for peaceful purposes, and everything will turn out right.

Work

In August, your ruler, Mercury, will be in retrograde, which is why you may be lacking in logic and consistency in everything you do. Remember, you can't do without either of these qualities!

Business owners and managers will face trouble with someone highly placed, or perhaps government agencies, while employees will clash with management. In any case, you may have met your match, and find that neither party is willing to back down. This may lead to a breakdown in your relationship or even being fired. If losing your job is not part of your plans, keep your head down and find another workaround.

Your relationship with colleagues in other cities or abroad is developing with varying success.

You might take a trip or be busy with negotiations or meetings with former colleagues and old friends.

Money

Your finances are not looking very bright this month. You will not see any special milestones here, but your expenses are inescapable. Keep any unnecessary expenses at bay and watch your budget.

Love and family

Your personal life is no walk in the park, either. Many Geminis will face trouble involving their parents or elderly family members.

Your loved ones may be going through a rough patch and require your help. Alternatively, you might have a serious argument with them. Perhaps it will be over real estate, so give these matters your utmost attention.

Your relationship with relatives is also turbulent and troublesome, which makes perfect sense given the instability this month.

Many Geminis will go on a trip and visit relatives who live in other cities or abroad. If you are planning on traveling for leisure, choose a place you have been to before, at the urging of Mercury, which will be in retrograde nearly the entire month.

Health

August is a difficult and confusing time, but you have no reason to fear falling ill. This month is anxiety-inducing, and by September, your energy will be sapped. The stars recommend that you keep your emotions in check and avoid any hasty decisions. Be very careful driving and traveling. If you are, it will make August much better and calmer.

CANCER

Jupiter's, Mars's, and Saturn's aspects are in conflict, which may make August one of the most difficult months of the entire year. The stars recommend that you resolve any problems as they come, avoid rushing anything, and hold back if things don't go as you hoped and planned.

Work

This summer month, many Cancers who are part of the working world will face problems with roots in the past. You might see old legal issues rear their ugly heads again, which will open up some unpleasant circumstances for you. Alternatively, you will face unexpected complications involving colleagues in other cities or abroad, which will halt your cooperation for some time.

Employees would be wise to avoid any office gossip and rushing to take sides. Things might not be as they seem, so think hard before opening your mouth or making any moves.

Any Cancers would be wise to remember that this month will highlight your shortcomings, rather than your achievements. Your enemies and those who secretly wish you ill might take advantage of that. Expect intrigue, unnecessary conversations, and various disagreements to set the stage for this month. Be ready for all of August's turbulence and remember that after the storm, comes the sun.

Money

Your bank account leaves a lot to be desired this month. You won't end up penniless, but you will have a lot of expenses, which may be related to either business or your personal life.

Love and family

Cancers who are more focused on their personal life might face trouble, too. For various reasons, your relationship with relatives might grow more complicated. Perhaps you will disagree over money or become dissatisfied with an increasingly difficult relationship.

Couples will be disappointed in one another and face serious quarrels. Perhaps ill-wishers will meddle in your relationship to the point of you separating.

Be careful and watch your back. Remember that there will also be attempts at dragging your skeletons out of the closet.

Health

Those who are able to escape any work-related or personal strife unscathed might instead suffer health problems.

This month, you are feeling low, so there is a likelihood of old illnesses or unexpected new ones impacting your health.

August is also a month with a high chance of injuries. Be careful when traveling and driving and avoid any risky situations.

For everything, the second half of the month is the most dangerous time.

LEO

It seems the tranquility of July is over. Instead, you will have to climb obstacles, so buckle up!

Work

Leos who are part of the working world will have to resolve various important tasks this month. One of them will be smoothing over some financial issues, while another will be your thorny relationship with a colleague. Perhaps these two matters are related. Though the first half of the month will be relatively calm, the second will bring problems in full force.

During this time, expect conflicts with business partners and to spend time troubleshooting money problems. You might also find that your challenges are so serious that other business partners will have to walk away.

This might also involve your friends, or someone highly placed in society, in addition to colleagues.

Do everything in your power to mitigate things here, but there will be some issues you are unable to fix this month.

Employees would be wise to keep an eye on their duties and ask management for nothing. Put off any big decisions for a better time, and you will be grateful later on. Mercury will spend most of the month in retrograde, right in your sign. Expect a lot of stormy skies and difficulties with communication, as well as things standing in the way of a direct dialogue. Remember this and don't beat your head against the wall, because this time, it is made of steel.

Money

Your main problems this month are related to money, which means that you are not going to be able to relax here. You may have to settle old debts, or perhaps respond to claims from a VIP. Get ready for the onslaught – it's going to be long and ferocious.

Love and family

Cancers who are focused on their personal lives will also face difficulties. Most couples will find their relationship under attack from the heavens, including married couples who have been on the rocks for a while, now.

After the calm of July, you will find yourself repeating earlier mistakes, and the results will be serious. If that sounds like you, remember the past and that you will be able to steer things your way this time.

Divorcing couples will face trouble with their children, and the strife might be emotional as well as financial.

Health

In August, you are feeling sluggish – the nervous, anxious atmosphere impacts your body. If you are unable to handle your emotions, remember that a good night's sleep is very calming for the mind and body.

VIRGO

August will not exactly be the most successful month of the year for you. You may face opposition, clashing opinions, and even outright aggression. This may be work-related, or possibly something in your personal life. Get ready to defend yourself on all fronts!

Work

There is no doubt about your professional success, but not everyone is pleased with it.

In August, you may face aggressive business partners, who have an eye on your business and its future development.

The most difficult time will be after August 15, but things will be brewing in the first half of the month.

You may also have a challenging relationship with colleagues from other cities or abroad. Your partners from far away want to remind you of their position and you will have to deal with this in August, as well as into September. You may also have secret enemies, who will start rumors about you. This is true for all Virgos, regardless of what field they work in.

Employees should be adaptable and put all efforts into resolving conflict through diplomatic means. There is also another alternative – many Virgos will take some vacation time this month and focus on themselves. You will certainly have an opportunity to do just that.

Money

Naturally, with the way things are going, you can expect money trouble. However, you can count on a small sum on August 8, 9, 18, 19, 26, and 27.

Love and family

Your personal life is difficult, especially if you have had trouble here before. After several weeks going your way, you will see several problems appear, and you will be grappling with them until mid-September.

Divorcing and separated couples might return to the past, falling back into old patterns and conflicts.

Stable partners will also feel tension in their relationship. You and your partner will have seriously clashing views or opinions on something, which might lead to serious arguments or be a major factor as things cool off between you.

Things will be compounded by an unstable legal situation, especially if you recently moved abroad.

Health

This month, you are noticeably less energetic than you have been, and that often leads to the reappearance of old illnesses or new health problems. Be careful when traveling and driving.

LIBRA

You are entering a difficult month, and when it rains, it pours. Remember, that he who seeks shall find, as you make your way toward victory.

Work

This month, you will be dealing with a suddenly difficult relationship involving colleagues in other cities or abroad. After a relatively calm period here, you have seen challenges reappear. In addition to outright hostilities, you will also have to deal with underhanded games at the hands of your adversaries.

Managers and business owners would be wise to keep an eye on subordinates, who might not be as loyal and genuine as you might need them to be.

Get ready for legal trouble or a visit from audit agencies.

Employees might find themselves in a sticky situation, which may be due to foes among their colleagues or a tense atmosphere on their team.

The second half of August will be difficult, as will most of September.

During the first half of the month, you will be able to lay the groundwork, as future problems start to reveal themselves.

During these troubled times, you can expect support from friends, but it may not be enough, and at the end of the day, you can only count on yourself. Don't get up when the going gets tough! The stars assure you that this too shall pass!

Money

Financially, August is not very stable. You have a lot of expenses, and they may be related to work or your personal life. However, this trend will not continue, and by fall, things will be under control.

Love and family

Libras who are focused on their personal life should also steel themselves.

Those who are moving somewhere far away might face challenges from official bodies, especially if you are headed abroad.

In August, you will probably not be able to overcome all of your obstacles, and in many cases, they will continue into September.

Clashes between Mars and Venus will have a negative impact on all of your personal relationships.

Couples, whether married or not, will have trouble agreeing on the simplest issues. Many Libras will see skeletons dragged out of the closest, so if you have something to hide, be very attentive and tread lightly.

If you plan on taking a vacation this month, avoid going anywhere far away. Things may be unpredictable, and you will probably not be able to resolve any issues the first time around. The second half of the month will be particularly challenging, though it doesn't hurt to be careful during the first half, as well.

Health

In August, you are feeling energetic, but the stars still urge you to be careful when traveling and driving. There is an extremely high risk of accidents this month.

SCORPIO

August will have you facing off with a series of unrelated tasks. So keep yourself in check, concentrate, and keep everything under control. After all, you can do it!

Work

You are busy at work, but things aren't easy.

Business owners and leaders will have to resolve difficult financial issues, as well as challenging relationships that may have developed among close friends.

You might also face setbacks at work, difficulties with auditing agencies, or someone highly placed in society. Alternatively, you may not have the people you need when you need them.

Employees will be seeing changes at work, and perhaps there will be changes to management or the direction your employer is headed. During this time, the stars recommend that you work meticulously on your own duties and keep an eye on any important paperwork.

Mercury will be in retrograde for most of August, which heightens the risk of mistakes, misunderstandings with your contacts, and that can be reflected both at work and in your relationship with many people.

Money

August will be ruinous. You will be bleeding money in every direction, while earning less.

However, you can count on receiving something on August 4, 5, 13-15, and 29-31.

Love and family

Scorpios who are focused on their personal life are also in store for unpleasant surprises. Parents will face trouble with their children, and this will involve a lot of expense, too.

Perhaps, your child will be going through a tough time, and you will have to support him or her, both morally and financially.

Alternatively, you might find yourself having blowouts with your partner.

Couples will face a series of stressors, which will reach a crescendo during the second half of the month.

Most Scorpios should remember that by mid-August, your anxiety will be on the rise, and you will need to keep yourself in check, which will not be easy. If you want to hold onto your relationships, do not react. The stars recommend that you keep a cool head and act diplomatically.

If you have been on the rocks with your partner for some time, however, and you have no desire to continue with him or her, then just let things play out.

Health

This month, your main problem will be your emotions and turbulence, which will literally permeate the atmosphere. That might leave even the strongest Scorpios feeling shaken, so spend more time in nature and remember wise King Solomon, who said that to everything, there is a season.

SAGITTARIUS

August will bring a series of discoveries, most of them unpleasant. However, it is worth remembering that clarity is more important than the fog as it is the only way for you to resolve all of these problems.

Work

Your main task this month might be your relationships with certain partners. You might disagree over how your business should develop, or perhaps its financial circumstances.

You might also clash over major property or real estate, and this argument might drag on for a long time. What's more, your relationship with colleagues in other cities or abroad will also become very complex. Your business partners from far away might not complete their end of the deal, or perhaps will produce conditions that are far from what you had agreed on.

Employees might face competition and gossip among their team members, and it will be hard to keep this under control. The stars recommend that you keep your mouth shut unless you've really thought your words through and keep your temper under control in order to avoid harsh consequences.

Overall, this is a difficult month, and it is worth limiting your regular projects, as any serious launch might be rife with challenges.

For almost the entire month, Mercury will be in retrograde – from the 5th to 28th, and this is not the best time for trying to move forward. The best thing you can do is get your affairs in order, shore up your position, and finish up what you've already started.

Any business travel needs to be carefully planned, and if you can, try to stay close to home or at least go somewhere you've been a few times before.

Money

This month, your finances are not looking very healthy. You have low expenses, but your income is also going to drop. You can count on a small amount on August 6, 7, 16, 17, 24, and 25.

Love and family

In many cases, the lion's share of August's events will take place in your personal life.

During the second half of the month, tension will reach a crescendo, and there will be a high risk of conflict between couples and spouses. In many families, arguments will break out over their home, apartment, summer home, or other real estate.

Your partner's position looks stronger, and you will have to give in somewhat.

If you have to make a choice between two relationships, think things through long and hard, and don't make any decisive steps until next month. Any decisions you make while Mercury is in retrograde may turn into something you reconsider later on.

Many Sagittarians will face trouble with their relatives, and you might expect a serious argument or perhaps elder family members grappling with major difficulties.

Health

In August, you are feeling rather energetic, but you might have to take care of your parents or elderly family members.

If you are planning on any travel for leisure, the best choice you can make is to head somewhere you've been before. Otherwise you might end up dealing with a series of obstacles.

CAPRICORN

August is hectic and chaotic, and your main task is to meet the challenges thrown at you by the unpredictable stars. You've got grit, though, and you are able to keep an open mind as you roll with the punches, which means you'll make out just fine.

Work

In August, lay as low as you can at work and limit yourself to simple tasks that are easy to understand.

Many Capricorns will face trouble from colleagues in other cities or abroad, which will lead to significant setbacks at work. You can expect the unexpected when it comes to auditing agencies, so get ready in advance.

Any trips planned this month might be canceled or not turn out the way you expected.

Either way, be very cautious with any business travel, as there is a risk of unpleasant and even dangerous situations.

Your relationship with your team will also leave a lot to be desired, and employees and business owners should remember that. You may be dealing with a stressful atmosphere all month long, no matter what. Alternatively, you might clash with colleagues, who are starting to play by their own rules.

Be very careful with any information you come across and be sure to verify it very meticulously. It may be mistaken or even outright lies.

Money

August is difficult for your wallet. Most Capricorns will have less income but spend more money along the way.

That may be due to unfinished business at work, or alternatively, your personal life.

Love and family

The stars' influence this month is anxiety-inducing when it comes to your personal life. Many Capricorns will face significantly more difficulties with their relatives, and that may include unpleasant surprises after a relatively peaceful July. This time, things will be serious, and any arguments will probably have longstanding consequences.

Those with real estate in another city or abroad might once again face trouble, which is probably legal in nature. International circumstances might get in the way of making your plans and intentions come true.

Confrontation between Mars and Venus will do no favors to couples, whether they are married or not, and this month. You're damned if you do, and damned if you don't, and this month that is truer than ever.

Health

August is not an easy time for you, and you may be noticeably more tired, and probably feel an urge to get away from it all.

However, if you plan any travel somewhere far away, think things through carefully, as it might not turn out the way you would have liked. The stars recommend that you stick to places you know this month.

Be very careful driving during the dark days from August 12-31!

AQUARIUS

This month, you might face real trouble with discipline, logic, and concentration – just the skills you need! You're in for a rough ride in August.

Work

The astrologist predicts that this beautiful summer month may not be a good time for you at work. The only thing you can do is study your relationships with partners and make the adjustments you need.

You have several unresolved issues, and they might involve real estate or other major property. It is worth steeling yourself, as partners may walk away from fixing things, or perhaps, time will run out.

Employees might take a well-deserved break from work and spend most of the time with loved ones.

Money

For most Aquarians, August is a time for financial devastation. You will be bleeding money, and your family and personal life are probably the culprits.

Your income is low if you even have any.

Love and family

Your personal life might be taking most of your attention in August, as it is full of turbulence. Your relationship with your spouse might cool down a bit, and you might expect disagreements over real estate.

Another source of tension may be your children, and they will probably take up the lion's share of your family budget.

You may also have to provide support to your youngest family members, which is what you should do, of course, when it comes to their education, starting a new business, or something else related to their future development. But if they are simply being capricious and demanding, reconsider.

August will be unbelievably difficult for unmarried couples, as well. The stars will seem to be putting you to the test, and few will pass. The conflict between Mars, Venus, and the Moon might leave a mark on relationships, unless they are truly steadfast.

The second half of the month will be hard for all relationships, and it is worth remembering that any problems that you encounter may continue into September.

Health

During the second half of August, many Aquarians will be lacking in self-confidence and cheer.

Those who are elderly or weakened should pay close attention to their health, as there is a risk of old conditions coming back or unexpected new illnesses appearing.

Remember that your health comes first, and act accordingly.

PISCES

This year, August is a time of instability. For you, and everyone else, it will bring stress and worry. But Saturn is right in your sign, which means that you in particular have to think things through carefully and make the right calculations.

Work

Pisceans who are part of the working world will have to deal with a series of uniquely complicated tasks.

One of these tasks might include issues related to real estate, land, or other major property. You may disagree with business partners, and you will be unable to resolve the problem this month.

The second problem may include an increasingly difficult relationship with colleagues in other cities or abroad. You may need to finish up some things, and reconsider others.

Those who are moving somewhere far away might also have to grapple with foreign laws, and you will have to learn to adapt to a new reality. Perhaps that will involve changing your plans to remain on the right side of the law in another country.

Business owners would be wise to also be attentive toward their subordinates, as their shortcomings may seriously complicate things for you at work.

Employees should be cautious with any documents and paperwork, and generally be more focused at work.

Mercury will be in retrograde from August 5 to 28, which usually means we can expect mistakes and unfinished business, which will have consequences you will have to overcome. Any Pisceans who are part of the working world should also get ready for visits from auditing agencies.

The most difficult time will be the second half of the month, when various problems will come at you, full force.

Money

It would be hard to describe August as stable for your finances, but you can count on a modest sum on the 4th, 5, 14th, 15th, 22nd, and 23rd.

Love and family

In many cases, Pisceans will be more focused on their personal lives than anything else in August.

Spouses might unexpectedly start arguing, and that situation is in danger of becoming chronic. You may be lacking in flexibility, diplomacy, and the desire to resolve the conflict through peaceful means. You might spurn or simply ignore any of your partner's initiatives.

If you have been thinking of repairs or buying a new home, there is no point in starting that process in August. Mercury is in retrograde most of this month, and any major purchases or consequential decisions would be best put off for a later date.

This rings true for all Pisceans, especially those who have hitched their plans to another country.

Divorcing couples might have blowouts over how to divide their shared property or home.

Health

During such an unlucky month, many Pisceans might feel significantly weaker than usual. Those who are elderly or weakened are under intense pressure from the heavens. They should get ready for this difficult period ahead of time, and that includes prophylactic measures against chronic illnesses.

Those who are young and strong should lead a healthy lifestyle and be careful when traveling, and especially behind the wheel. The second half of the month is the riskiest.

September

New York Time			London Time		
Calendar Day	Lunar Day	Lunar Day Start Time	Calendar Day	Lunar Day	Lunar Day Start Time
01/09/24	28	4.51 AM	01/09/24	28	4.16 AM
02/09/24	29	5.52 AM	02/09/24	29	5.25 AM
02/09/24	1	9.56 PM	03/09/24	1	2.56 AM
03/09/24	2	6.51 AM	03/09/24	2	6.32 AM
04/09/24	3	7.49 AM	04/09/24	3	7.39 AM
05/09/24	4	8.47 AM	05/09/24	4	8.45 AM
06/09/24	5	9.45 AM	06/09/24	5	9.51 AM
07/09/24	6	10.43 AM	07/09/24	6	10.57 AM
08/09/24	7	11.43 AM	08/09/24	7	12.04 PM
09/09/24	8	12.42 PM	09/09/24	8	1.11 PM
10/09/24	9	1.42 PM	10/09/24	9	2.17 PM
11/09/24	10	2.40 PM	11/09/24	10	3.19 PM
12/09/24	11	3.34 PM	12/09/24	11	4.14 PM
13/09/24	12	4.23 PM	13/09/24	12	5.00 PM
14/09/24	13	5.06 PM	14/09/24	13	5.37 PM
15/09/24	14	5.44 PM	15/09/24	14	6.07 PM
16/09/24	15	6.19 PM	16/09/24	15	6.33 PM
17/09/24	16	6.51 PM	17/09/24	16	6.56 PM
18/09/24	17	7.23 PM	18/09/24	17	7.18 PM
19/09/24	18	7.56 PM	19/09/24	18	7.40 PM
20/09/24	19	8.31 PM	20/09/24	19	8.05 PM
21/09/24	20	9.11 PM	21/09/24	20	8.35 PM
22/09/24	21	9.56 PM	22/09/24	21	9.11 PM
23/09/24	22	10.46 PM	23/09/24	22	9.55 PM
24/09/24	23	11.42 PM	24/09/24	23	10.49 PM
26/09/24	24	12.42 AM	25/09/24	24	11.51 PM
27/09/24	25	1.44 AM	27/09/24	25	12.58 AM
28/09/24	26	2.45 AM	28/09/24	26	2.07 AM
29/09/24	27	3.45 AM	29/09/24	27	3.16 AM
30/09/24	28	4.44 AM	30/09/24	28	4.23 AM

You can find the description of each lunar day in the chapter "A Guide to The Moon Cycle and Lunar Days"

ARIES

You might sum up this first month of autumn as "working on our mistakes"- both yours and others'. It's not easy, but you can do it.

Work

During the first half of September, many Aries will have to overcome challenges that began in August – first and foremost, disagreements with colleagues from other cities or abroad, which will once again break down your earlier agreements.

These kinds of tricks have come up before, so you already know how to respond to them. Closer to the end of the month, things will improve, and by October, you will be enjoying a short peace once again.

You may have to bring in supporters and allies in over to get through this. Their influence on your adversaries might be priceless.

Business owners and managers might also deal with tensions on their team, or behavior from certain associates that inspires you to incite a purge. In addition, the stars recommend that you keep any documents in order and be ready for visits from auditing agencies.

You are dealing with a wide range of problems this month, and it's best to be prepared for the whims of the unpredictable heavens.

Employees will face trouble on their teams as well, along with hostile colleagues – who may be operating in the open or in the shadows.

This time, it may be worth bringing the situation to your managers' attention, as they will help you and provide support.

Money

Despite the hectic nature of September, your bank account is looking good. You have a significantly higher income, which allows you to successfully resolve problems and keep a bold eye toward the future. Expect to receive the largest amounts on September 2-4, 12, 13, and 19-21.

Your expenses might be personal in nature.

Love and family

Those who are exclusively focused on their personal life will also have to deal with a range of difficulties this month. Aries who are moving somewhere far away will have to grapple with a foreign country's laws, as well as underhanded games by all types of officials.

Alternatively, you will deal with problems involving your relatives, perhaps drawn-out arguments that began in August.

In any case, you can be sure to count on your spouse or a loved one, whose influence will be crucial in any family conflict.

Many Aries will also be dealing with minor home repairs, and in many cases, that will take place somewhere far from your hometown.

The most turbulent time is the first half of September, after which your problems will slowly fade away.

Health

In September, you are feeling vigorous and that will be especially noticeable during the New Moon on September 2-3, and the Full Moon on the 16th-17th. This time, the Full Moon falls on a lunar eclipse, and its influence might be negative.

Elderly and weakened people may be most sensitive to the influence of the heavens, and they would be wise to stay active and observe their body carefully.

During the first 20 days of September, be careful when driving or traveling. It is best to avoid traveling, whether near or far, from September 2-4 or 16-18.

TAURUS

Your Ruler, Venus, will be in a strong position all month long, which means that you will be able to escape any difficulties with your head held high. After all, God only gives us a load we can carry.

Work

Many Taureans will face challenges that began last month. Perhaps the problem is money or financial matters, and it is a thorn in the side of your relationship with friends or someone highly placed.

You can count on your adversaries being unyielding, both in business and in reaching a compromise. Here, the most difficult time is the first 20 days of the month, and after the 20th, things will slowly but surely come to a resolution.

Your relationship with colleagues in other cities or abroad is developing in your favor, overall. You might go back to old cooperation or hold meetings with old friends and like-minded individuals.

In anything you do this month, business owners and managers can be sure to count on their subordinates, and employees can lean on their colleagues.

Money

Your finances are not looking stable in September. You will have a hole in your pocket, for various reasons. You may have to settle old debts, or perhaps cover your children's and family's needs. However, you will not end up in the red, and you might periodically come into a modest sum. Expect to receive the largest amounts on September 5-7, 14, 15, 23, and 24.

Love and family

Many Taureans will be busy with their personal matters this month.

Parents will face a lot of strife involving their children's needs and will probably spend huge amounts on them once again.

Couples might continue a disagreement that began in August. The full moon and eclipse on September 18 will bring clarity to your relationship, and perhaps what you learn will not be pleasant. Many will draw a red line for a relationship that is growing increasingly stressful and bothersome with each passing day.

Your relationship with relatives will be somewhat better, and you might visit family that lives in another city or abroad.

Health

In October, you are feeling energetic, and that will come in handy as you get through this very difficult month.

GEMINI

Jupiter is still in your sign, which means that you are able to hold on tight through the storm, even with the waves crashing around you!

Work

For most Geminis, September is a time of great strife. Your trouble at work is not letting up, and most of the time, it has gotten even worse. Business owners and managers will still face disagreements with government agencies or a VIP.

Employees might not be able to make peace with management's position and think about leaving for greener pastures. In all of your relationships, expect difficulties during the first 20 days of the month, when all of the challenges that began in August will make themselves known, and loudly.

The eclipse on September 18 will shed light on everything, and only then will emotions begin to simmer down. If you face similar problems in one way or another, remember that things are not so bad anymore, and when one door closes, another one opens. That rings true for you right now.

Money

Despite all the issues at work, you are just fine when it comes to money. Expect the largest sums to come in on September 7, 8, 16, 17, 24, and 25.

Your expenses are low and most of them are related to your personal life, work, home, and your family.

Love and family

Geminis who are more focused on their personal lives will also face difficulties during the first 20 days of September. You might clash with your parents or an elder family member. Alternatively, one of your parents might go through a tough time and you will have to provide support in both words and deeds.

Many Geminis will have to deal with issues surrounding their home. Perhaps you will have to redo something or come up with additional funds to pay for it all.

Couples who get along will resolve these incidents together, relying on their wisdom and undying love. Those whose relationship leaves much to be desired might argue and even have divorce on their mind.

Those who recently began a romantic relationship will be able to flourish, which is good for those who spent a long time looking for a partner, but bad news for those who have a family already. The astrologist has every reason to believe that this new love will replace old attachments.

Your children will bring you joy, and they will be on a very positive streak this month.

Health

This month, you may find yourself in a stressful, anxiety-inducing atmosphere. Geminis are very emotionally vulnerable, and the stars recommend that you remember that this too, shall pass, and there will be a light at the end of the tunnel by late September.

CANCER

Mars is in your sign for nearly all of September, which means that you will be bursting with energy. Your only responsibility is to use it for peaceful purposes.

Work

Cancers who are part of the working world will have to deal with yet another month of vigorously fighting back. You still have to deal with old legal issues, which may take a nasty turn, this time.

During the first 20 days of September, your foes may bring to light something you desperately wanted to keep quiet. That will have a major impact on the way things are going for you at work and tarnish your reputation.

Alternatively, you will face a very difficult relationship with colleagues in other cities or abroad, and in some cases, your cooperation will break down. Is that temporary or permanent? The astrologist predicts it will not last. In a few months, things will calm down and everything will fall back into place.

In September, you will do everything you can in order to resolve anything that comes your way, and you will have at least some success.

When things are looking difficult, lean on a friend for support, or someone highly placed in society. Their help is important, but the lion's share will fall on you.

Money

Financially, September is not great. Things look gloomy, and you may find yourself with absolutely no glimmers of light anywhere. However, things aren't all bad. In eight months, things will change for you. You just have to get through it right now, and there's no question you can do it.

Love and family

Cancers who are more focused on their personal life can expect problems that began in August to continue. You might not have resolved a disagreement with your relatives, or perhaps you will fight once again during the eclipse.

The darkest days are during the Full Moon from August 17-19, when the stars recommend that you be careful about what you do or say, in order to avoid any ruinous consequences. Mars in your sign might predispose you to conflicts, so remember that any peace is better than a good fight. Let that be your guide right now.

If you have any legal disputes involving family members, September is the best time to resolve them, as there is a high chance of losing in court is rather high.

Alternatively, a relative might fall ill or experience serious challenges, and will therefore need help in both words and deeds.

Health

In August, you have no reason to fear falling ill, but the stars urge you to be careful when driving or traveling.

The most difficult time is the first 20 days of the month, with the absolute worst on September 3, 4, and 16-19.

LEO

Happiness isn't about money, but how much of it you have! That may be your guide all month long. Here, you might experience successes or failures. So keep your finger on the pulse of things and get your reserve parachute ready!

Work

Until September 20, most Leos will have to overcome trouble that began in August.

Once again, you are dealing with financial matters, or perhaps material demands from certain business partners. This is nothing new to you, so you know where things are headed this time. You will be able to smooth things over closer to the end of the month, through both official and nonofficial channels.

Your relationship with colleagues who live in other cities or abroad is coming along nicely, and you have no cause for concern here.

Employees will be pleased when their relationship with management becomes somewhat smoother, and you might even conclude productive tasks and reach a full understanding.

Money

Expect a lot of financial difficulties. Many Leos will have to pay back old debts or shoulder commitments they have taken on.

You will not wind up penniless, however. You will periodically receive a modest sum, which will partly compensate for all of your pain last month. Expect to receive the largest amounts on September 2-4, 12, 13, 20-22, 29, and 30.

You will spend heavily during the Full Moon and eclipse on September 16-18.

Love and family

If your interests – and problems – are more aligned with your personal life, buckle up for a turbulent September.

Divorcing couples will yet again have to deal with financial matters, and your partner's demands may be eye-watering. You may have to give in a little, but it is worth standing your ground here.

Couples who get along might work together to overcome their money troubles.

Your relationship with relatives is harmonious, and perhaps a family member will come to your aid. Even if that is just moral support, it is valuable. You might also see family members who live in other cities or abroad.

Health

In September, you are not feeling particularly energetic, and that may be most noticeable during the Full Moon and eclipse from September 16-19, as well as during the New Moon from September 2-4. Steel yourself for some difficult days and remember that your health comes first, and the rest will follow.

VIRGO

In September, you will have to face others' opinions, and they are likely to clash with your own. In some cases, that may happen at work, and in others, your personal life.

Work

Virgos who are part of the working world will spend over half of September grappling with problems that began in August. That will probably include disagreements with partners over shared business, as well as future business development.

You might also have to address each partner's role, job descriptions, and financial investments in your shared endeavor.

Everyone will have their own opinion here, so there is no avoiding disputes. Your adversaries will dig into their position, but you're plenty stubborn yourself, so you may have finally met your match.

The first 20 days of September will be far more difficult here, and things will start to slowly resolve themselves after that. You may have to lean on old friends to act as intermediaries, but things aren't so simple. A few months down the road, this story will repeat itself.

Your relationship with colleagues in other cities or abroad is coming along as you had planned. That is thanks to your efforts alone, but you can be sure they will pay off in dividends.

Employees will face competition and ill will from foes hoping to minimize their contributions. Be attentive when you talk to management. Demand less of them and refrain from asking any questions, even if you know you are right. Keep your head down, do your work, and remember that you will be highly appreciated and in demand.

Money

Venus, the planet of small victories, will spend nearly all of September in the financial sector of your sky, which means that you will not find yourself in the red. Expect to receive the largest amounts of money on September 5, 6, 14-16, and 22-24.

Love and family

If your interests are more aligned with your personal life, and if you have few blemishes in your past, you might expect a variety of problems to come your way this month. After a relatively peaceful July and difficult August, September is looking like a turbulent time. Though you can count on full or partial financial victories, the moral side of the equation will be very difficult. Your partner might become harsh or unyielding, appear that they no longer have feelings for you, or the fire has simply gone out.

Alternatively, a loved one will face problems, and that may be irritating or cause you tension.

Those who are moving somewhere far away might successfully manage challenges that cropped up in August.

Health

This month, you will have more strength, which means you will be able to successfully grapple with all of September's challenges.

LIBRA

All month long, you would be wise to keep your guard up. Things may not play out exactly the way you have planned, and you will need to be prepared from the get-go.

Work

Your problems from August are not only continuing in September, but they are growing more difficult.

Business owners and managers will once again have to deal with unpredictable behavior from business partners in other cities or abroad. In addition, outright aggression and underhanded intrigue will seriously hamper everything at work.

What's more, you may experience disagreements with your subordinates, who will prove themselves to be either lazy or incompetent, and you will have to have a serious conversation with them.

If you have had legal trouble in the past, expect to find yourself dealing with it again, and you may not like the results.

You will also have to resolve a series of administrative and organizational tasks, and here, you will be able to cover a lot of ground.

For those who are part of the working world, the first 20 days of September will be the most difficult. After the 20th, many of these challenges will start to resolve themselves, thanks to you and your efforts alone.

Money

Financially, September is a neutral month for you. You can plan on receiving some income, but no more than the minimum. If you feel some financial pressure, your spouse or another loved one will come to your aid.

Love and family

Your personal life looks like smooth sailing. Venus will be in your sign nearly all month long, which always harmonizes things here. Spouses will work together to resolve household tasks, and even if you recently had an argument for some reason, now, things will start to quiet down.

Your relationship with your children is also harmonious, and everything here looks under control.

Health

This month, you will barely have enough energy to face your very busy schedule. Young and healthy Libras might be feeling less than confident and cheerful, while those who are elderly and weakened might face a relapse of old illnesses, so it is worth leading a healthy lifestyle and taking care of yourself.

In all relationships, the most critical period this month is during the Full Moon and lunar eclipse, from September 16-18. During this time, you might face all kinds of trouble in your life, so try to try to be very careful during this time.

SCORPIO

During the first month of Autumn, things are not exactly going your way, and your problems from August will have to be resolved, one way or another. The pendulum will not swing in the other direction until late September, so hold your defenses, if you are unable to go on the offense just yet.

Work

For most Scorpios, your main task at work is still financial in nature. You might face demands from business partners, friends, or someone highly placed in society. Most of this is likely to be clearly material in nature, and you will have to reckon with it one way or another.

Employees should refrain from any criticism of their managers or arguing with colleagues. You might not be entirely objective, but even if you are in the right, it is worth defending your position diplomatically and avoiding any conflict or quarrels. That recommendation goes for all Scorpios, regardless of your field.

Your relationship with colleagues in other cities or abroad is coming along well, and in mid-September, you might take a trip, where you will hold a series of favorable and very necessary meetings.

Money

September is a ruinous month for your pocketbook. You might be bleeding money in every direction, and lots of it. You may need to settle old debts and shoulder your material obligations, or alternatively, you will be putting up the lion's share of the resources for your business development.

Those who are not part of the working world will spend money on their children and loved ones.

Love and family

During this quiet month, many Scorpios will be more focused on their personal life.

Parents will continue to deal with problems involving their children, who will require large amounts of spending. It is impossible to predict what will happen in each individual case, but there is reason for concern here.

Be attentive to the younger members of your family and be sure to provide extra support for the elder ones, who may be going through some difficulties right now. Gloomy Saturn, which is spending a long time in the sector of the sky responsible for the new generation, is to blame.

Couples might find themselves constantly arguing, and one of these spats may be your last. The eclipse and Full Moon will bring tension to all relationships from September 16-18, and these are days full of excessive emotions, when any slip of the tongue may provoke an all-out conflict. Remember this and think 100 times before you open your mouth or make a move. Scorpio is an emotional sign, and all of its representatives would be wise to heed this advice.

During the last part of the month, or perhaps early in October, you might take a trip or meet with loved ones who live in another city or abroad.

Health

This month, you are not feeling particularly energetic, but if you live a healthy lifestyle, you will not face any complications.

SAGITTARIUS

Your range of interests – and concerns – is running high this month! Your business, family, and loved ones will all require your attention. Don't overdo it, don't rush things, and everything will work out!

Work

Sagittarians who are part of the working world will have to deal with strong opposition from business partners or even aggressive foes. Your disagreements and open struggle might continue all month long and not be resolved until October.

During this difficult time, you might count on help from friends, or also people who are highly placed in society. Their influence on hostile opponents will be priceless and go a long way toward smoothing things over.

Use all of your contacts, as your adversaries have dug in, and it will be difficult to find a way out of this situation without any help.

Employees would be wise to avoid approaching management unless it is absolutely necessary. Any requests or demands would be best put off for another time. It's not that far off – you can hold off until next month – October.

Your relationship with business partners in other cities or abroad is coming along successfully, and this part of your working life looks busy, yet harmonious.

Money

Your financial situation is overall stable, and here, things are going according to plan, no more, and no less. Expect to receive the largest amounts on September 2-4, 12, 13, 21, 22, 29, and 30.

Love and family

Many Sagittarians will spend most of their energy on personal matters and family in September.

Married couples might face a series of challenges involving real estate. If you are getting divorced, you will be dividing up property or arguing over the future of your home or perhaps repairing it. You might disagree over how to sell something that is very valuable to both parties.

In some cases, you might also argue with parents or an elder family member.

As far as your overall emotional backdrop, this month is rather difficult, and you can expect a series of mistakes. The stars recommend that you try to have a little more tact than usual, which is difficult for such a direct and passionate sign like Sagittarius. Follow this advice in all of your communications, whether business or personal. It will continue being useful in October, when the emotional overload slowly begins to ease up and fade away.

Health

In September, you are feeling rather energetic, and the stars urge you to only use this for peaceful purposes.

CAPRICORN

September will feel like a breath of fresh air after August, but not everything will be positive. The eclipse, which will impact the most important parts of your sky, is to blame.

Work

After a troubling August, with huge consequences for your wallet, September is looking up and much more attractive. You have a lot of work, and your paychecks reflect that.

Everything might be going well, but the fly in the ointment will be a difficult relationship with colleagues in other cities or abroad. This will be an issue despite your efforts, and it will be negative. Your plans may be disrupted, especially if are trying to cooperate with someone from far away.

Things will reach a crescendo during the Full Moon and lunar eclipse from September 16-18, before slowly stabilizing.

Alternatively, you may see a continuation of business audits or old legal problems come back to life.

In order to resolve all of these issues, you might need to turn to an intermediary, who will help you smooth things over. However, you will also be able to cover a lot of ground on your own.

In some cases, you will have trouble on your team if you are an employee, and you will have to turn to your managers. This time, you can count on their loyalty, empathy, and understanding.

Money

Your bank accounts are looking healthy in September. You will have regular earnings, and significantly more of them. Expect to receive the largest amounts on September 5-7, 14-16, 23, and 24.

Your expenses after such a devastating August will be significantly lower this month.

Love and family

Your personal life is looking steadier this month. Your relationship with your children and loved ones will significantly improve.

However, your relationship with your parents is still far from ideal, and you can expect conflict to continue here, and many other family members may get drawn into the fray, as well. It will be hard for you to fix this alone, but you might lean on your spouse or a loved one for help. Their influence will mitigate things to a degree but is unlikely to actually provide a solution.

It is hard to give a prognosis for this conflict, but the roots lie in the distant past, and you are well-aware of the arguments at hand by now.

Any travel, whether business or personal in nature, would be better for another time, as anything that takes place in September is unlikely to turn out as you might have hoped.

Health

In September, you are starting to feel better, but the stars still urge you to be careful when traveling and especially when driving. Expect trouble all month long, especially during the New Moon, from September 2-4 and the Full Moon, which falls during the lunar eclipse from September 16-18.

AQUARIUS

If you can solve it, there's no sense in worrying about it – keep that in mind as you sail stormy seas all month long.

Work

For anything work-related, the first 20 days of September do not hold much promise. You will be able to review your assets and prepare the groundwork for a more productive time beginning in October.

Those who work in construction or real estate will do well- this month, you will be the "King of the World"!

Other Aquarians will be busy with various organizational and administrative tasks. You will have a chance to get away from work and relax for a few days, as well.

The last 10 days of September will be more exciting, and you will receive an interesting snippet of information from a colleague from afar, and you might take a trip or start planning one.

Money

Your finances are shaky. You may be heavily spending all month long, and the stars predict that most of it will be related to your personal life and your children's and family's needs.

Love and family

Your personal life can be described as a series of wildly fluctuating trends. Parents will still be handling their children's affairs and ready to invest a large sum of money in their education or development.

Many Aquarians will be busy with minor repairs or other home improvements, and this time, things will go as planned. Your relationship with your spouse will be somewhat better, but you might periodically argue over money.

Couples will have to get through a tough time. Aquarians are not known for their patience (especially male Aquarians), and it is precisely what you need right now. There is a danger of making a big decision rashly, without thinking things through.

This is the case all month long, but especially during the Full Moon and eclipse from September 16-18. These are difficult, emotional days, when it is best to keep a cool head and not get over-excited.

It is a good idea to abide by this advice during the eclipse, regardless of your marital or family status or your field at work.

Health

In September, you are feeling a bit sluggish, and the New Moon from September 2-4 and the Full Moon and eclipse from the 16th-18th are the hardest days. During this time, you might feel significantly worse, and you can expect dangerous and risky situations.

PISCES

This month, you will have to start tackling your problems head on and think outside the box to do it. There's no other way out!

Work

In September, the Sun is in conflict with Jupiter, Saturn, and Neptune, and these celestial battles will be reflected in both your personal and professional lives.

During the first 20 days of September, you might have a serious disagreement with business partners, and the cause will probably be over real estate, land, or other major property. You will not be able to reach an agreement right away, but friends, relatives, or someone highly placed might act as mediators. Thanks to your joint efforts, you will find a solution, possibly by late September or October.

Your relationship with colleagues in other cities or abroad is coming along well, and this is a bright spot for those planning on opening a business somewhere far from home, or who recently began taking steps in that direction.

Money

September is a neutral time for your bank account. You have enough income to cover your expenses, and at the end of the month, you will be in the black.

If you need help, you might be able to turn to your parents or a loved one. You might also come into favorable terms of credit.

Love and family

This month, the lunar eclipse on September 18 will play a major role in matters of the heart. On this day, and on the days approaching it, be careful and do not provoke any conflicts. If your partner is the provocateur, be diplomatic and show restraint.

You might be dealing with an apartment, home, or other real estate. Some time later, any acute issues will be resolved, if you recently decided to get divorced or separate.

Those moving somewhere far away might have difficulties dealing with matters related to real estate.

In any difficult situation, do not be afraid to ask your friends, relatives, or well-wishers for help. They will support you and smooth over a lot of the difficulties you face.

Spouses who are fighting might reconcile for their children, who need a peaceful family.

Health

In September, you are not feeling particularly energetic. You might be sensitive to the harsh influence of Saturn, which has been in your sign for some time now. This stern planet demands attention to yourself and your body and will severely punish any negligence and apathy. Heed Saturn's demands and live a healthy lifestyle if you want to avoid problems, both now and in the future.

October

New York Time			London Time		
Calendar Day	Lunar Day	Lunar Day Start Time	Calendar Day	Lunar Day	Lunar Day Start Time
01/10/24	29	5.42 AM	01/10/24	29	5.30 AM
02/10/24	30	6.40 AM	02/10/24	30	6.35 AM
02/10/24	1	1.50 PM	02/10/24	1	7.50 PM
03/10/24	2	6.38 AM	03/10/24	2	7.41 AM
04/10/24	3	7.36 AM	04/10/24	3	8.48 AM
05/10/24	4	8.36 AM	05/10/24	4	9.55 AM
06/10/24	5	9.35 AM	06/10/24	5	11.02 AM
07/10/24	6	10.35 AM	07/10/24	6	12.08 PM
08/10/24	7	11.32 AM	08/10/24	7	1.11 PM
09/10/24	8	12.26 PM	09/10/24	8	2.07 PM
10/10/24	9	1.16 PM	10/10/24	9	2.55 PM
11/10/24	10	2.00 PM	11/10/24	10	3.34 PM
12/10/24	11	2.39 PM	12/10/24	11	4.06 PM
13/10/24	12	3.14 PM	13/10/24	12	4.33 PM
14/10/24	13	3.46 PM	14/10/24	13	4.56 PM
15/10/24	14	4.18 PM	15/10/24	14	5.18 PM
16/10/24	15	4.50 PM	16/10/24	15	5.40 PM
17/10/24	16	5.24 PM	17/10/24	16	6.03 PM
18/10/24	17	6.02 PM	18/10/24	17	6.31 PM
19/10/24	18	6.46 PM	19/10/24	18	7.04 PM
20/10/24	19	7.36 PM	20/10/24	19	7.46 PM
21/10/24	20	8.32 PM	21/10/24	20	8.38 PM
22/10/24	21	9.32 PM	22/10/24	21	9.39 PM
23/10/24	22	10.34 PM	23/10/24	22	10.47 PM
24/10/24	23	11.37 PM	24/10/24	23	11.56 PM
26/10/24	24	12.38 AM	26/10/24	24	1.06 AM
27/10/24	25	1.38 AM	27/10/24	25	1.14 AM
28/10/24	26	2.36 AM	28/10/24	26	2.20 AM
29/10/24	27	3.34 AM	29/10/24	27	3.26 AM
30/10/24	28	4.31 AM	30/10/24	28	4.32 AM
31/10/24	29	5.30 AM	31/10/24	29	5.38 AM

You can find the description of each lunar day in the chapter "A Guide to The Moon Cycle and Lunar Days"

ARIES

October is a busy and relatively peaceful time for you. Remember that a bad peace is better than a good argument.

Work

Your main task this month is to smooth over a relationship with your business partners. First and foremost, that means colleagues from other cities or abroad, with whom you have had difficult ties since August and September of this year.

This time, things are looking clearer and more like something you can overcome, though you will probably need to call in some intermediaries, allies, and like-minded people if you want to fix things entirely.

Business owners and managers will have to deal with organizational and administrative tasks. You might be setting up new production spaces, or perhaps you began this process recently.

This time, you will have to deal with the finer details of things, which is necessary if you want things to move ahead quickly and without a hitch.

Employees will have to work in a team in order to achieve results more easily. This is not a weakness by any stretch, but rather an opportunity to look at things from another perspective. When the time comes, you will be able to step out of the shadows and take charge yourself.

Any trips planned for October will turn out very well, especially if you are planning to go during the first half of the month.

Money

Financially, October is not a bad time at all for you. Your expenses are in line with your income, and you are earning significantly more, too.

In addition to your usual earnings, you can also count on financial support from your partners, favorable terms of credit, or help from a sponsor.

Those who are not part of the working world can count on help from loved ones.

Love and family

This peaceful trend is also taking hold in your personal life in October. Spouses who get along will improve their home, and perhaps have a minor spat here or there, which is something that happens from time to time. You might spend some of your money on your spouse or loved one.

Your relationship with relatives is also improved, and here, the dove of peace might be none other than your spouse or partner.

Those who are single can count on an interesting encounter among close friends. If you are looking to change your life, the person who will take you by the hand and show you the right path is sure to appear this month.

Any travel planned for the first half of the month will be a remarkable success. You can count on new acquaintances and a lot of attention on all sides.

Health

During the first 20 days of the month, you will feel energetic and have no reason to fear falling ill. Your energy levels will significantly weaken during the last 10 days of October (this is a much less successful time overall), so the stars recommend laying low and focusing on yourself.

TAURUS

Fortune is on your side once again in October, but you need to earn her gifts. You are doing just that, after all, it's not for nothing that you're considered the most persistent sign of the Zodiac.

Work

It's time to focus on work right now. You are climbing the career ladder, but you are also probably busier than ever. The solar eclipse on October 2 will do wonders to help you advance on the most difficult tasks here, as well as anything financial in nature.

One pleasant surprise in October will be that your relationship with people in positions of power and influence will significantly improve.

Any thorny issues surrounding money will be nearly resolved, and any loose ends will not get in your way of calmly completing your tasks.

October's favorable outlook will also include much stronger ties to colleagues from other cities or abroad. Though there are still questions here, the forecast looks sunny.

Employees will often be working on a team, which will allow them to cover much more ground as far as their goals are concerned.

You might also take on additional responsibilities, and the stars predict that this will be extremely useful later on, whether in the form of financial compensation, respect from your peers, or building a bridge to a promotion later on. All of this may take place in October.

Money

Your financial position is growing stronger. You will have income coming in regularly, and significantly more of it. Expect to receive the largest amounts on October 2, 3, 12, 13, 20, 21, and 29-31.

Love and family

The solar eclipse predicts that the most important thing in your life this month will be work. However, your ruler, Venus, might also make some adjustments to this rather harsh verdict.

Venus's transit ensures that work is work, but you can't do without love. October will give couples a unique opportunity to reconcile, especially if you recently had an argument.

Spouses' relationships will also grow softer and generally improve, especially if you keep a lid on your hot temper. Feelings are fickle, they can unexpectedly appear out of nowhere or simply vanish at any time. If that has happened to you, try to work on yourself, as October is a wonderful time for just that.

You are speaking much more with family members, and you might see loved ones who live in another city or abroad.

Any trips, whether for business or pleasure, are sure to be a success in October.

Health

In October, you are not feeling as energetic as usual, but that is especially the case if you are elderly or weakened. If that is you, you would be wise to take care of yourself and take it easy during the New Moon and eclipse on October 2-3.

Younger Taureans should lead a healthy lifestyle and remember the importance of diet and getting enough sleep.

GEMINI

This month, you are feeling free in a way you did not in August and September. It seems that the stars are finally coming to their senses and starting to help you. Go for it!

Work

The solar eclipse, which takes place on October 2, will draw special attention to you as a person. You can be sure of success at work, as well as with any official bodies that gave you trouble in August and September.

Business owners and managers can count on their subordinates, who will do everything in their power to help the working process move along. Employees will improve their ties to management, though in order for that to happen, you will need to display your skill and how irreplaceable you are. The stars believe that you will manage, and your work will be valued. You might even receive a new and attractive offer to work somewhere more promising.

October is especially kind to those who work in the creative fields – actors, artists, musicians, writers, and journalists.

Many Geminis will feel a tug at their creative spirit this month and will enthusiastically demonstrate their achievements to their colleagues and a wider audience.

October is a good time for any exhibits, performances, and presentations – your work will be noted and appreciated.

Money

Financially, this is not a bad time for you at all. You will be earning money regularly, and significantly more of it. Your expenses are also on the rise, mostly due to your personal life and the demands of your family and children. Your loved ones may be on a positive streak, which is always a good thing.

Love and family

When it comes to love and romance, October is fantastic, whether you are meeting new people or for your existing relationships, which will reach a greater level of love, trust, and closeness.

Parents will spend a lot of time with their children, who will bring them immense joy.

Many Geminis will seriously think about marriage and expanding their family.

Health

In October, you have the right amount of energy to handle everything Fate throws your way.

This is a great time for changing up your image, as well as making various alterations to your appearance.

CANCER

You are embarking on a calm, steady month, which will allow you to take care of yourself and relax after all the stress you've been through lately. Rather than rushing to the barricades, strengthen your position!

Work

In October, business owners and managers will have to grapple with a disagreement involving business partners, and most likely, it will be over large property or real estate. Here, you might see some success, especially if you keep your ambition in check and make an effort to resolve things by reaching a compromise both sides can live with. Otherwise, you might be met with a fierce response.

Employees would be wise to steer clear of management. Any personal communication might end in a blowout, and remember, management always wins. If you really have to approach your superiors, it's best to do so in writing.

You might also take a few days off and spend time with yourself and your loved ones. The world won't stop turning if you are away from the office for a few days.

Money

Your financial situation is relatively stable and uninteresting, though you might receive a healthy profit from a successful real estate transaction. Some Cancers might also receive help from parents or an elderly family member.

Your expenses are low, and most of them are related to longstanding financial obligations, old debts, and your personal life.

Love and family

The major events of this month will probably be related to your personal life and family relationships. Spouses who get along will be immersed in improving their homes, and any arguments here might be a constant in the background all month long.

Your children will bring you joy, and you are likely to go on a trip together or visit your children who live in another city or abroad.

Things look quite different between separated or divorced couples. Here, you might have arguments of an entirely different nature over your home. You might struggle to divide your house, apartment, summer home, or other real estate. If you happen to have a shared business, things will only get worse.

Many Cancers will be acquiring new property, as foretold by the solar eclipse, which will accentuate the sector of the sky responsible for homes.

Health

This month, you are not feeling very energetic, but if you lead a healthy lifestyle and take care of yourself, any autumn colds will pass you by.

L E O

In October, some challenges that came up in the past will unexpectedly resolve, and those that are left may no longer be such a big deal. Either way, you come out ahead, so grab the reins and charge forward!

Work

When it comes to work, this month will be more promising and easier than the last one.

The solar eclipse on October 2 will activate your ties with colleagues in other cities or abroad, and this time might bring you success. You might still have to deal with some difficult quandaries, but the general trend is positive.

You might take a trip, or perhaps your colleagues from afar will come to you, and you will be able to tackle a lot of issues. Your relationship with friends and those in high places will improve, and this trend will continue into the future.

You will also be able to deal with a variety of administrative and organizational tasks, including repairs, and other issues related to acquiring a production space. To summarize, one way or another, everything will be resolved, and you won't ever find yourself stuck.

Money

Any money trouble that was bothering you in the past seems to be resolved in October. In addition to your usual income, you might also receive additional profits from various real estate transactions or support from friends or loved ones. Your expenses are low, and your income is more than enough to cover them.

Love and family

Those who are busy with personal matters this month might resolve serious issues related to their homes. In many cases, this may take place in another city or abroad. You might take a trip or meet with old friends and people who you have not seen in a long time.

The friendship between Venus and Mars will help you smooth over relationships if you have been arguing a lot lately with your partner or spouse.

Divorcing couples will be able to find a compromise to get over difficult issues involving real estate.

You will spend significantly more time talking to relatives, and maybe one of you will visit the other.

After some recent stress, couples will try to repair their relationship, but it will only work if you are ready to own your mistakes and forgive one another. And that will only happen if your love is sincere. The ball is in your court!

Health

In October, you are noticeably more energetic, and even if you were recently ill, you will quickly recover in October.

VIRGO

You are in for a wonderful month! Your wishes will come true, and your spirit will feel calm. Times like this don't come very often, so take advantage of the stars' influence and do whatever you have in mind.

Work

When it comes to anything-work related, October is one of the best months of 2024! Things will move forward, and new projects and opportunities will come your way.

Business owners and managers will receive profits from work you completed earlier and lay plans for the future.

Employees can expect support from managers and a corresponding salary raise. You are likely to receive a new job offer with an enticing financial incentive.

Your relationship with colleagues from other cities is moving along the way you need it to. Here, you may find stability, though there might still be some trouble on the horizon. This month, however, you will be able to address it easily, by leveraging your sign's diplomatic skills.

Any trips planned for October will be successful, especially If they do not take place from October 15 to 17, when there is a high chance of accidents.

Money

The solar eclipse on October 2 will shed powerful light on the financial sector of your sky. That means that you will have more money, and this is a positive development that will continue into the future. You might even say that many Virgos will be on a golden streak when it comes to their income and material wealth.

Expect to receive the largest amounts on October 2, 3, 12, 13, 20, 21, and

29-31. Your expenses are not going anywhere, but they are well below your income, which is significantly higher.

Love and family

Your personal life is calming down. Divorced and separated couples might peacefully resolve difficult financial matters. Things will lean in your favor most likely when it comes to anything material.

The harsh mood of the second half of October can be smoothed over when you approach dialogue with tact and flexibility. This advice is valid for all Virgos, regardless of your marital status. Severe Saturn has dug into the sector of the sky responsible for long-term relationships and will make you pay for any mistakes you have made, either now or in the past.

If your partner is going through challenging times, it is worth supporting him or her in both words and deeds.

You are growing closer to relatives, and you might visit family members who live in other cities or abroad.

Your children will require attention and major spending right now, but that is not a problem. You can afford it all.

Health

In October, you are energetic enough, but it's not worth putting your body to the test. Lead a healthy lifestyle and everything will be just fine.

LIBRA

You are celebrating your birthday on full alert, but that's only natural – for a long time, you've been between a rock and a hard place, but you've still managed to move forward.

Work

The solar eclipse will take place on October 2, and this time, it is in your Zodiac sign, which means that many will have their eyes right on you. That means energy and success, so be bold and don't waste any time.

Your relationship with colleagues from other cities or abroad is reaching a stage of positive development and it's all thanks to you. You are the one who is able to settle down a shaky relationship with capricious business partners, and you can do it without incurring any damage yourself.

Difficult legal quandaries will also be resolved favorably, though you may have to deal with some frenetic tasks in order to get there.

The good news this month will be that a situation on your team will be significantly easier to deal with, whether you are a business owner or an employee.

Those who are hoping to open a business in another city or abroad, or those who are planning to find a job somewhere else can cover a lot of ground in achieving their goals.

Money

Your bank accounts will start to look significantly better, and not only will your income be regular, but it will also be noticeably larger. This will come in quite handy, because your expenses are also about to increase, whether because of business or your personal life.

You can expect the large sums to come in on October 4-6, 14, 15, 22, 23, and 31.

Love and family

Your personal life is full of administrative tasks, and here, things are going according to plan. If you have a family or are busy setting up a home, you can expect to have your hands full with these matters.

Couples and spouses will spend some time traveling together, and that will bring a fresh burst of life back into their relationship. From time to time, your romantic sign just needs a change of scenery or to step away from routine.

Those who are moving somewhere far away might be dealing with issues they were recently unable to resolve.

Health

In October, your energy potential is high enough, and you have no reason to fear falling ill. Despite the overall favorable backdrop this month, those who are weakened, or elderly should be incredibly careful and avoid overdoing it or putting their bodies to the test. These recommendations are relevant all month long, especially during the New Moon and eclipse on October 2-4.

SCORPIO

October promises to be a quiet month filled with administrative tasks, and an opportunity to shore up your position and find your footing, both at work and in your personal life.

Work

In October, you will be able to immerse yourself in getting your affairs in order at work. Business owners and managers may find themselves climbing mountains, especially if you are currently expanding your business or busy with construction and repairs. After a busy August and September, the heavens are giving you a chance to do everything you need to do.

Your relationship with colleagues in other cities or abroad is moving along in your favor, and you might get back into touch with old acquaintances or build new ties as well. Any trips planned for October will be an enormous success.

Employees will spend most of October focused on family issues, where you will also be fairly busy. You might have to take some days off and spend time on household matters. If you have to remain at the office, lay low and avoid getting on management's nerves.

Money

October is stable when it comes to your finances, but no more. You won't come into any windfalls, but you will also not find yourself broke. Your expenses are significantly less than before, which is a positive trend set to continue into the future. You might see healthy profits from real estate transactions or favorable terms of credit.

Those who are not part of the working world can count on support from their loved ones.

Love and family

The stars predict that many Scorpios will spend most of this month focused on their personal lives and various family events.

You will be setting up a home or conducting various real estate transactions. You can expect any of these tasks to run smoothly, without any trouble or setbacks.

A tricky situation involving your children recently arose, and here, your woes seem to be easing and you are able to make a lot of progress. Most likely, things look less urgent than before. You might see your children who live in other cities or abroad.

The friendly contact between Mars and Venus will significantly improve your relationship with your partner. If you have any desire to rekindle a relationship that has cooled off, that will not be a difficult endeavor, though you will have to make the first step. If you are clear that you are willing to meet your partner, you will be pleased with his or her response.

Health

This month, you are not particularly energetic, but you have staunch support from Venus, which means that you are probably spared any serious illnesses. In any case, during the New Moon and eclipse from October 2-4, lay low and take care of yourself.

SAGITTARIUS

October will bring many opportunities, which you should use wisely. Don't be afraid to start a new business, and the excitement and originality of your decision will help you find the best options, which no one else could have possibly seen.

Work

Be sure to do your most important tasks during the first 20 days of October, which is the best time for anything work-related. During this time, you can count on support from friends, as well as VIPs, and their help will be both useful and necessary. You will be able to significantly strengthen your position and resolve any issues that have been concerning you, while also becoming well-known in your circle and even further afield.

During the first 20 days of the month, you can expect to renew old contacts on a positive note, as well as meet new people who will prove themselves valuable.

You will also be able to tackle various organizational tasks, as many businesspeople will see for themselves.

Employees will also do well, their authority will grow, while their relationship with colleagues improves.

The only drawback this month might be your relationship with certain colleagues and subordinates who may be envious of your success and periodically try to throw a spanner into the work. But it's just a tempest in a teacup, and life will go on.

During the last ten days of October, things will settle down, and you will be able to step back from all the stress and work on the things you had been setting aside for "later."

Money

October is also not bad for your bank account. In addition to your regular earnings, you may see additional income, perhaps profits from successful real estate

Those who are not part of the working world can count on help from loved ones.

Love and family

Only good can come to your personal life this month. Couples who have been together for a while will be able to make fateful decisions on marriage or living together.

Those with families will significantly improve their relationship, which recently hit a rough patch. You might get along as you work on setting up your home.

Those who are single might fall under Cupid's arrows, as there is a higher-than-average chance of torrid affairs this month, so be sure to spend time out where there are a lot of people and always look your best.

The first 20 days of the month are a good time for shopping, whether small finds or a whole shopping spree, presentations, and visiting friends.

Health

During the first 20 days of the month, you are healthy, energetic, and leaving quite an impression on everyone Fate throws your way. After October 20, you might start to feel run down from all of the activity this month, so try to find the time to relax and generally take care of yourself.

CAPRICORN

October is a fantastic time. You will be able to solve problems in your favor, you are on the right path, and it is smooth and even. The stars promise you undeniable success!

Work

The most important victories this month will take place at work, and here, you will be leading the charge. Business owners and managers will be able to show off their achievements to colleagues and a wider audience, as well as close new deals in their favor.

Employees will be on management's good side and can count on a new job offer with great promise for the future. A more modest and likely alternative is that you may simply be given a raise.

Your relationship with colleagues in other cities or abroad will look more optimistic this month. You might reconnect with old friends or colleagues who live in other cities or abroad. Any trips planned for October will be a success.

The fly in the ointment, however, might be your relationship with certain business partners. Here, you may face competition, hostility, and even obvious envy. Remember that his bark is worse than his bite, though, and act accordingly.

Money

Financially, October is one of the best months of the year. You will have regular income coming in, and significantly more of it than usual. Expect to receive the largest amounts on October 2, 3, 12, 13, 20, 21, and 29-31.

Your expenses are low and mostly related to your personal and family life.

Love and family

Much of the activity this month will be work-related, and your personal life may fall on the back burner. But you can't live without love and romance, so no one is stopping you from heading somewhere beautiful with your partner.

You might meet up with an old flame living in another city or abroad.

Spouses will face some more difficulties. If your relationship has cooled recently and you are simply living together out of habit, in October, get ready for a fight. As usual, however, it will head nowhere and just amounts to minor disagreements, old grudges, and maybe boredom... In that case, spend more time out in public and try to get some new interests in your life.

Your relationship with relatives will improve, and if you have any longstanding arguments, you might be able to negotiate. However things turn out, it's better than nothing.

Health

In October, you are feeling energetic and have no reason to fear falling ill.

AQUARIUS

You can celebrate – this month, things will turn out your way. You can expect a surge of energy, speed, and original ideas. Dive in!

Work

For Aquarians who are part of the working world, the main idea this month is developing your relationship with colleagues in other cities and abroad. The solar eclipse on October 2 is pointing toward this.

Your relationship with colleagues, subordinates, and VIPs is improving, and you are also seeing sunnier skies in general when it comes to work. You might be able to show your achievements to an audience and see your popularity grow within your own circle. This is a good time for resolving any legal issues, disagreements, and dealing with any auditing agencies or official bodies. If you wish to start something new, there's no better time than now.

Those who work in creative fields can expect particular success, with a popular tour, as well as accolades and love from those around you.

Money

Your wallet is looking fatter this month, which is a positive trend that will continue into November. Your income is growing while your spending is dropping, which will be one of October's many gifts. You can expect the largest amounts to come in on October 4-6, 14, 15, 22, 23, 30, and 31.

Love and family

There are some contradictions in your personal life. Whether you have just met, have started a recent romance, or have been bound by holy matrimony for years, the stars are offering you an opportunity to fix any problems on your own.

Those who are single will be able to easily find a partner, and that might happen while you are traveling or among people who have come from far away. Recent romances will start to develop favorably, and you might meet with loved ones who live in other cities or abroad.

Many will be busy dealing with issues related to their home. If you have any thorny situation involving real estate, there is no better time than now to tackle them.

A tricky situation involving your parents or elderly family members will almost be resolved, and they may even lend you a helping hand.

Your children will bring you joy, and their positive streak will continue into the future.

Health

In October, you are feeling great, and even if you have recently been ill, you will recuperate quickly. October is an ideal time for shopping, updating your wardrobe, and also cosmetic procedures, from minor to major. If you want to undergo plastic surgery, there's no better time.

PISCES

The difficulties you faced in August and September are now a thing of the past. You have faith in yourself and support from someone powerful but unseen – the stars, of course!

Work

October is more of a time for relaxation and dealing with family issues, but if you are an incurable workaholic, you might also find some things to do this month.

Those planning on expanding their business to another city or abroad will be able to significantly strengthen their position. You might be busy with construction, repairs, and other real estate operations that you began earlier. This also applies to those who are expanding their business at home.

Your ties with colleagues in other cities or abroad are coming along favorably. You might take a trip or hold peaceful negotiations and reach a highly productive partnership.

Employees will face a dilemma – whether to stay at work or take some vacation time? Many will choose the latter and spend time on personal matters.

Money

October is a neutral month for your bank account. If you need anything, you can be sure that your business partner or a loved one will lend a hand. You might receive loans or credit on favorable terms, or else profit from successful real estate transactions.

Much of your spending will be related to your children or loved ones in October.

Love and family

The stars predict that the major events of October will be personal in nature. Many Pisceans will be busy improving their home and cover a lot of ground here. In some cases, which may be taking place in another city or even abroad.

October might also bring you some time for relaxation, which you will spend somewhere you have been before.

Parents will have to spend a lot of time with their children, and you might take a trip together and enjoy one another's company.

Spouses whose marriage is on the rocks will come together thanks to their children, who will have a healing influence on the home.

This month, couples might also take a trip together, which will ignite their emotions for one another.

The peaceful tone of this month will be felt literally everywhere, so be sure to take advantage of the stars' wonderful October influence and reconcile with anyone you love.

Health

In October, you are feeling somewhat sluggish, and that might be especially noticeable during the New Moon and solar eclipse on October 2-3, and during the Full Moon on October 16-17. During these periods, take it easy and take care of yourself while avoiding any excess.

Spend more time relaxing and remember the power of meditation, yoga, and self-care.

In October, many Pisceans will feel their intuition grow stronger, and they may experience prophetic dreams, which they would be wise to pay attention to.

November

New York Time			London Time		
Calendar Day	Lunar Day	Lunar Day Start Time	Calendar Day	Lunar Day	Lunar Day Start Time
01/11/24	30	6.29 AM	01/11/24	30	6.45 AM
01/11/24	1	7.48 AM	01/11/24	1	12.48 PM
02/11/24	2	7.29 AM	02/11/24	2	7.53 AM
03/11/24	3	8.29 AM	03/11/24	3	9.00 AM
04/11/24	4	9.27 AM	04/11/24	4	10.04 AM
05/11/24	5	10.23 AM	05/11/24	5	11.03 AM
06/11/24	6	11.13 AM	06/11/24	6	11.53 AM
07/11/24	7	11.58 AM	07/11/24	7	12.34 PM
08/11/24	8	12.37 PM	08/11/24	8	1.08 PM
09/11/24	9	1.13 PM	09/11/24	9	1.35 PM
10/11/24	10	1.44 PM	10/11/24	10	1.58 PM
11/11/24	11	2.15 PM	11/11/24	11	2.20 PM
12/11/24	12	2.45 PM	12/11/24	12	2.40 PM
13/11/24	13	3.17 PM	13/11/24	13	3.02 PM
14/11/24	14	3.53 PM	14/11/24	14	3.27 PM
15/11/24	15	4.33 PM	15/11/24	15	3.57 PM
16/11/24	16	5.20 PM	16/11/24	16	4.35 PM
17/11/24	17	6.15 PM	17/11/24	17	5.22 PM
18/11/24	18	7.15 PM	18/11/24	18	6.21 PM
19/11/24	19	8.19 PM	19/11/24	19	7.28 PM
20/11/24	20	9.23 PM	20/11/24	20	8.39 PM
21/11/24	21	10.27 PM	21/11/24	21	9.51 PM
22/11/24	22	11.28 PM	22/11/24	22	11.01 PM
24/11/24	23	12.27 AM	24/11/24	23	12.09 AM
25/11/24	24	1.25 AM	25/11/24	24	1.15 AM
26/11/24	25	2.23 AM	26/11/24	25	2.21 AM
27/11/24	26	3.21 AM	27/11/24	26	3.27 AM
28/11/24	27	4.20 AM	28/11/24	27	4.33 AM
29/11/24	28	5.20 AM	29/11/24	28	5.41 AM
30/11/24	29	6.21 AM	30/11/24	29	6.49 AM

You can find the description of each lunar day in the chapter "A Guide to The Moon Cycle and Lunar Days"

ARIES

November is an ideal month for spiritual searching, creativity, and organizational tasks. Try to select what is most important to you!

Work

November is a highly unusual time for you. It is hardly an unlucky time, but you may run into some roadblocks along the way.

For example, be careful when talking to your managers or any VIPs. Right now, they are on your side, but you run a high risk of losing that support if you become too unyielding, demanding, or hasty. Ideally, if you have any requests or requirements, relay them through a diplomatic intermediary. You will have no trouble finding the right person for that.

Many Aries who are part of the working world will be busy with administrative and organizational tasks, and they will add their own creative flair to their work.

Your relationship with colleagues in other cities or abroad is coming along with varying success. Some things will go your way, while in other areas, you will have to slam on the brakes. Overall, November will require restraint, meticulousness, and modesty. Remember, there's no "I" in "team", and you will need your team to get your desired results.

Money

This month, your finances are looking great. In addition to your regular income, you can also count on serious support from business partners, sponsorship, and favorable terms of credit.

Of course, there are always expenses, but they are predictable and reasonable.

Love and family

Your personal life will be full of important events, as well. You might be working on minor construction jobs, for example, and many will be trying to have their homes ready by the holidays.

Spouses will get along this month and support one another in everything they do.

Unmarried couples might find that their relationship mirrors the capricious autumn weather, but then again, a ray of light may replace the rain. Don't give into these mood swings, trust in one another, and everything will turn out as you had hoped and dreamed.

Your relationship with relatives is not easy, but if you don't get bogged down in the details, perhaps you will avoid any conflict.

Health

In November, you are not feeling particularly energetic. Take some time to rest and be sure to get a good night's sleep. November is a great time for relaxing spa procedures, meditation, and perhaps going to confession or any other activities that will bring peace to your soul.

TAURUS

Taureans are known for their patience, but in November, yours may be wearing thin. Don't throw any tantrums, don't be stubborn, and learn to listen to others. If you follow this advice, you will be able to avoid any trouble.

Work

This is an exciting but difficult time at work, when your main task is to strengthen your relationship with business partners and people whose position is higher up than yours.

A certain level of flexibility might restore your relationship with former colleagues and old friends.

What's more, many Taureans will have to handle important financial and organizational tasks. Getting what you want will be exceedingly difficult here, and you will have to show some real ingenuity in order to avoid disappointment.

Your relationship with colleagues in other cities or abroad might become turbulent, but things will not reach a critical level. Here, you need to weigh the possibilities before you and assess what you need, and what you have to do to achieve it. You are sure to find a solution.

Money

November is a month full of major spending. You will be bleeding money constantly, but that will be either due to work or perhaps your personal life and family's and children's needs. Be careful with your savings, as this trend will continue into December.

Love and family

Many Taureans will be primarily focused on home and family this month. You may have to resolve important household tasks, but you may not have the same opinions as your spouse here when it comes to money matters. You can expect to disagree over ethics, and there is likely no way out of a conflict here.

This is a difficult time for couples. One of you may like something that the other cannot support, which will lead to a clash. Your sign is known for being unusually stubborn, but your partner is hardly going to give in here, either. Remember that and that a bad peace is better than a good fight.

This advice also applies to spouses whose feelings for one another may have cooled a bit.

Health

This month, you are not feeling particularly energetic, and that is especially noticeable during the last 10 days of the month.

In order to avoid any physical or emotional suffering, spend your weekends in any type of nature. There's no bad weather in nature, after all, and that is more relevant now than ever.

GEMINI

The disagreements you have faced over the last few months are slowly fading away. The stars are telling you that is time to put your nose to the grindstone, and that is what November is all about.

Work

November is a great time for you at work. Your brilliant ideas deserve to be taken seriously in the very near future.

Despite achieving some plans and projects, you might also run into some difficulties, but if you take the bull by the horns, you will be able to overcome many of them.

Business owners and managers will put together a strong team and brick by brick, use their help to build a strong foundation for future business development.

You will improve your standing in the eyes of influential people this month. Not everything will be a walk in the park, but you are in a strong position, and in the end, victory will be yours.

The stars also have some advice – all Geminis, regardless of what field they work in, should trust their intellect and do what they feel they need to, and not allow themselves to be led astray by "well-wishers", much less the criticism of others.

Money

Your wallet is growing fatter, you have more money, and it is all thanks to your own honest work. You might also have additional income and profits from projects you recently completed. Some Geminis will receive payment for old debts or find money that had disappeared somewhere.

Your expenses are low, and all of them are predictable and reasonable.

Love and family

November will be heavily focused on professional activities, and your personal life might be on the back burner. However, for those who are primarily immersed in family and romantic affairs, this is a time to tread lightly.

Married couples might have differing opinions on major family matters, and you are unlikely to avoid an argument this month. Meddling by family members or your parents will only make things worse.

But no one is preventing you from sharing your perspective, though doing that is always a delicate task requiring a lot of tact. If that is you, you will be able to share your side with all of your relatives.

Closer to the end of the month, you will be speaking more frequently to relatives, and you might see family members who live in other cities or abroad.

Health

In November, you are not feeling particularly energetic, so avoid any bad habits and remember to get enough sleep. Sleep is just what Geminis need to heal themselves of many illnesses.

CANCER

In November, you would be wise to exercise caution. The path ahead is still long and winding, so remember that walking softly will take you a lot further.

Work

You are experiencing a somewhat difficult streak at work. Business owners and managers might find themselves audited, or legal trouble from the past may resurface, and your victory might be in doubt. If you can, put off any difficult decisions for a better time, that is, another six months, when the stars will be in a better position to help you.

You might experience minor friction within your team, which will get in the way of your productivity at work.

Employees' colleagues will gossip, and they may try to drag something you would rather keep quiet into the light.

The good news is that you will be busy developing your ties with colleagues in other cities or abroad. You will do everything you can in order to reconnect with old business partners living far away, and here, you can enjoy the tailwinds.

Money

Financially, November is full of challenges and turbulence. Your expenses are low, but your income is quite modest. You will be able to count on money coming in, however, on November 3, 4, 12, and 13, and the largest sum on 21-22.

Love and family

Your personal life looks sunnier, despite what is happening at work.

Parents will spend a lot of time with their children, which will bring them great joy. You might take a trip together, which will combine both business and pleasure, while also giving you new perspective on many situations. Even your expenses related to vacation and your children are not overwhelming, as you are able to take full advantage of everything.

Many couples will go on a trip together.

Rumors and gossip may cast a pall over November and set the stage for the entire month. Everyone has some skeletons in the closet, but you would be wise to make sure that yours stayed there, especially when it comes to people whose opinions you respect. This may begin in November and continue next month.

Health

This month, you may feel just like the capricious autumn weather.

You might feel amazing some days, while others, you may feel weak and fragile. You are able to stabilize this situation if you remember the importance of leading a healthy lifestyle and getting enough sleep.

LEO

After a busy, stressful couple of months, you have an opportunity to make a bit of a transition. Unless, of course, administrative tasks or family matters make you work up a sweat.

Work

In November, Leos who are part of the working world will be able to resolve a mountain of administrative and organizational tasks. You might be dealing with various real estate transactions, minor office repairs, or even rebuilding production spaces. Here, everything depends on the scale of your business, and you can count on positive results.

On one hand, you will be patient enough to overcome any potential challenges, but also disciplined and pragmatic enough to avoid any major mistakes.

Even with these qualities, however, nothing is ever easy. In mid-November, business owners and managers will clash with influential people or even business partners.

Things will not become catastrophic, but they might drag on until December.

Employees will disagree with managers during this period. Overall, things will be less than stellar for those who work for others. Instead, channel your energy into taking care of your family and household affairs. This is plenty of motivation to take a few days off and get away from it all.

Money

Financially, November is not particularly auspicious. You may be spending heavily due to your children, loved ones, and various household needs.

Your income this month is low, and part of it will stem from real estate transactions.

Young people can count on help from parents or older family members.

Love and family

Many Leos will be primarily focused on their personal life in November.

You will continue to be busy with real estate transactions that you began in the recent past.

Some Leos will be getting their house in order, selling their old home, or moving to a new one. Some will be dealing with their children's or grandchildren's homes.

Couples will experience a lot of ups and downs this month, especially from the 8th to 19th. The reasons for your disagreement are unimportant but if you do not clarify things now, this situation will continue into December.

Health

In November, you are feeling sluggish, so take care of yourself and practice moderation. You may have to care for a family member in ill health, which will be an additional burden.

Be sure to manage your time well so that you are able to relax. With some clever maneuvering, you will manage.

VIRGO

November is a time of contrasts for you. There will not be any dark periods, but you can certainly expect alternating clouds and sunshine. There is not much you can do about this – c'est la vie!

Work

Your main task in November is to reconnect with business partners with whom your cooperation may have suffered over the last year. The positive steps you began in October will continue into November, but in some cases, you will have to turn to intermediaries to help smooth things over.

An attorney or perhaps a kind soul from your inner circle may play this role.

Your relationship with colleagues in other cities or abroad is coming along nicely, and you may hold promising negotiations or take a successful trip.

The difficulties this month might include some disagreements over real estate, land, or other major property. This situation might continue into December.

Employees should be careful when it comes to their job, and if you can, avoid arguments with management. Here, some tension and unpleasant interactions are inevitable.

Mid-November is a time of conflict, as is next month.

Money

Financially, November looks fairly neutral. Your income will be average, and your expenses will be low. You can count on receiving some money on November 8, 9, 16, 17, and 25-27.

Love and family

In many cases, the main events of November will take place in your personal life. Divorcing and separated couples might continue to argue over their joint property, especially real estate. In order to overcome these difficult issues, you will have to lean on relatives, old friends, or a well-wishing friend.

Your children will bring you joy, and they may serve as a bridge between couples who are fighting or already divorced.

You might take a trip, which will make your relationship stronger, as long as there is something left to fix.

Those who are moving to a faraway place might have difficulty securing a place to live, and here, the spanner in the works might be official government bodies and red tape.

Health

In November, your energy is high, and you have no reason to fear falling ill.

LIBRA

November is an incredibly lucky time for you. Nothing is ever perfect, but thanks to your efforts, you will be able to overcome any difficulties. The road belongs to he who walks it!

Work

This month, most Libras will be busy with organizational and financial matters and might cover a lot of ground in this area.

Business owners, managers, and employees will receive a handsome profit for work they completed recently and will continue being busy with new projects.

The dark side of November might be yet another difficult period involving colleagues in other cities or abroad. This is not the first time you have encountered such a situation, so just take it as another day at the office.

Keep in mind, however, that problems involving business partners somewhere faraway may continue for some time and come to a head in December.

Business owners and managers should be cautious as they monitor this process, as your subordinates will not be reliable this time. They may show themselves to be incompetent or unscrupulous, or perhaps both.

Money

November is not bad at all when it comes to your bank account. You will have regular income coming in, and significantly more of it.

Some Libras might receive payments for old debts or come into money they had forgotten about. You might also profit from various real estate transactions. Expect to receive the largest sums on November 1, 2, 10, 11, 18-20, and 27-29.

Love and family

This month, there are a lot of surprises in store for you when it comes to your personal life, and some of them will be very pleasant.

You can expect positive developments as you set up your home, perhaps somewhere far from your hometown, or right in the same neighborhood.

Those who are moving somewhere far away would be wise to be very meticulous when filling out official papers and follow foreign laws to a T. Here, you have a lot of arduous work ahead, not only this month, but also in the future.

Your relationship with relatives might become a bit more complicated, perhaps over old grudges or mutual complaints. You will be able to smooth over the situation, however, and it is worth doing that to nip this conflict in the bud.

Spouses' relationships will be stable, and they will be able to resolve any household issues and support one another in everything together.

Health

In November, you are feeling sluggish, but if you lead a healthy lifestyle and do not put your body to the test or turn to any sorts of excess, you will be able to avoid the worst.

SCORPIO

It's common to celebrate your birth month as you ward off problems from all sides – at home, at work, and in your inner circle. But God only gives us what we can handle, so you will manage!

Work

Your main task this month will be resolving financial trouble. Business owners and managers will have to find a lot of resources in order to expand their business, but this process will continue in your favor. You might need to carry out the challenging task of reorganizing your business, which will occupy you for the near future.

Employees will see changes underway at work and be able to leverage them. This may become clear a bit later, but there are definitely opportunities on the horizon.

Your relationship with colleagues in other cities or abroad is developing the way it should, and that will be noticeable in mid-November. You might take a trip or start preparing for one.

Money

You are in for some financial turbulence this month. Everyone will need money – your loved ones, children, your house!

You will spend a lot expanding your business, especially if you are a business owner.

You will still have income, but it will be barely enough to cover your expenses, and close to the end of the month, your wallet will be looking mighty thin.

Love and family

Your personal life is unstable right now, as well. Once again, parents will have to deal with trouble involving their children, and once again, you will have to spend a lot of money to resolve it all. You will do everything in order to fix this and be largely successful.

You might see your children who live in another city or abroad.

Spouses will once again be busy with household tasks, and perhaps even work on building a new home.

This might seem like a Sisyphean task right now, but the stars predict that within six months, many of these quandaries will be resolved, and favorably! In the meantime, you are working in this direction and have more than enough resources to get it done. Remember, it costs money to save money.

Couples will experience some stormy seas. You will do everything you can for your partner to get over his or her anger, and you will have some success here. Things will continue to be unstable here for a long time to come, so you will need some patience.

Any travel with your partner in November will go well and might improve things, whether you are married or not.

Health

This month, you are feeling noticeably more energetic and any illnesses from October will fade away.

SAGITTARIUS

November is not an easy time for you, but there's still hope. You will get some of what you want, but not all. However, the planets will surely give you another chance, and this time, you won't let it pass you by. After all, you're the one holding the bow and arrow!

Work

Your main achievements in November will involve active organizational tasks, clearing the rubble, and dealing with problems that you've been putting off.

Business owners and managers will get their office in order, along with production space and your team in general.

Employees will calmly carry out their job, but find time for household issues, too. Many Sagittarians might take some time off in order to do just that.

The dark clouds this month will be a relationship with business partners from afar. Your overtures will be spurned, and in mid-November you might even have a serious argument.

This may be over real estate, land, or other major property. Resolving your problems is not in the cards this month, and most likely, they will continue into November.

Closer to the end of the month, you will be spending more time talking with colleagues in other cities or abroad, and this positive trend will continue into December.

Money

November is a great time for your wallet, and you will have significantly more money coming in regularly. In addition to your usual earnings, you can count on profits from successful real estate transactions or support from business partners or other loved ones.

Love and family

Your personal life will come first in November. Many Sagittarians will be busy with household and organizational tasks, and you might have the desire and opportunity to start getting your house ready for the holidays.

Spouses might argue, as they each have their own vision of how that should look. Here, the stars recommend that you show some flexibility and openness and listen to one another's ideas.

Alternatively, you might have a more serious argument over your home, as the consequence of longstanding problems, or perhaps your relationship has cooled to the point you are planning a divorce.

We cannot predict emotions. They come and go, and might return. Remember that and avoid any extremes.

Health

In November, you are at your most exhausted, so be careful with your body and avoid getting any colds.

The New Moon on November 1-2 and the Full Moon on November 14-16 will be the most difficult period, when you should lay low and avoid putting your body to the test with any excesses.

CAPRICORN

You will continue to move forward. Right now, you are able to find support wherever Fate takes you. Isn't that great?

Work

November is a great time for meeting new people and reconnecting with old ties. Of course, this trend began in October, and is now reaching a logical continuation.

Your ideas are popular with influential people, and everyone around you. Your relationship with colleagues in other cities or abroad is also coming along nicely and you might take a successful trip.

The first half of November is a great time to show off your achievements to like-minded people and a wider audience.

However, despite the overall favorable tone this month, nothing is ever perfect. This time, a disagreement with an associate or subordinate may become a thorn in your side. The most difficult time here is mid-November. Keep an eye on all processes and don't try to let things just work themselves out, as the problems that begin in November are likely to worsen in the future.

Money

Financially, November is not bad. You will have income coming in regularly. No more, no less.

Your expenses are not going away entirely, of course, and most of them are related to your children or loved ones, as usual. You might also be spending on fun and leisure activities.

Love and family

Your family life is quiet and harmonious, and spouses are unlikely to argue at all this month.

In mid-November, you might disagree with your children. Each specific case will look differently, but here, it all depends on how old they are as well as recent situations. You may have to deal with old problems that are coming back yet again. But in any case, all you need is attention and money.

In mid-November, many Capricorns will have some trouble involving relatives. Perhaps you will learn something upsetting about your family members. Your relationship with loved ones is not that great to begin with, and this will only throw fuel on the fire. Steel yourself and you are less likely to be upset by it all.

Health

During the first 20 days of November, you are feeling energetic and have no reason to fear falling ill.

During the last 10 days, however, you might feel fatigued from all of the running around, work, and daily grind. Find some time to relax and remember that your health comes first.

AQUARIUS

November brings a continuation of the positive developments from October, and the stars are doing everything to support your endeavors. Good luck!

Work

November is one of the busiest months for you at work this year.

Business owners and managers will resolve the most difficult problems on their current projects, and might start new projects, as well.

Employees will improve their position at work, and in many cases, this is reflected in your paycheck.

All month long, most Aquarians who are part of the working world will be successful and effective in resolving any task.

However, when it comes to your relationship with friends or someone influential, it is worth treading lightly. You might disagree over money or have clashing views on your business development. This is most pertinent for business owners, as well as executives. If you have any trouble, shore up your arguments and be ready with facts.

The best time for anything work-related is the first half of November, and most of your challenges will arise from the 12th to the 24th.

Money

Your finances are looking good in November. You will have regular earnings and significantly more of it, too. Expect the largest sums to come in on November 1, 2, 10, 11, 19, 20, 28, and 29.

You have a lot of expenses, but your income is more than enough to cover them. The stars predict that most of your spending will be related to your personal life-children and loved ones.

Love and family

Despite your full dance card at work, many Aquarians will find time for their personal lives, as well. And here, unlike at work, you can expect an onslaught of problems in every direction.

Parents might face trouble involving their children, which will require a lot of resources to resolve. In the best-case scenario, you will have to spend money on their development and education, and in the worst case- you will argue with your adult children over ethical or financial matters.

Couples might find themselves frequently fighting, with November 12-24 as the most acute period.

It is not worth it to run your mouth during this time- you are not always known for your tact or diplomacy. Rein it in and remember that no one has ever been canceled for being too polite.

This advice is also valid for married couples on the warpath.

Health

In November, you are surging with energy and "tired" might not be part of your vocabulary anymore. What's more – the more energy you expend, the more you create.

PISCES

This month, your usual restlessness and ingenuity are back. And with these qualities up your sleeve, you are ready to move mountains!

Work

In November, you will have a burning desire to act, and every specific case will look different.

Many Pisceans will be busy reconnecting with colleagues in other cities or abroad and perhaps going on a trip. You might be at the start of a new phase in your business, especially those who recently decided to move or start a new job.

In any events planned for November, you can count on support from old friends and VIPs.

Business owners and managers will continue to face intrigue over major property, possibly real estate. Expect arguments over this from November 12-18.

During this time, employees would be wise to be very meticulous at work and not annoy management. If you are absolutely sure you are in the right, choose the first half of November, when your initiatives are likely to be welcomed.

Money

Financially, November is a wonderful time for you. You will have money coming in regularly, and significantly more than usual. Expect the largest sums to come in on November 3, 4, 12, 13, 21, and 22.

Your expenses are low and mostly related to your personal life, your home, and your family's and children's needs.

Love and family

You are unlikely to see any changes in your personal life. Many Pisceans are still busy setting up their home, and in some cases, this is taking place in a new city or abroad.

Couples who are on the rocks and those who are already separated or divorced might still be dealing with thorny negotiations over real estate or their children's future. These arguments are unlikely to end in November and will probably continue into the future.

Any trips planned for this month will be a smashing success, but the stars recommend that you avoid traveling from the 14th to 18th of November. These days promise nothing but conflict and injury.

Health

This month, you are healthy, energetic, and leaving quite an impression on everyone Fate sends your way. However, from the 14th to 18th, be careful when traveling or driving.

December

New York Time			London Time		
Calendar Day	Lunar Day	Lunar Day Start Time	Calendar Day	Lunar Day	Lunar Day Start Time
1	01/12/24	1.22 AM	01/12/24	1	6.22 AM
2	01/12/24	7.21 AM	01/12/24	2	7.56 AM
3	02/12/24	8.18 AM	02/12/24	3	8.57 AM
4	03/12/24	9.11 AM	03/12/24	4	9.51 AM
5	04/12/24	9.58 AM	04/12/24	5	10.35 AM
6	05/12/24	10.39 AM	05/12/24	6	11.11 AM
7	06/12/24	11.15 AM	06/12/24	7	11.40 AM
8	07/12/24	11.47 AM	07/12/24	8	12.04 PM
9	08/12/24	12.17 PM	08/12/24	9	12.25 PM
10	09/12/24	12.46 PM	09/12/24	10	12.45 PM
11	10/12/24	1.16 PM	10/12/24	11	1.05 PM
12	11/12/24	1.48 PM	11/12/24	12	1.28 PM
13	12/12/24	2.25 PM	12/12/24	13	1.54 PM
14	13/12/24	3.07 PM	13/12/24	14	2.27 PM
15	14/12/24	3.58 PM	14/12/24	15	3.08 PM
16	15/12/24	4.55 PM	15/12/24	16	4.01 PM
17	16/12/24	5.58 PM	16/12/24	17	5.05 PM
18	17/12/24	7.04 PM	17/12/24	18	6.16 PM
19	18/12/24	8.10 PM	18/12/24	19	7.29 PM
20	19/12/24	9.13 PM	19/12/24	20	8.42 PM
21	20/12/24	10.15 PM	20/12/24	21	9.52 PM
22	21/12/24	11.14 PM	21/12/24	22	11.00 PM
23	23/12/24	12.12 AM	23/12/24	23	12.07 AM
24	24/12/24	1.10 AM	24/12/24	24	1.13 AM
25	25/12/24	2.09 AM	25/12/24	25	2.19 AM
26	26/12/24	3.08 AM	26/12/24	26	3.26 AM
27	27/12/24	4.08 AM	27/12/24	27	4.34 AM
28	28/12/24	5.09 AM	28/12/24	28	5.42 AM
29	29/12/24	6.08 AM	29/12/24	29	6.46 AM
30	30/12/24	7.04 AM	30/12/24	30	7.44 AM
1	30/12/24	5.27 PM	30/12/24	1	10.27 PM
2	31/12/24	7.54 AM	31/12/24	2	8.32 AM

You can find the description of each lunar day in the chapter "A Guide to The Moon Cycle and Lunar Days"

ARIES

December is an unusual month. All of the difficulties you have been dealing with recently are suddenly getting even worse. What can you do? There's only one answer: Don't give up. Remember the wise words of Winston Churchill – Never give in, never give in, never, never, never...

Work

This month, two of the most crucial planets, Mercury and your ruler, Mars, will be in retrograde, which will be reflected in any work you aim to do.

Many who are planning to cooperate with colleagues in other cities or abroad will run into trouble here. Your colleagues from afar might shirk their responsibilities which is likely to happen for various reasons. Perhaps the world stage will suddenly become more complicated, or you will face some other kind of force majeure.

In any case, there is no way to avoid trouble here, and it is worth laying the groundwork for alternatives for business development. For example, you might focus your efforts on the here and now, in your own town.

It is not worth trying to rely on any support here this month. You will have to bear the brunt on your own, though you overcome a few blips with the help of influential people. This is especially the case for business owners and managers. Employees can be sure of support from their managers and certain colleagues.

The good news is that this month, you will improve your relationship with business partners in your own country.

Money

Despite all the chaos at work, things aren't actually so bad when it comes to money. You will periodically receive a healthy sum in your account, which gives you hope for the future and your ability to get through these otherwise tough times.

Your expenses are low, and some of them might be unpredictable. Having a financial safety net is a blessing, but you have to have built it up ahead of time!

Expect to receive the largest amounts on December 4, 5, 12, 13, 20, and 21.

Love and family

Your personal life is looking messy. Clashes between Venus and Mars will be heavily reflected in your relationship with your partner, and you might find yourselves frequently fighting, and even deciding to separate.

If you are married, your marriage might also be on the rocks this month, though less extreme than if you are not. You will quickly reconcile and in the end you will reach a mutual understanding.

Many families will run into difficulties involving their children, and the older they are, the more troublesome their problems will become.

Your relationship with relatives will also require special attention. A situation that arose in August of this year may repeat itself. The conflict might reach a new level this time, and you will have a hard time finding common ground.

Carefully plan any travel this month, and if it isn't absolutely necessary, it might be better to just stay home, whether you are thinking of traveling for business or leisure.

Health

In December, you are feeling energetic enough to withstand all of the challenges this month throws at you.

The stars still urge you to be very cautious when traveling and driving. All month is a risky time, especially the first half.

TAURUS

You are embarking on one of the most difficult months of the year. Literally everything is in flux – try to keep a stiff upper lip as you face an ever-changing world. You are strong and you'll get through it.

Work

Your main task at work will be material or financial in nature, as this will be the source of a conflict involving a VIP or old friend. You've been here before - in August of this year, in fact, so you have a good understanding of what's at play.

Business owners and managers will deal with trouble involving real estate. This will dragon and might not be resolved until 2025. If you have problems at work, employees might count on support from managers, but that might not be enough to smooth things over entirely.

Things will improve somewhat by the end of the month, but you will not be able to tackle the lion's share until next year.

Money

Your finances look like a tragedy this month. You will be bleeding money, and lots of it.

Despite the fact that you will have some money coming in, by the end of the month, you might even be in the red.

You can expect to receive something on December 6, 7, 14, 15, 23, and 24.

Love and family

Your personal life, which is more important to you than work, is also a mess. Spouses who get along will work together to overcome their problems and be able to lean on one another when the going gets tough.

Couples who don't get along, however, and those who have already decided to separate or divorce, might clash over shared property, most likely their home. Nothing will be resolved now. This will drag on for months, so learn to be patient and gather all of your necessary documents.

Couples will have trouble holding onto one another. Your better half will be full of complaints. Only you can decide how to respond to this, but your relationship is unlikely to last.

Health

Those who manage to escape any professional or personal strife might instead suffer in their health.

You can expect old illnesses or new ones to rear their ugly heads, so take care to avoid any winter illnesses or colds and stay away from any risky situations.

GEMINI

This month's events will have lasting consequences, so avoid any unnecessary risks and stay on the straight and narrow. Don't rush anything – haste makes waste.

Work

Your relationship with other people is the most important theme of this month. This includes business partners, official government bodies, and of course, your superiors.

For various reasons, your relationship with those around you is significantly more complicated right now. You may not be at fault, this time, but it is what it is.

However, either way, there is a strong psychological component here. For a long time, now, you have been agreeing to something that is no longer making you happy. This will cause you trouble. What's more, the stars recommend taking precautions – Mercury, your planet, is in retrograde, so you might be anxious, tense, and have a hard time making the right decisions.

You will also have to work on your relationship with colleagues from other cities or abroad this month. This is hard but not impossible. You are capable of making things work with them, though in some cases, you might have to rely on an intermediary.

Employees might argue with management and think about leaving for greener pastures. You will receive a new job offer in about three months- by the end of February or March 2025, and it's worth keeping this in mind.

Money

December is not the best time for your wallet this year. You have lower income than usual, and your expenses are climbing. This situation will continue until January 2025.

Love and family

Your personal life is no bed of roses, either, especially if this is what you value the most. Couples, whether married or not, might argue constantly, though you will not get as far as breaking up. You will find common ground and your loved ones will be able to put your broken world back together. A relative will prove influential on bringing the warring parties back together, and back to normal.

Be especially careful if you plan on traveling this month, and if it is not absolutely necessary, maybe just stay home instead.

Health

In December, you are feeling energetic enough and have no reason to fear any winter colds. The stars still advise you to be careful traveling and driving. The riskiest days are December 1, 2, 6, 7, 12, 13, 18, 19, 25, and 26.

CANCER

This month you would be wise to keep your ambitions in check, and generally be more modest. Your number one goal is to shore up your position and protect yourself, like any experienced warlord under siege.

Work

You are in for a turbulent month. Business owners and managers might run into audits, which will bring some skeletons in your closet to light.

This might involve old dealings which have unexpectedly taken on a new hue. Many Cancers will also have to grapple with old legal issues, and here, it is worth remembering that all of the failures you have faced in the past might repeat themselves once again. If things drag on, however, which is the most likely scenario, the best days ahead of you will start in April 2025.

What's more, managers are likely to have trouble involving subordinates, who might fail to carry out their responsibilities or clash with one another.

Employees can expect to disagree with colleagues or face intrigue and gossip or other breakdowns on their team.

Those planning any cooperation with colleagues in other cities or abroad will also face challenges this month. Business partners from afar might endure force majeure, which is becoming increasingly common in our world. You won't be bored in December, as you ward off attacks on all fronts.

Money

Financially, December is a difficult time for you, but things aren't entirely hopeless. You will have your normal income, and you can expect to receive the most money on December 1, 2, 10, 11, 18, 19, 28, and 29.

Love and family

Those who are primarily focused on their personal lives will have to deal with some tough times this month. You might see your relationship with relatives significantly worsen, and you may even have a serious argument or go your separate ways from a family member after a major misunderstanding.

Spouses will likely clash over money or how to raise their children. In December, it is a good idea to be attentive to one another, and if something goes wrong, you will have to simply accept it and get through it. This way, things will turn out better.

Those with real estate or other assets abroad will also be in for some turmoil.

In each specific case, it is impossible to predict what will happen, but there will definitely be cause for concern. Look at all potential options, and if you can, take steps ahead of time.

Any trips planned for December might be complicated or not turn out the way you had hoped and dreamed.

Health

Those who manage to get through December unscathed at work or at home might instead suffer in their health. You might see old illnesses resurface, or new ones unexpectedly appear. If that sounds like you, remember that carelessness toward yourself will turn out poorly this month, so if you run into any trouble, see a good doctor.

Be careful when traveling or driving.

LEO

This month, you may feel like you are in a never-ending maze. Your strategic task is therefore to make it out without any losses, so come up with a detailed plan of action and stick to it.

Work

The spotlight this month is on your relationship with those around you. Business owners and managers might disagree with someone influential, and naturally, the culprit will be money or other material assets. This is not the first time you have been here in 2024, and you may things from August repeating themselves, only more seriously this time.

You can expect a colleague to be a thorn in your side.

Employees will be wise to keep their ambitions in check and not draw any attention from management or ask for anything, much less make any demands.

For all Leos, the general advice this month, regardless of your field, is to try to be flexible and don't beat your head against the wall, because this time, it's made out of reinforced concrete.

Money

December is not a good time for your bank account. You might be bleeding money, and at some point, it will be clear that you might not have enough. You may have to repay old debts or cover your family's and children's needs.

Things will start to look up when you receive small amounts on December 2, 5, 20-22, 30, and 31.

Love and family

Your personal life is not going to let you rest, either, this month.

Parents will be worried about their children's future, education, and upbringing. If your children's affairs are not yet in order, remember that no one but you can help them, and act immediately.

Naturally, that will cost money, and your family budget will be threadbare.

But those same children will become the link between squabbling spouses, including those in the middle of a divorce.

Couples will also feel a lot of ups and downs, though you can smooth things over, especially if you both have the desire to meet one another halfway. Even if your loved one starts to act cold and aloof and you have to take the first step, there's nothing wrong with that. In the end, it is for everyone's benefit, so swallow your pride and act accordingly.

Health

In December, you are feeling energetic, which will allow you to overcome all of this month's hurdles.

VIRGO

In December, your ruler, Mercury, will be in retrograde, which means you may be lacking in logic, patience, and inner calm – which also happen to be the very qualities you have always been known for. Remember that inner peace is the key to success in everything and do not give into emotional triggers.

Work

For Virgos who are part of the working world, December is a supremely difficult time.

You have been hoping for a breakthrough at work, and it may not happen quite the way you hoped. Instead, you might have to overcome challenges, and it won't be easy.

Business owners will once again clash with business partners, in a more acute version of the events from August. This time, you may disagree over your shared business, or perhaps how to divide it up. You might also run into trouble involving real estate. What's more, your work may come to the attention of various auditing agencies.

Employees might find themselves under an onslaught of criticism from management and office gossip. Any attempt to defend your side of the story will be counterproductive at best.

The stars recommend that you don't go into any open battlefield. Keep restraint and be cautious. At the very least, avoid any major decisions and hold tight. This applies to any Virgos, regardless of your field.

Money

When it comes to finances, December is relatively stable for you. You will have your regular earnings, and you can expect the largest sums to come in on December 6, 7, 14, 15, 23, and 24.

You still have expenses, and they may be related to either business or your personal life.

Love and family

This month, your personal life is no less important than work, but it is just as turbulent. After a temporary calm, spouses whose marriage is on the rocks will once again unleash war on one another. There is plenty of reason for this, including old grudges, and your better half's unwillingness to come to an understanding. Similar situations are likely for couples who are divorcing. In any case, the crux of the matter may be real estate or shared business (or how to divide it up). You will resolve this later on, but right now, there is no hope of a compromise.

Things might look difficult, and it is unpleasant, but some skeletons may be dragged out of the closet – either yours or your partner's. Perhaps you both have secrets that will come to light.

Health

Those who manage to escape any professional or personal strife might instead be hit with health problems. If you have suffered from various illnesses in the past, they might come roaring back. That may be facilitated by the tense, emotional backdrop this month, so take care of yourself, and remember that your nerves are behind any illness. Nothing is more important than your health, the rest will follow.

LIBRA

There are times in life when we have to make a choice between two options, and neither option is particularly appetizing. Will you find a third? After all, there's a reason they say that he who looks for something will always find it.

Work

Libras who are part of the working world will run into a whole series of problems this month. Your cooperation with business partners in other cities or abroad is once again giving you headaches. This time, things run deep, though, and in many cases, it will lead to a breakdown in your relationship.

You will manage to find common ground with a colleague abroad, however, and it will be exclusively thanks to your efforts. You may find a situation from August repeating itself from time to time this month, so a lot of this is old news, and you know how to handle it.

Your relationship with friends and like-minded individuals will also require special attention as you are likely to run into disagreements here.

Perhaps someone from your circle will be eying your place in the sun and be willing to do anything to realize his or her ambitions. You are in a strong place, however, and will be the victor in the end.

Money

December is not your best month when it comes to money. You will be spending constantly, maybe on business, or perhaps your personal life.

Love and family

Your personal life will see a continuation of processes that began in November. Your relationship with your relatives is looking rocky, and there may be mutual grudges here, or alternatively, you will have to deal with a difficult situation involving a close relative.

Families will have to deal with trouble involving their children, and this may look different, depending on how old they are, and what sort of trouble they have faced in the recent past. You can be sure that all of your children's issues will be resolved favorably, however, and in the end, they will fade away.

Your relationship with your partner is significantly more difficult than previously, and in mid-December, you can expect a serious row. Unexpectedly, it will become clear that you and your partner have very different ideas about certain events, people, or your relationship in general. This will guarantee disappointment and arguments. Only time will tell how serious it is, but there is a chance that your relationship will survive.

Health

In December, you are feeling vigorous, and the stars urge you to be attentive when traveling and driving.

The stars also recommend that you avoid any travel for leisure. Why test fate during such a difficult time?

SCORPIO

December may yank you from one extreme to another, giving you whiplash. The stars urge you to be adaptable and solve problems as they come. That is how you will win this battle.

Work

December has you busy at work, but this month is also a whirlwind, and you will have to put a lot of effort into getting what you want.

Business owners and managers will continue to expand their business, but this is difficult and will require a lot of elbow grease and huge investments on your part, as well.

Your relationship with colleagues in other cities or abroad is also developing, and in general, things will go well. By the end of the month, you will be talking about traveling or preparing to do just that.

Employees will see their employer continue to undergo changes, and in some cases, that may be cause for concern. If you want to leave, your job search will continue until the middle of 2025, so it is futile to try to rush things now.

Money

December is not a good time for your finances. Everyone needs money-your children, loved ones, and you might also have to make major investments in your family's needs.

Businesspeople will have to make peace with the fact that their initiatives, and business in general, will require greater resources. .

You will not end up in the red, however, and you will periodically receive some money. Expect the largest amounts on December 1, 2, 10, 11, 18, 19, 28, and 29.

Love and family

Many Scorpios might be more focused on their personal life, which will require a lot of attention this month.

Parents will continue to grapple with problems involving their children and resolving this will take time, nerves, and of course, money.

Those planning various events related to improving their home, construction, or repairs might have a hard time continuing what they started earlier. Many families might argue over money and differing views over how things should look. It is worth remembering that each person wants to do things the best they can, so there is reason to listen to one another's positions and reach a compromise.

Unmarried couples may be edging toward the brink of a breakup, and only a miracle will help them avoid it. Of course, a miracle includes love and a mutual desire to remain together.

Health

This month, you are feeling sluggish, but you have no reason to fear falling seriously ill, as long as you lead a healthy lifestyle and don't give into emotional outbursts and mood swings.

SAGITTARIUS

Conflict in the aspects of Mercury, Mars, the Sun, Jupiter, and Saturn promise anything but a peaceful December. Sometimes, life is like this, so it is worth steeling yourself for the stars' capricious behavior. After all, fighting it is futile.

Work

Your biggest problem this month will be your relationship with a business partner. Disagreements that began in recent months have taken on a new, nastier shape. You might clash over real estate, land, or other major assets.

Your relationship with colleagues in other cities or abroad will also be troublesome. Your partners from afar might shirk their responsibilities or create circumstances that threaten your cooperation.

So long as Mercury is in retrograde, right in your sign, Sagittarius, you may be lacking in logic, patience, and sometimes, endurance.

When you need to act, you might hit the brakes, and when you need to stop and listen, you might jump the gun or even get aggressive. This kind of rash behavior might weaken your position as you face off with your business partners.

The stars recommend that all Sagittarians, regardless of their field, avoid any major projects, signing any important documents, or counting on people who came into your life only recently. The best strategy for you is to tie up loose ends and keep an eye on your partners.

Money

Financially, December is neutral for you. Your expenses and income are as usual, and you can expect the largest sums to come in on December 4, 5, 21, 22, and 28-30.

Love and family

If you are more focused on your personal life, trouble is inevitable here, too. Spouses might argue over important issues related to their home or other major real estate.

Alternatively, married couples might work together to overcome various challenges related to their home or other real estate that someone else is trying to claim is theirs.

Your relationship with relatives looks complicated as well. A major argument may erupt among your close family members, and everyone else will be dragged into the fray. On the other hand, this may lead to a reconciliation – someone will act as a mediator, and by late December, the family will have reached a fragile ceasefire.

Health

In December, you are a little sluggish, perhaps because of the anxiety-inducing atmosphere all month long. Lay low and don't try to second-guess the stars. The planets are clear- there is no way around this difficult period.

CAPRICORN

During this last month of the year, you will be put to the test. This is a difficult time, when any expectations seem like a trick, whether in your personal life or at work. Hold on tight!

Work

In December, it's not worth it to try to dive into any major projects. It is better to finish up what you started earlier and shore up your position. That is especially true for any managers or business owners, who may face serious trouble on all fronts.

Your relationship with colleagues in other cities or abroad is seriously difficult right now, as once again, they are behaving inappropriately, if not aggressively. You may also have to contend with obstacles on the world stage that throw a wrench into any international cooperation.

In December, it is worth preparing for your work to come to the attention of various audit agencies, which may bring to light things that you'd rather keep quiet.

Employees might run into office gossip, while managers might face off with competitors, who might act out in the open, or perhaps under a veneer.

All of the difficulties this month offer you an opportunity to strengthen your defenses. Once December is over, things will start to settle down once again.

Money

This month, your financial situation is also difficult, which is only natural after the way things are going at work. You are spending heavily, particularly in mid-December. You need to make sure that you are able to earn money so that this month doesn't bankrupt you.

Love and family

Your personal life is also seeing a continuation of the events that began in the recent past. Your relationship with relatives is more difficult, and in many cases, you may even go no contact with one another.

You might also learn something about a family member, or perhaps your own secrets will be dragged into the light. Alternatively, your family members will continue to experience serious trouble, and you will have to provide them with both moral and financial support.

Spouses will be busy with their children's affairs, and once again, that will require a lot of spending.

The heavens are capricious right now, and that is reflected in many couples. People with ulterior motives might meddle in your relationship, and you might be in for some serious gossip and rumors – it will not be easy to shake this off.

The astrologist advises you not to believe wagging tongues, which may embellish the truth. If you have any questions, sit down, and have a heart-to-heart talk with your partner.

Health

Capricorns who are elderly or weakened might have serious health problems this month. Be attentive to any changes, and if you feel unwell, turn to a good doctor instead of trying to treat yourself. This is a difficult month, and even young and healthy people might feel under the weather or less than cheerful. Lay low, don't try to put your body to the test, and be very careful behind the wheel!

All Capricorns can expect trouble on the road this month, as there is a high risk of accidents. Avoid any traveling, either near or far.

AQUARIUS

This month, you will be incredibly determined, or perhaps even downright belligerent. However, your attempts to act tough will be met with a tough response. You will manage to find trouble anywhere you go.

Work

Many Aquarians will have to come back to some tasks that you have recently finished. Perhaps, there are disagreements with friends or influential people over money or other financial assets. Your position is strong, but your partners have no intentions of giving in, either.

Therefore, expect negotiations, debates, or arguments to last all of December.

Perhaps the issue is real estate, land, or another major asset.

At some point, you will realize that being confrontational here is not working in your favor, and you will spare no efforts to reach a peaceful conclusion to your negotiations. You will get what you want, too, and be pleasantly surprised by your partner's response.

The stars recommend this strategy for employees facing challenging managers, as well

Money

This is not a good time for your bank account. You will be spending constantly, and much of it will be related to your personal life and the needs of your children or loved one.

Your income is lower than usual, and by New Year's your wallet will be empty.

Love and family

Many Aquarians will be primarily focused on their personal lives in December.

Parents will face trouble involving their children, and that may look different, depending on how old they are, as well as the recent past. In any case, however, you will have to lend a hand in words, deeds, and of course- money.

You will do everything to keep the situation under control, and you will be successful here.

December is also a difficult time for most couples, as once again, their relationship is on the rocks, and in order to avoid celebrating the holidays alone, you will have to meet your loved one halfway. This will go a long way to calming him or her down, and lowering the tensions that characterize this month. Married couples who don't get along can expect the same.

Health

Much of December will have you feeling energetic, and you have no reason to fear falling ill. You might experience some fatigue at the end of the month, so it is best to keep your holiday celebrations low key.

PISCES

In December, you will be bursting with energy, but the stars urge you to use this for peaceful purposes. You should avoid risks and accidents this month, so avoid rushing anywhere.

Work

You are busy at work, but you are also on a difficult streak right now.

Business owners and managers will be reorganizing their business, and in some cases, that will be forced on them.

Perhaps you clashed with an official government agency or someone influential. In some cases, you might be dealing with a dispute over real estate, land, or other major property.

You are not going to resolve all of this in one fell swoop this month. It will likely drag on into 2025. You will be able to smooth some rough edges, though, as long as you aren't ham-fisted in your efforts and instead opt for a roundabout way. Through circumvention, you will be successful.

Employees will also see changes at work, and that may make you nervous. The stars recommend that you avoid opposing your managers or try to fight what is happening. The train has left the station.

Try to accept things and remember that any changes are generally for the better, this time.

Money

Despite all the trouble at work, your bank account is looking good. You will have your usual earnings, and somewhat more money will be coming in. Expect to receive the largest amounts on December 1, 2, 10, 11, 18, 19, and 28-30. Your expenses are low, and you have more than enough income to cover them.

Love and family

Expect your personal life to bring you turmoil and strife, potentially revolutionary scenarios, when you are stuck between a rock and a hard place. Most likely, that involves couples whose relationship has been waiting to erupt for some time, now.

You might be talking about divorce, real estate, or your children's future- this will be the backdrop for the last month of 2024. Old friends might exert their influence to smooth things over a bit, but this is unlikely to be a silver bullet.

Saturn is in your sign, and that is driving you to seek justice, so be bold if you are absolutely sure you are right. If not, then try to understand your partner's point of view, and meet him or her halfway. This is relevant for couples, as well as those who have been arguing with their parents or elderly family members lately.

Health

In December, you are bounding with energy and have no reason to fear falling ill.

Description of Zodiac Signs

ARIES DESCRIPTION

Sign. Masculine, fire, cardinal.

Rulers. Mars and Pluto in retrograde.

Exaltation. Sun.

Temperament. Choleric, impulsive, aggressive.

Positive traits. Logical, self-confident, decisive, determined, vigorous, persistence, proactive, entrepreneurial, ambitious, optimistic, dynamic.

Negative traits. Irritable, excitable, impulsive, intolerant, stubborn, grumpy, reckless, a tendency to exaggerate and sensationalize, unchecked passion, aggressive, despotic, tyrannical.

Weaknesses in the body. Head, brain, central nervous system, face, eyes, ears, teeth, tongue, nose, mouth, upper jaw, chin.

Metal. Iron.

Minerals. For a talisman, red jasper. Generally: rubies, carnet, diamond, Indian carnelian.

Numbers. 5, 7, 9.

Day. Tuesday.

Color. Red.

Aries's Energy

Aries opens the Zodiac and is first in the circle of signs. This is reflected in life, as Aries always tries to be first with everything – and he manages to do it, too! Aries is a fire sign, which symbolizes the material embodiment of the spirit, power, and transformation. In the trigon of fire signs, it is the first manifestation of cosmic fire – a fire of life that erupted, giving way to obsession and the desire to unleash one's natural potential.

Aries is ruled by Mars, which gives its children incredible energy reserves and enviable creativity. This planet is named for the mythological hero associated with victory and incredible powers; in ancient times, he was depicted as an angel with a magic sword cutting through the darkness. The energy of both Mars and Fire makes Aries the most active and powerful sign of the zodiac, with the greatest chances of conquering the highest mountains.

Astrological portrait of Aries

Anyone born under this sign believes in self-affirmation: "I am." He takes initiative and is a sure leader and moves forward, and doesn't worry about the consequences (those who follow will do that for you), guided by ideas that inspire and encourage – this is Aries' highest cosmic task.

Aries is symbolized by a ram, an animal that is direct and courageous as it tackles the challenges thrown at it by Fate. Aries are no different. They conquer the world with strength, assertiveness, and aggression. They are courageous and fearless. They cut straight to the chase, pushing any obstacles out of the way. Aries are never discouraged, they are always moving ahead as they dive into work with a passion, making waves, learn from the school of hard knocks, and in the end, are victorious.

To an Aries, life is a battlefield, and he is ready for anything, has no fear of insults or humiliation, and will not stop in the face of failure or difficulties. Fearlessness often drives an Aries to risk, and for the right cause, an Aries might even risk his or her life. But once in a crisis, Aries has strong intuition, and therefore can rule and cope without any outside assistance.

All of Aries' excess fire makes him or her active, always striving to be the first and the best in everything, with a thirst for fame and recognition. Aries lights up at the sight of a new business and begins to radiate joy and electrify those around him. He is capable of leading large crowds with almost magical influence; this is why he is always in a position of power – either physical or psychological.

Aries is self-absorbed and views the world around him as an extension of himself. The feelings and interests of others are of little interest, and he does not know how to tap into the secrets of the human soul. It is not worth blaming him for that. Aries is able to succeed precisely because of this individualism. However, Aries has something that the other signs do not have – he is honest, noble, and absolutely sincere in every way. Lies and deceit are unknown to an Aries, which softens some of his selfishness. Another valuable quality is Aries' ability to always come to the rescue in times of suffering and need. He is a strong shoulder to lean on during tough times. Once Aries has lent a hand in a difficult time, he will do it again and again, though he may feel hurt if his own worries and concerns go unnoticed.

For all of Aries' bravery, assertiveness, and aggression, he is a very sensitive and defenseless child underneath. It is easy to insult or offend him. However, he quickly gets over any such attacks, as long as you provide him with praise and affection. Despite having a short fuse (Aries can descend into boorishness, scandal, and even fights), Aries will quickly walk away, and he will not waste much sulking before forgiving the offender, especially if he or she has a kind word to say about him.

But don't hold your breath waiting for an Aries to discover tact and the ability to smooth over disagreements and avoid outbursts. These qualities are not on his list of virtues. To an Aries, diplomacy means directness, ingenuity, and honesty. Thanks to their incredible work ethic, Aries tend to be wealthy, though they are never stingy and are willing to share it with others. After all, despite their selfishness, one of Aries' most fundamental needs is to bring joy to others. What's the point of wealth if there's no one to share it with?

How to recognize an Aries by appearances

There are two types of Aries: strong and muscular, or weak and sickly, which is what happens to them if they do not live in harmony with their sign, which requires a healthy diet and constant physical activity. Aries is lively in appearance, speaking quickly and in imperative tones, moving around decisively.

Aries is distinguished by a ruddy complexion. Mars, the red planet, bestows this on its children. Aries' face has a certain roughness, stiffness, and a pronounced nose. Aries women are somewhat masculine in their appearance, with a strong torso, broad shoulders, a narrow waist and hips, and a low, often hoarse voice.

Charting Aries' Fate

Generally speaking, Aries' fate is positive, though his path in life is unlikely to be called "smooth". There will be many changes, crises, and acute situations. Usually, Aries have had a restless youth and later settle down as adults. They always achieve anything they set their mind to, and their dreams and plans come true. But their success is theirs alone – Aries are workaholics, unafraid to take a risk, take great chances in life, and never fixate on past failures. They take Fate by the horns, and will not surrender, no matter what is thrown their way. They simply know no fear and ignore their failures. This, along with their self-confidence are Aries' trump cards.

Aries' impulsivity and scatterbrained nature may become obstacles to success. Aries is inspired by many ideas and perpetually rushing around and has a difficult time focusing on just one thing. They want to do it all, and right now. Therefore, they often do not see things through.

The root cause of this is a lack of inner grounding and discipline; Aries is stubborn though and will replace them with stubbornness. He simply keeps charging forward, sometimes without even looking where he is going, until he is running into serious obstacles. In order to overcome this problem, he must:

- Find the right way to channel this energy into something inspiring.
- Create a set of behavioral rules for himself. He needs to be educated, have high standards for himself, but not be too strict, as being too hard one himself will be counterproductive), that is, to show both love and high standards at once, while occasionally indulging himself;
- learn to think first and have a clear behavioral standard. He can start small – count to 10 before saying or doing anything;
- Do away with black and white thinking – mine-yours, friend-enemy, good-bad) and expand his mind;
- Occasionally look within and reflect on his spiritual impulses and do a "debriefing". Aries is the only sign that does not fall into depression triggered by self-discovery.

TAURUS DESCRIPTION

Sign. Feminine, Earth, fixed.,

Ruler. Venus.

Exaltation. Moon.

Temperament. Melancholic, slow.

Positive traits. Persistent, patient, restrained, diligent, thorough, careful, a good judge, consistent, honest, a good temperament.

Negative traits. Stubborn, willful, overly sensitive, pessimistic, lazy, apathetic, sluggish, conservative.

Weaknesses in the body. Neck and internal organs. Thyroid gland, tonsils, frontal sinuses, vocal cords, trachea. The esophagus. Occipital and cerebellum.

Metal. Copper.

Minerals. For talisman – carnelian orange. For general wearing – hyacinth, coral, pink quartz.

Number. 6.

Day. Friday.

Color. Yellow-orange and bright green.

Taurus's energy

It is great fortune to be born under the sign of Taurus, and receive the energy of Venus, the ruler of beauty, harmony, love, and prosperity. Taurus is made to flourish and prosper in everything – in love, with money, friends, knowledge, and spiritual values.

The Earth element means that people born under Taurus are practical, incredibly patient, strong, and tenacious. These are their trump cards. Taureans know exactly what they want, and they are determined as they work toward their goals, and these efforts are not in vain! Often, Taureans manage to become wealthy and well-known, with few exceptions.

Astrological portrait of Taurus

Taurus's motto is "acquire, accumulate, possess". They are extremely practical, and their goal is to take ideas in the spiritual phase and make them take shape by creating, building, and strengthening. In everything Taureans do, they are guided by common sense. They are materialists and pragmatists who place great importance on comfort, satisfaction, and prosperity. They are ready to overcome any obstacles on the way to financial stability – but they are not driven by greed or a passion for hoarding wealth, but rather a need to feel comfortable in this world. This is the only way a Taurus can be effective in life, when she feels the ground beneath her feet. The best support you can give a Taurus is material possessions or monetary savings. Taurus is distinguished by her poise and emotional stability – it is hard to get him/her to lose control, and even harder to prove something to her.

Taureans will hold onto certain beliefs until they have been disappointed. They are stubborn, though they would not agree with that description. Taureans are willing to gain strength, experience, and knowledge over a long time in hopes of achieving their goals and then make an overnight breakthrough to see unprecedented results.

Taurus is patient, reliable, responsible, and consistent in everything. As long as this determination lasts, she can withstand just about anything. She is loyal to friends, business partners, and loved ones, so long as they are honest with her.

Taurus still has some shortcomings. First of all, she is conservative. On the other hand, however, conservatism can be necessary and even a virtue in serious matters. That is why if Taurus shows a healthy level of conservatism, that is only an advantage. Taurus's desire to follow the established order also means she is capable of achieving great success.

Taurus also has some unusual qualities. She is hypersensitive. At her highest level of spiritual development, she will literally achieve the state of being a medium, perceiving objects in her world at the most subtle levels of energy. Many Taureans are often soothsayers, psychics, and healers who are capable of accumulating natural energy. J.R.R. Tolkien describes the highest level of Taurus in Lord of the Rings. Hobbits are true Taureans, capable of having fun, living an earthly life, and also guarding eternal values. Other Taureans should strive for the same.

How to recognize Taurus by appearances

A typical Taurus is calm, charming, and friendly, with a harmonious build, though she may tend to gain weight. Men tend to be large and robust. Taureans inspire confidence and authority. One might describe them as "well-cut and well-stitched". Women are extremely attractive, with big, beautiful eyes to lose oneself in, curved eyelashes, a flirtatious, upturned nose, and irresistible dimples. They have a dense build and a rounded shape and are always surrounded by admirers.

Charting Taurus's Fate

A young Taurus is restless, and usually needy, deprived, and her own worst enemy. But during the second half of life, she will see a period of prosperity. Taureans are business-minded, practical people who plan life several years in advance. They are methodical as they move toward their goals, and in the end, their persistence pays off, as they get everything they have been striving for. Everything that Taurus dreamt of is sure to come true. It might not be right away, but gradually, with enormous effort, they will soar to new heights!

Generally speaking, Taurus is healthy, with enviable strength.

GEMINI DESCRIPTION

Sign. Masculine, air, mutable.

Ruler. Mercury.

Exaltation. Mercury, Ascendant Lunar node.

Temperament. Sanguine, nervous, easygoing, volatile.

Positive traits. Intelligent and intuitive, very perceptive, quick to react, agile, observant, very imaginative, curious, honest, full of good will.

Negative traits. Superficial, unreliable, immodest, talkative, scattered, cold, reckless.

Weaknesses in the body. Hands. Respiratory organs. Tongue. Nervous system. Grey matter of the brain. The psyche.

Metal. Mercury.

Minerals. For a talisman – gold topaz, yellow beryl. Generally: topaz, tiger's eye, chrysoprase, carnelian.

Numbers. 5, 12.

Days. Wednesday.

Color. Orange-yellow and yellow green.

Gemini's energy

Gemini's personality is formed by the energy of Mercury, the closest planet to the Sun. It rotates far more quickly than the other planets. One side of Mercury is constantly facing the Sun, while the other side faces away from it with temperatures far below zero. This speed and duality are also a good description of Gemini. Geminis rush through life at the speed of light, constantly afraid of not having time to do something, and are reminiscent of Julius Caesar, who was known for being a master multitasker. Gemini is an air sign, which means that he has the gift of communication, along with inconsistency and a bit of a tendency toward the superficial. It is very difficult for a Gemini to focus on one thing at a time and see things through to the end. However, that is not too much of an obstacle in their lives.

Astrological portrait of Gemini

Geminis are cute, attractive, and a pleasure to spend time with. Their best qualities are their energy, mental alertness, intuition, and insight.

They are observant, capable of easily and quickly grasping information, and process it just as quickly. Mercury rules the mental processes, among other things, meaning that Gemini is the sign of intellectuals. People born under this sign achieve great success and have incredible public speaking skills. Coming from them, just about anything can seem true, and they are able to convince anyone of anything. Gemini's duty to himself is to not waste these qualities, and channel them in the right direction instead.

Gemini is restless, temperamental, and inconsistent. He rushes around from one extreme to the other, is in constant motion, and always looking to meet new friends and make new connections at every level. He eats breakfast, lunch, and dinner at the same time, has office romances at work, talks about work issues with their spouse, especially at night, when it is time to go to bed. A Gemini's mood changes from one second to the next. He might be prone to acting irrationally when he is in a bad mood, only to later regret it.

Geminis have a double nature. They can be both happy and sad at the same time. Everything in their lives exists in a duplicate – apartments, families, friends, girlfriends or boyfriends, lovers, and work. Things change with astonishing speed. You might say that to a Gemini, the purpose of life is trying it all.

One of Gemini's more troublesome qualities is inconsistency. If astrologers could rename Gemini, they might refer to this sign as a chameleon, which changes colors in order to camouflage and protect itself. We might add sensitivity to that inconsistency, as Geminis have a tendency to exaggerate the most minute details. They are known for emotional restraint, but this is not out of callousness, but rather a defense mechanism against other peoples' criticisms.

All Gemini tend to hide their true intentions. You will never know what a Gemini is really thinking deep down, even after living with him for decades. They are prone to fantasizing, have rich imaginations, and are inclined to embellish everything. But even in a lie, Gemini is harmless. He is not seeking revenge or to humiliate anyone in order to raise himself up in his own eyes. He is simply protecting his personal space and secrets. He is always interested in those he communicates with, reaching out and easily making a connection. With Gemini, you can always reach an understanding.

How to recognize Gemini by appearance

A typical Gemini is of average height, slim, agile, sociable, and charming. He has thin, pointed facial features.

Charting Gemini's Fate

Gemini's Fate reflects his nature. His life is an endless series of ups and downs. It is very difficult for Geminis to focus on just one thing, even if it is very important. Failing to address this can feed into Gemini's fatalism- they often let things float away from them.

Gemini tends to have an unstable family life, due to his overwhelming desire for new experiences. This sign is not exactly adapted to marriage, at least in the traditional sense.

Nature has bestowed Gemini with many talents. If he manages to harness at least a modicum of perseverance, he will achieve incredible success. He should avoid throwing himself into things or making hasty decisions.

CANCER DESCRIPTION

Sign. Feminine, water, cardinal.

Ruler. Moon.

Exaltation. Jupiter and Neptune in retrograde.

Temperament. Melancholic, with a tendency toward phlegmatic.

Positive traits. Adaptable, sensitive, romantic, intuitive, emotional, purposeful, patient, persistent, responsible, thrifty, caring, soft, restrained, imaginative, has a good memory.

Negative traits. Irritable, violently reactive, a tendency toward exaggeration, fearful, hysterical, cowardly, resentful, capricious, volatile, lazy, moody, passive, arrogant.

Weaknesses in the body. Stomach, digestive organs, pleura, mucous membranes, breasts, mammary glands, lymph.

Metal. Silver

Minerals. For a talisman – chrysoprase and emerald. In general: pearls, moonstone (selenite), opal.

Number. 5.

Day. Monday

Color. Bright green and purple.

Cancer energy

The volatile Moon changes phases four times in a month, making its children sensitive, easily influenced by their emotions, and mood swings. When Cancers are in a good mood, they are friendly and benevolent, but when their mood shifts to bad, it is best to avoid them. Cancers are forgiven for any mistake. What else would they do? After all, they are surprisingly cute and charming.

Despite the fact that Cancers are confident in themselves, they reach out to others. They have an undeniable talent for attracting others, because they need support and emotional energy from others. This is no surprise, given the fact that they are ruled by the Moon, which reflects the light of the Sun.

Cancer is a water sign, giving her an astuteness and intuition bordering on clairvoyance, as well as real skills at making money. Few others on the Zodiac are as adept at handling people and leveraging the energy of money. Cancers have turned this into an art form.

Astrological portrait of Cancer

Those born under Cancer are the most sensitive and emotional signs of the entire Zodiac. They have a rich spiritual life, which is always changing, just like the Moon, which is born, grows, climaxes, diminishes, and dies in order to do it all over again. Frequent mood swings are one of Cancer's traits. When Cancer is in a good mood, she is sweet, charming, and friendly. When she is in a bad mood, she has a tendency to slip into a long depression.

Cancer's motto is "I feel, therefore, I am". However, this does not mean we should assume that Cancer's heart is inherently warm or that she tends to feel sympathy for others. Cancers take much more than they give, and mainly have empathy for themselves. They will come to the rescue only when they can be convinced that there is no other option. Cancer seeks to be loved and cared for. However, she remains a bit of a mystery and will never fully reveal herself.

Cancers are vulnerable and sensitive to criticism and will react sharply to ridicule and sarcasm. Cancer is easily offended by a "wrong" look or tone. However, she is capable of defending herself. Cancer's self-defense mechanisms are very strong. A typical response is to lurk silently. Do not think for a second that she will forget or ignore what has happened, however. Cancer rarely forgives insults but believes that revenge is a dish best served cold. She might take a long time to come up with a plan for retaliation, and then leverage a convenient situation. It is best to stay neutral with a person like this.

Cancers tend to be successful people. They are not given to impulsivity or haste, but rather are cautious and risk-averse. Before doing anything, Cancer weighs the pros and cons. Only rarely will she listen to anyone else's advice. She prefers to resolve everything on her own and is not afraid of responsibility. Cancers do what they say and succeed at it. Mistakes are a rarity, thanks in large part to their outstanding intellectual abilities. Cancers perceive all nuances of what is happening around them. All of this is the influence of the Moon, which perceives and reflects the light of the Sun. Much like the Moon, Cancer perceives the outside world and immediately reflects it back.

Cancer's intuition is more developed than most other signs, meaning that she is excellent at understanding how other people are feeling and anticipating how situations will play out. Cancer is able to build a strong cause and effect relationship and find the root causes of certain problems, facts, and phenomena.

It is almost impossible to deceive a Cancer, and they should be treated with kindness. Pressuring them is useless – Cancer has developed a multi-stage defense mechanism, and the only way you can influence a Cancer is to pique her interest.

Cancers are persistent and assertive. If they have decided to do something, nothing will stop them. But in setting a goal, Cancer will never get straight to the point. Rather, she will bide her time, circle around the target, and keep an eye on it until she manages to reach it.

Despite Cancer's love of changes, novelty, and travel, they are strongly drawn to the home and their loved ones, especially their mother and children. To a Cancer, children are the world's greatest gift. Cancer is a home-bound and family sign, the keeper of family traditions. She adores her home and does not feel as relaxed and comfortable anywhere else.

If a Cancer is unable to achieve normal intellectual development, she might develop negative traits such as stinginess, childishness, or become conniving.

Cancers are often spilling over with emotions: it is normal for them to speak in loud tones, argue, or experience bouts of melancholy and even depression. This heightened sensitivity and vulnerability can eventually develop into complexes or neuroses. Cancer tries very hard to fulfill the ideal and be a strong person but continues to feel vulnerable.

Cancer is capable of seeing the true nature of the world around her and its essence, and carries higher ideas, and is a great zealot and creator. She passes all of the dirtiness in the world through her soul but holds onto her own pure soul. This is why it is wise to pay attention not only to a Cancer's outward appearance, but also her essence when dealing with her. If you manage to lure her out of her shell, you will be repaid in the highest form. After all, Cancer is not always on her best behavior, and not because she harbors any ill will. At her core, she is kind and selfless, due to her heightened sensitivity. Her soul cannot withstand the cruelty of the outside world. This might break Cancer, so she is forced to defend herself. If you cannot get her to open up, you will have to deal with her as though she were a child.

How to recognize Cancer by appearances

Cancer does not like to draw attention to herself, though she is very sociable by nature. She behaves modestly and exercises restraint. Cancers are rarely tall, and tend to be obese, though they often look more overweight than they really are, due to the roundness of their figure. They tend to have a round face, like the Moon, which may look childlike due to its puffiness. Their eyes are framed by long, thick eyelashes. They tend to gaze around themselves, often with a slightly sad look. Their thick eyebrows often meet over their nose, and their nose tends to be slightly upturned. Their lips are not distinctive, though often a bit smudged, puffy, and "sensual". Their hair is usually dark and curly, with pale skin and small hands.

Charting Cancer's Fate

Up until about 30-35 years of age, Cancer is fickle, full of worries, disappointments, and conflicts. They do not always succeed in marriage – divorce and separation are possible. Cancers are sensitive, vulnerable people, who depend on the opinions of others. They are characterized by volatile emotional outbursts. All of this may be a red flag to potential partners. This is why Cancers should be taught to reign in their temper from early childhood.

In adulthood, Fate rewards Cancers for all of the challenges they have faced. They will reach a decent position in society and earn a sizeable fortune.

It is important for Cancers to remember that in order to move forward, they need to always be looking backward, that is, to come back to their roots and build on the past. Roots are our first home and family. Build your own nest, and the rest will fall into place. Without a strong home, Cancers lack the support they need to succeed in society.

Excessive caution and suspiciousness can throw a wrench in Cancer's ability to succeed. Cancers are often prone to building safety nets where there is no threat.

LEO DESCRIPTION

Sign. Masculine, fire, fixed.

Ruler. Sun.

Exaltation. Pluto

Temperament. Slightly choleric, with a strong sense of self-esteem.

Positive traits. Proud, self-confident, noble, indulgent, ambitious, determined, passionate, bold, loyal, honest, efficient, eloquent.

Negative traits. Arrogant, insolent, vain, conceited, nervous, cruel, treacherous, demands attention, in love with luxury.

Weaknesses in the body. Left eye in women, right eye in men, upper back, heart, aorta, cardiovascular system, back, spine, spinal cord, ribs, spleen, diaphragm, arterial circulation.

Metal. Gold.

Minerals. For a talisman- rock crystal. Generally- diamond, ruby, chrysoberyl, gold quartz, beryl, jasper, hyacinth, chrysolite.

Numbers. 1, 4, 9.

Day. Sunday.

Color. Purple-red and yellow green.

Leo energy

The Sun is Leo's celestial ruler. It bestows Leo with qualities such as endurance, powerful creative potential, and an incredible range of both soul and generosity. Leo can also be rather vain, however. His ambition means he will not simply stop and rest on his laurels. Leo has a truly regal gaze and is always looking ahead. He has enough innate qualities to satisfy himself. Leo is the sign of winners and rulers. Figuratively speaking, Leos have a special mission, specifically to light the spark of God in themselves to ignite a divine cosmic fire and lead others to the height of spiritual evolution and develop their best qualities. They must understand that the power given to them carries great responsibility.

Astrological portrait of Leo

Leos are born leaders. They aspire to exert control over everything and everyone. Leos like to wear the purple mantle and laurel wreath of a victorious leader in society, and to share this generosity with their neighbors. There are some Leos who do not wish to rule over anyone. These people are individualists who rule themselves and their own destiny. They do not impose their will on anyone, but will not allow anyone to command them, either. No Leo will tolerate orders from someone else. Even if he may occasionally make a concession, he will gradually gain the upper hand by any means necessary.

Usually, Leos do not actively try to take power. Rather, they have been given this job from the very beginning. They are never climbers, and do not push others around. They are totally convinced of their own uniqueness, and subconsciously try to stand out and show others what makes them special. They radiate sunshine and tend to act through intermediaries or assistance. People are drawn to Leo, as they are drawn to the sunlight.

Leos stand out for their great physical and spiritual strength. They are capable of great achievements, and constantly seek to do more. However, they do not openly reveal this, and almost seem embarrassed of their own drive. As far as a Leo is concerned, for the right cause, he is capable of putting it all on the line and going for broke. Fortune is always smiling on him. When it seems that there is no way out, Leo will suddenly find that his supporters and allies open the door to new horizons, seemingly out of thin air.

The most important thing in a Leo's life is his career. He is ready to give it his very all. Family is also very important. Often, Leo views his home as another office. Most Leos have extraordinary talent, and great creative potential. These qualities are on display when Leo manages to fully realize himself. Leo is sincere, trusting, and honest, but also easily influenced by others and prone to ending up in a sticky situation. Leo does not tolerate betrayal in others and is intensely loyal himself.

They are intensely self-sufficient and will never ask anyone else for help, though they are happy to lend a hand to others. They reject anyone's advice, and might make a mistake, but will never regret the experience. Leo simply continues his climb to the top and will eventually conquer his goals. Leo loves the good life, expensive, high-quality things, pleasures, and sports. Physical activity helps him get rid of negative emotions and tension while increasing his energy.

Those born under Leo tend to be friendly and polite, with deep, sincere feelings. They are capable of being very chivalrous, and will never finish off a defeated enemy, just because they can.

Leo's greatest shortcoming is his vanity and pride, which make it difficult to capitalize on all of his virtues. Leo is constant in everything, even his delusions; pressuring him only makes him grow more stubborn, and he has zero humility. As far as Leo is concerned, there are only two opinions – mine and the wrong one. If Leo were to start acting more democratic toward others and treat them with just a little more patience, they would automatically do his bidding. Developing that humility is Leo's great challenge, though he is equipped with the intelligence and drive to win this battle with himself.

Leo feeds off of attention from others. He suffers when no one noticed him. He is easily swayed by flattery, meaning that it may not be difficult to deceive him. If for some reason, Leo is unable to realize his rich potential, he might fall into a real depression and become locked in a vicious cycle.

For this reason, from an early age, Leo needs to be taught to manage his emotions and get used to the idea of rolling up his sleeves and getting to work. Do not encourage him if he is trying to humiliate his peers or tries to prove his point through tantrums and physical violence.

How to recognize Leo by appearances

A typical Leo has prominent, bright features, and a large figure. Their incredible energy is palpable. They are always being noticed, even if discreetly dressed. Generally, they are medium height or tall, with beautiful, almond-shaped eyes, a straight, aristocratic nose, and long, graceful arms. They often have light hair, and men might tend to experience male pattern baldness from a young age. Their body is well-developed, muscular, and usually top-heavy. They have a direct gaze, and a habit of looking right into the eyes of anyone talking to them.

Charting Leo's Fate

Overall, Leo has a good chance of achieving success. When Leo was born, there was a feast in heaven, and God, who was feeling generous, showered Leo with many blessings. Leos may be known as the favorites of Fortune, but that does not always mean they go through life laughing. They pay a high price for their success, and only gain the strength and opportunities they need after making it through several taxing trials. Even if a Leo does not have any particular talent, he will eventually reach the summit thanks to incredible perseverance. Leo is the sign of victory! He should remember that nature has been very kind to him, and he needs to use his gifts.

VIRGO DESCRIPTION

Sign. Feminine, earth, mutable.

Ruler. Mercury.

Exaltation. Mercury.

Temperament. Melancholic, restrained, cold yet anxious.

Positive traits. Hard-working, business-minded, intelligent and with a great memory, teachable, methodical, punctual, pragmatic, neat, dignified.

Negative traits. Formal, petty, thoughtless, anxious, indecisive, self-centered, self-interested, cunning, prone to flattery, resentful, capricious, greedy, vain.

Weaknesses in the body. Gastro-intestinal tract, solar plexus, pylorus, duodenum, cecum, pancreas, spleen, liver, gallbladder, autonomic nervous system, abdominal cavity.

Metal. Brass.

Minerals. For a talisman- yellow agate and jasper. Generally- yellow sapphire, amber, citrine, chrysolite.

Numbers. 5, 10.

Day. Wednesday.

Colors. Bright green and yellow brown.

Virgo energy

Virgo's personality is colored by the energy of two planets – Mercury and Proserpina. Mercury impacts Virgos differently than it does Geminis, creating a calmer, less independent character. One might say that Proserpina's unhurried effect "slows down" Mercury's influence in Virgo. Virgo and Gemini share a brilliant intellect, but Proserpina is a powerful planet that unleashes the swirl of time. She endows her children with a sense of duty, punctuality, clarity, analytical abilities, a tendency to study the root cause of any problem, grow, and transition to a higher state. In order to that to happen, though, the conscious must work, which is what Virgo has been doing her entire life. Virgo is an Earth sign, making her a practical materialist guided by logic and common sense.

Astrological portrait of Virgo

Virgo is a sign associated with work, service, and duty. It is a sign that is capable of overcoming difficulties. This is why Virgo is always concerned with her health and does not hesitate to seek medical attention. Virgos are willing to work tirelessly for a good cause. Their goals are clear and real rather than simply theoretical ideals. Virgos do not build pies in the sky, and their work is what gives life meaning. Virgos cannot tolerate laziness in others and will not aid those who refuse to work.

Virgos analyze. They are rational, with perfectly developed logic. They have a clear mind, with few illusions about life or other people. Even in love, they are capable of seeing their partner's shortcomings and turn to various methods to correct them. This does not mean that Virgos are devoid of emotions or purely driven by logic, however. Virgo's feelings are there, but she will only rarely reveal them. Even love is first and foremost a duty to Virgo. If someone is truly in need, she will happily step up and do whatever is necessary. Virgo is an intellectual sign, and people born under it constantly strive for new knowledge. They are skilled at absorbing information and memorizing facts. This is why many Virgos are known to their friends as a walking encyclopedia. They seem to know everything and give intelligent, practical advice on any topic. When asked about anything, it is as if they had a file in their head storing complete information on whatever topic is at hand, and they will not be satisfied until they have informed you of all of it. Virgo seeks knowledge to subdue matters with their mind – this is their great, cosmic task.

Virgos are thorough critics. But they are also extremely ambitious and painfully sensitive to any comments. If you start criticizing a Virgo, she will refute all of your arguments, and you will come to regret ever starting the discussion. Virgos are pedantic, judgmental, and calculated, and their ability to impose their opinion on others mean they are impervious to criticism.

Virgos may lack intuition and creativity. They have a need to touch and see everything with their own eyes, and it is difficult for them to grasp the abstract. They subject the entire world to excellent analysis but are less gifted at synthesizing what they perceive. This means that Virgos might have a tendency to miss the forest for the trees. Virgo's home is usually in perfect order. Less pleasant traits may be her coldness and emotional rigidity.

At her highest level, a Virgo is an erudite person full of information, but her greatest battle will be her own pedantry.

How to recognize a Virgo by appearance

A typical Virgo is a slender person with a somewhat disproportional figure. In adulthood, Virgo women may tend to lose more weight than they gain, and will stay in good physical shape, even in old age. Virgos have wide bones, and their facial expressions are serious and stern. They tend to be tall but are rarely excessively so. Their faces tend to be long, as is their nose, which thickens into the shape of a water droplet. Their features are thin and well-defined. They have small eyes. Virgos are modest and often shy, and do not seek to draw attention to themselves, even if they are famous.

Charting Virgo's Fate

In childhood and adolescence, Virgos will face great difficulties. Later, they will manage to reach stability and security. Virgo builds her own happiness through decades of hard work and trial and error. Virgos tend to suffer a crisis in their personal life between the ages of about 18 to 29. They may experience marriage followed by divorce. Perhaps it finding a suitable partner seems impossible. Virgos reach personal harmony rather late in life, after the age of 36, and in some cases, as late as 42.

LIBRA DESCRIPTION

Sign. Masculine, air, cardinal.

Ruler. Venus.

Exaltation. Saturn, Uranus.

Temperament. Sanguine.

Positive traits. Diplomatic, intuitive, loves harmony, idealist, romantic, friendly, tender, fair, noble, light, refined, drawn to beauty, needs a partner.

Negative traits. Lacks self-confidence, volatile, unbalanced, sensitive, weak-willed, detached from reality.

Weaknesses in the body. Groin, uterus, bladder, kidneys, thighs, skin, veins.

Metal. Copper.

Minerals. For a talisman- orange topaz. Generally- hyacinth, orange corundum, diamond, rock crystal, coral.

Numbers. 6, 8, 12.

Day. Friday.

Color. Red-orange and green blue.

Libra energy

Libra is ruled by two planets – Venus (the planet of love, beauty, and prosperity) and Chiron (the symbol of balance and justice). Venus is known to astrologists as "small happiness" (Jupiter is known as "big happiness"). Venus's energy brings Libras good luck, but behind the scenes, Libras need to work hard. They achieve much thanks to their talents, charms, persuasiveness, and ability to smooth over any contradictions. Chiron gives them the key to all kinds of information. Libras can combine that which seems incompatible – they manage to work two jobs, bring enemies and friends together, and maintain a balance, all the while.

The element of air starts off active, before getting carried away. It brings Libra the ability to keep a cool head, remain calm, and seek compromises while getting along with others and avoiding causing a conflict.

Astrological portrait of Libra

Libras are connoisseurs of beauty, aesthetics, and they strive to find the golden mean in everything. Their contradictory natures make it difficult to achieve complete harmony. Libras love people but hate crowds. They are kind and sociable while also experiencing long bouts of depression. They can be intelligent but naïve. Restless and mobile, but never in a hurry. They do not tolerate rudeness but are capable of saying a harsh word in their hearts. It is worth noting that this kind of behavior is just a mask to hide their insecurities. In fact, Libras are good-natured, and any rudeness is contrived rather than their nature. Libra's character is constantly changing, balancing, and rushing from one extreme to the next. From the outside, they may seem to be connected to two totally different people, and they might even appear confused with their own beliefs.

Libras seek stability, comfort, companionship, and partnership. However, they are selective in their contacts, and always keep a relationship with the powers that be. People lacking in intelligence are not attractive to a Libra.

Libras can only flourish in an environment of benevolence and approval. Disharmonious and stressful situations drive them to depression and illness. They try to avoid conflicts and remove any negative energy from themselves. During a heated debate, they will usually side with the winner. At his highest level, Libra is a talented diplomat. Many politicians who manage to straddle two positions at once or provoke two sides in order to benefit from their hostility are also Libras. Despite their conflict avoidance, Libras love to argue for any reason. They take to debates like a fish to water, and always have the last word.

Libras often face contradictory situations. They have a hard time making a choice life puts in front of them. Libra's indecisiveness can be felt everywhere. They hesitate for a long time before making the right decision, and prefer to wait until things have resolved themselves, if they can.

Libras' coldness and detachment can cause them great harm. A lack of positive emotions and rigidity can have a negative impact on their Fate. A Libra's cosmic task is to learn to be sensitive and strike a balance.

Disharmony and imbalance have a very negative impact on Libra. They need to learn the essence of the phenomena around them and understand the cause-and-effect relationship. Chaos takes this ability away from Libra, and they cannot find harmony.

Most Libras have a perfectly developed ability to concentrate in order to make the right choices. They tend to be very wise people, especially in terms of life experience.

Libra's most serious shortcoming is a tendency toward stereotypical thinking and a rigid commitment to principles.

How to recognize Libra from appearances

The only thing that would distinguish a Libra from the other signs by appearance is a charming smile – it is soft, gentle, and mysterious. Libra's figure is balanced, and as a rule he does not tend to put on weight. His appearance is elusive. Wherever he goes, he changes to fit his environment, like a chameleon. Libra is careful with his appearance and is always dressed tastefully. Female Libras need to remember not to get carried away with makeup.

Charting Libra's Fate

Libra is constantly shifting from one direction to another, and so periods of happiness and prosperity are replaced with moments of sadness or disappointment. Libras tend to find prosperity in the second half of their lives. By and large, Fortune is on Libra's side, but Libra's task is to realize this and accept what he has been given.

SCORPIO DESCRIPTION

Sign. Feminine, water, fixed.

Ruler. Pluto, Mars.

Exaltation. Pluto.

Temperament. Phlegmatic, easily choleric, sarcastic.

Positive traits. Passionate, self-confident, restrained, deliberate, determined, persistent, resilient, has high self-esteem, fair, seeks recognition, is able to see an opponent's weaknesses. Richly imaginative, sensitive, a sound judge, prophetically gifted, talented.

Negative traits. Irritable, excitable, willful, critical, deceptive, rude, vindictive, insidious, passion is unbridled, excessively sexual.

Weaknesses in the body. Lower abdomen, groin, reproductive system. Organs of secretion. Bladder and renal pelvis. Gallbladder, veins.

Metal. Iron and bronze.

Minerals. For a talisman – sarder. Generally – ruby, red carnelian.

Numbers. 4, 9, 14.

Day. Tuesday.

Color. Bright red and black.

Scorpio Energy

Scorpio is a water sign ruled by Mars and Pluto. The energy of these two planets is related, and both give off sexuality, fearlessness, determination, and the ability to make decisions in extreme situations. Scorpio is capable of withstanding any battle, making the necessary changes within and rising from the ashes to a new life. Scorpio's main driving force is her incredible sexual appetite, which she gets from both Mars and Pluto. This is reflected in self-expression, love, and creativity. One's sexual energy tends to be expressed outwardly, but the water element holds it back in Scorpio, meaning that her passions live within and rarely splash out.

Astrological portrait of Scorpio

Scorpio is the most complex, mysterious, and sexiest of the Zodiac signs. It is also the strongest sign psychologically – Scorpios are considered to be innate magicians. They possess incredible intuition, and have a real talent for guessing others' thoughts, along with an ability to get those around them to speak frankly and openly. Scorpio is a sign of transformation, perfection, and rebirth. Scorpio's entire life consists of ups and downs, and the lower she falls, the higher she will climb.

Scorpio is mocking and snide, and to her, there are no secrets in human nature. Scorpio's loved ones are open books that she can easily read. Generally speaking, they strive for self-improvement, with a strong will and emotions. Few notice these emotions, however, as they burn inside, given that Scorpios are actually secretive and reserved by nature.

Scorpios are fearless and can tolerate the toughest conditions and recover from any crisis. They despise any weakness in themselves or others, and this is a constant struggle for them. By nature, Scorpios are loners and sometimes, they find it difficult to connect with others. Their personalities are very attractive and charismatic – social, active, and diplomatic, capable of controlling the powerful energy that nature has given them since birth and unwinding the collective energy to subordinate their will onto others. Scorpios are capable of achieving great things in life.

Scorpios are always consistent – in their views, in love, affection, and what they dislike. They can tend toward being overbearing or even authoritarian, but occasionally allow themselves to be manipulated. Scorpio's hardest task is coping with her passions and inner contradictions.

On one hand, Scorpios are strict (both with themselves and others), suspicious, and secretive. On the other, however, they are seeking spiritual transformation and knowledge, and are persistent, determined, fearless, and soft-hearted. This is probably why Scorpios are so attractive, too. They are capable of making a real impression and drawing everyone's attention. They are witty, but that wit can be sharp and even wound. Keep that in mind when communicating with a Scorpio.

Despite Scorpio's secrecy and distrustfulness, she can often be sincere and frank with those close to her. That trust is not easy to earn, however. This is why Scorpios tend to have a very small circle of friends they have known since childhood.

Scorpios must learn how to restrain their passions and angry outbursts. It is very difficult for them to control themselves and their temper. They need to channel that energy into something constructive, preferably creative.

How to recognize Scorpio by appearances

Outwardly, Scorpio does not appear to be particularly strong. Her strength is, after all, spiritual, rather than physical. She may appear to be rather ordinary, but there is something fascinating about her, and it not related to her external beauty.

Scorpios always look right into their partners' eyes. This is a serious, burning, and penetrating gaze. They tend to be ironic and mocking, and over time, develop characteristic crows' eyes.

Female Scorpios are easy to spot by their clothes. They love red and black (they also dye their hair these colors). Often, they prefer tight, revealing clothing, however you will rarely find a Scorpio woman who looks vulgar or tacky.

Charting Scorpio's Fate

A Scorpio's youth is a time of excitement and fateful changes. They reach success slightly later in life – after 30. Marriage is beneficial to them. This is a very sensual sign. When alone, Scorpio becomes an ascetic, channeling her sexual energy into professional endeavors.

The quality of a Scorpio's life depends on how she uses her energy. She can channel it into one of three ways.

The first path is the "Scorpian path". Scorpios here have a hard time finding their place in society. In time, they become aggressive and even dangerous. Their worst qualities take over – insidious, treacherous, a lack of empathy, unclear moral principles. They become vulnerable to many vices and dangerous addictions and get into self-destruct mode.

The second path is that of the "eagle". A Scorpio who takes this journey is aware of her power and authority. "I am so strong that I don't need to attack anyone!" is her attitude to life. Such a Scorpio becomes wise, powerful, and fair, and her energy drives her creativity. She is sociable and gifted, great company, an advocate and a fighter against injustice.

The third way is the path of the "grey lizard", or the path of least resistance. Here, Scorpio's energy does not find a worthy channel. She is dissatisfied with herself and others but does nothing to change things, becomes pessimistic, and loses her vitality.

SAGITTARIUS DESCRIPTION

Sign. Masculine, Fire, Mutable.

Ruler. Jupiter, Neptune.

Exaltation. Descending lunar node.

Temperament. Choleric, impulsive.

Positive traits. Strives for freedom and independence. Honest, fair. Persistent, and has good will. Intuitive, a good judge, and has ambitious goals. Optimist, reasonable, compassionate, generous. Is able to manage skills, brave, energetic, enthusiastic, ambitious, and lacks prejudice.

Negative traits. Craves power, fame, and respect in society. Always wants more. Impatient with any restrictions, oppressive, violent, coercive. Tends to exaggerate, charm, seduce, and build a good opinion and impression of themselves. Loves pleasures, entertainment, and joyful feasts. Tends to be a risk taker, seeking romance and adventure. Excessively polite, sociable, makes rash decisions, direct, abrupt, adventurist.

Weaknesses in the body. Hips, pelvis, back muscles, tendons, and ligaments. Autonomic nervous system.

Metal. Tin.

Minerals. For a talisman – chalcedony. Other good minerals are turquoise, topaz, heliotrope, lapis lazuli, emerald, hyacinth, chrysolite.

Numbers. 3,4, 15.

Day. Thursday.

Color. Indigo.

Sagittarius energy

Jupiter is the planet of luck. Astrologists refer to it as "big happiness". It bestows its children with a special charisma and good luck. Success comes easily to Sagittarians, and they are admired people of honor. But before Sagittarius receives these gifts, Jupiter will put him to the test, and he will have to cross the seven seas in order to find his ideal, which, in the end, will turn out to be within himself. And yet, Sagittarius is incredibly lucky. Jupiter is generous, and Sagittarius always manages to be in the right place at the right time. The fire element gives Sagittarius his organizational skills, energy, and zest for life. Naturally, life reciprocates.

Astrological portrait of Sagittarius

Sagittarians are reckless, life-loving, and open-minded people. They are always positive no matter what the circumstances are, and manage to keep their chin up, so Fate is on their side. Many people envy Sagittarius's success – often people cannot understand how life can be so kind to him. What they do not know is that Sagittarius carefully plans his future success, and always knows his next move in advance. He may give off the impression of flying by the seat of his pants, but in fact, he has a rigid structure and clear life plan. What's more, Sagittarius is highly principled and slightly conservative. He is used to acting intelligently. Yet, he can at times be impulsive and rash. Sagittarius would be wise to learn to wait and analyze his own behavior.

Most Sagittarians are sociable and open. They are characterized by independence and seek to throw off any restrictions they may face – whether internal or external. Sagittarius is incapable of engaging in deception. Intrigue and trickery are not for him, and he is straightforward and open, which those dealing with him need to understand. Sagittarius is not known for being tactful or delicate, though in his mind, he is a model of politeness and diplomacy. He is well-meaning and generous, though he is also capable of standing up for himself. He does not allow anyone to infringe on his rights or property.

Sagittarius is always charming, and that is usually not due to his appearance. Sagittarius's smile lights up a room. His natural charm is an aid as he gains authority and climbs to high positions, which are his main aspirations in life.

Sagittarius is in need of recognition, and it is important for him to be admired by those around him and that they listen to what he has to say. Sagittarians are very good at this, as being in charge and running things is their calling.

Sagittarians travel a lot. They crave new experiences, have a thirst for learning, and want to try everything before their earthly journey is over. It is difficult for them to sit still. They tend to accumulate large libraries, learn on their own, and are excellent teachers, lecturers, and religious leaders. Spiritually, they are open and want to share their ideas with everyone and teach others. At their best, Sagittarians become highly spiritual and might devote themselves to religious activities, missionary work, or simply preach spiritual knowledge.

If Sagittarius does not receive a normal spiritual and intellectual development, he may tend to become authoritarian and arrogant, with a weakness for awards and accolades. He will not tolerate defeat or the slightest criticism.

Sagittarius's most difficult task is to fight his own weaknesses and shortcomings. The most important thing is that his human nature wins, rather than animal nature. After all, Sagittarius is a centaur – half animal (horse) and half human.

How to recognize Sagittarius by appearances

Sagittarians are medium height to tall, with a dense figure and broad bones. They tend to be obese, and so they need to keep an eye on their physical shape from a young age. They have a certain robustness to them. If you see someone who seems like he would be a great boss, he is probably a Sagittarius. Jupiter places great importance on one's figure. Sagittarius's face is round, but proportional and harmonious. They tend to have a big head, round face, bushy eyebrows, and a good-natured smile. They prefer expensive, brand name clothes. Sagittarius is always surrounded by many fans, and knows how to communicate, tell a story, cheer someone up, and he is not afraid to be funny.

Charting Sagittarius's Fate

In his youth, Sagittarius is full of excitement and anxiety. Sometimes, he experiences personal troubles, but he quickly finds financial prosperity, either by marrying well, receiving an inheritance, or influential patrons who give them a leg up on a strong position. Living off of their own labor is not for Sagittarius. Overall, they are successful people both professionally and in their family life. There is a danger of incurring large financial losses due to their naivete, but they always land on their feet. Sagittarius always manages to make the money back. There is a high chance things will end up in court, but Sagittarius will come out on top.

CAPRICORN DESCRIPTION

Sign. Feminine, earth, cardinal.

Ruler. Saturn

Exaltation. Mars, Pluto.

Temperament. Phlegmatic, with a strong tendency toward pessimism.

Positive traits. Goal-oriented, perseverance, has a strong endurance, restrained, has self-control, ambitious, proud, independent, industrious, efficient.

Negative traits. Selfish, capricious, ambitious, insidiousness, incredulous, cruel, greedy, is dissatisfied with herself, moody.

Weaknesses in the body. Knees, bones, skeleton, ligaments, tendons, digestive tract, liver, gallbladder, spleen, pancreas, skin, teeth.

Metal. Iron.

Minerals. For a talisman, black onyx. Generally – opal, blue sapphire, spinel, chalcedony, cat's eye.

Color. Black, blue-black, dark red.

Day. Saturday.

Capricorn energy

In ancient times, Saturn, the ruling planet of Capricorn, was associated with time. The ancient Aryans referred to it as Keyvan, the "lord of time". A calendar was built around Saturn's revolutions around the Sun (32 years), and it still survives today. The Saturnian calendar is not only for counting time, but also for spiritual protection from the heavens and gaining spiritual power. Saturn was revered as the god of the golden age. This means that every Capricorn is capable of rearranging the world, but it would be a mistake to assume that Capricorns are only focused on social revolutions. They start with their own world – their home, family, and themselves. Saturn's children tend to be withdrawn and isolated, as this is a planet of loners and ascetics. Capricorn's life is a journey of trials and self-improvement, but there is also a reward. Saturn allows individuals to slowly but surely achieve their goals through determination and patience. Capricorns always find their place in life and manage to settle down successfully. Capricorn is an Earth sign, and as a result is patient, practical, stable, and clear-headed. She will never miss out on any money-making opportunities, has her feet firmly on the ground, and a clear appreciation of reality.

Astrological portrait of Capricorn

Capricorn is fiercely independent. She is contemplative and analyzes and evaluates all of the events around her. She will not accept anything that she has not seen and heard with her own eyes and ears. She relies on her own strength and will not tolerate any meddling in her life. She is purposeful, and this may be Capricorn's most essential trait. She is very goal-oriented, and incredibly adaptable and tactical as she works to reach her target. She is never satisfied with what she has and continues to strive to reach the very top. She is brimming with ambition, and lives with a sense of higher purpose to achieve something special and change the world. Capricorn is steady as she moves ahead. She is very patient and not afraid of hard work. Sooner or later, almost all Capricorns end up in some sort of leadership position. They respect reliability, and to them, that means money. They are very good with money, never waste it, and always have savings. They aim for financial security and usually achieve it.

Many Capricorns are pessimistic or secretive, with high walls around them. Many are also ascetic and limit themselves in everything. But this is rooted in Capricorn's deep vulnerability. Despite her stiff upper lip and desire to be alone, Capricorn also needs affection. She suffers from her own isolation and is tormented by constant fears and pessimism. If that were not in her way, she might reach her goals twice as fast as she does.

Capricorn is high-minded and knows how to apply this to life. She is willing to sacrifice everything, including her own comforts, and to carefully plan her next step. She is able to worm her way out of anything, has a calm demeanor, and never loses control, no matter how tough things get. Many preachers, pastors, prophets, and missionaries are Capricorns. Her worst qualities are bitterness and irritability, as well as nagging doubt and indecision, along with a general distrust of others. From early childhood, Capricorn needs solid intellectual and spiritual development. Her life's path will be difficult, and for that, she needs personal strength as well as knowledge and money.

How to recognize Capricorn from appearances

Capricorns tend to be slender, but they are rarely very tall. They don't smile much and laugh even less. Their face seems rigid, even when they speak. They have pointed chins, and their eyes are either small and deep set or large. They usually have dark, sometimes curly hair. They are quiet and discreet, do not argue, and prefer to watch things play out from a distance as they draw their own conclusions. They don't talk about themselves much and are usually not the life of the party, though they are excellent at organizing and leading.

Charting Capricorn's Fate

It is unlikely that Capricorn will have a smooth journey through life. There are obstacles, ups and downs, worries, and fears. However, every cloud has a silver lining. Thanks to Capricorn's persistence, skill, and work ethic, she is able to achieve everything she plans, and even manage to enjoy her success, thanks to her longevity. As children and teens, they tend to be sickly, but this improves with age, as they become stronger and more resilient. Once they have overcome all of the hurdles in their way, Capricorns enjoy a period of prosperity that usually begins in middle age (40-50 years).

AQUARIUS DESCRIPTION

Sign. Masculine, air, fixed.

Ruler. Uranus, Saturn.

Exaltation. Neptune.

Temperament. Sanguine, agile.

Positive traits. Progressive, humanist, self-confident, intuitive, social, independent, optimistic, loyal to ideas, original, receptive, impressive, professional.

Weaknesses in the body. Tibia, calves, ankles, joints of the toes, periosteum, tendons, cerebellum, nervous system, blood, heart.

Metal. Uranium.

Minerals. For a talisman, turquoise and sapphire. Generally, aquamarine, falcon eye, obsidian, amethyst, zircon.

Color. Green-blue, grey.

Number. 2.

Aquarius energy

Aquarius is ruled by Uranus, which does not behave like other planets in the solar system. Its axis is deflected from the plane of orbit by 98 degrees, as though the planet were laying on its side. When the Sun is opposite to the North Pole, the southern half of Uranus sinks into the shadows for 20 years. These features of Uranus are a perfect metaphor for those born under its energy. Aquarians are known for their unconventional views and rebelliousness. They see a world thirsty for radical changes, but when push comes to shove, they tread carefully and tend not to get their own hands dirty, preferring instead to inspire others to act.

Astrological portrait of Aquarius

Uranus was revered in ancient times as the god of heaven, thunder, and lightening. Aquarius is not afraid of making changes to his life and is quick to make a decision and act. Uranus is the planet of freedom, spontaneity, and providence, after all. Aquarius is known for his originality, friendship, camaraderie with everyone, eccentricity, and stubbornness. He feels misunderstood, can be defiant, and is often offended. He is not entirely wrong on this count. Aquarius is the Zodiac's most obscure sign, and his behavior often raises eyebrows. He is always unpredictable, marches to the beat of his own drum, and lives based on his own lived experience. He does not always feel it necessary to share his motivations with others.

Aquarius's driving force is absolute justice, which he will defend, no matter whose rights have been trampled. He loves to express his opinions but never imposes them on others. He has respect for individual thought. He has no patience for flattery, hypocrisy, and lies, though he engages in all three. He will not follow the crowd or adjust his ways.

Despite all of this, Aquarius is not a loner or recluse. He loves his circle of friends and needs communication and human contact. These ties are shallow, though, and Aquarius does not let anyone into his soul, no matter how close they are. He is somewhat aloof, with a stiff upper lip and focused on practicality. Inside, however, Aquarius feels isolated and prefers to watch from a distance. He is not a fighter or aggressive in any way, though he will not give up his positions in the face of pressure.

Aquarius sometimes has spontaneous moments of revelation, bordering on prophecy. He can guess others' thoughts and is ahead of his time in his ideas. Aquarius is the sign with the most geniuses. But Aquarius can easily shift his own views and adopt those of his foes. He may not have a lack of clear principles, and a relatively lax attitude toward morality and public opinion, but thanks to his charm, he can be forgiven for many sins.

How to recognize Aquarius by appearances

Aquarius is original and unpredictable in everything, even outward appearances. There is always something extraordinary about him, and he manages to catch everyone's eye. He may be tall with long limbs, and be the picture of contrasts – for example, dark hair with light skin and light-colored eyes. His movements are impulsive and jerky. He is verbose, speaks quickly, and talks with his hands.

Charting Aquarius's Fate

Aquarius's life is full of changes. In his youth, he might spend a lot of time trying to find his path. In adulthood, however, this change becomes internal and therefore more manageable. Aquarians love to travel, especially overseas for long trips, and they bring good luck with them.

PISCES DESCRIPTION

Sign. Feminine, water, mutable.

Ruler. Neptune, Pluto.

Exaltation. Venus.

Positive traits. Highly imaginative, kind, adaptable, tranquil, peaceful, receptive, impressive, modest, compassionate, caring, delicate, gentle, idealistic, religious, deep.

Negative traits. Passive, shy, fanatical, impractical, fantastical, slovenly, volatile, unreliable, self-indulgent, overly sensual, malleable, submissive, dependent, moody, lazy, apathetic.

Weaknesses in the body. Legs – ankles, toe joints, toes. Tendons and ligaments. Digestive, lymphatic, and endocrine systems, heart and circulatory system.

Metal. Platinum and tin.

Minerals. For a talisman – amethyst and chrysolite. Opal, jasper, and coral are compatible.

Numbers. 3, 11, 19.

Day. Thursday.

Color. Purple and indigo.

Pisces energy

Pisces is influenced by the energies of both Neptune and Jupiter. In ancient cultures, Neptune was revered as the ruler of the seas. He represents the primal ocean and chaos where all opportunities lie, but nothing ever comes to life on its own. Neptune is the highest faith, psychic phenomena, hypersensitivity, deep and intuitive understanding of things and capacity for unearthly love. All of these traits are inherent to Pisces, and generous Jupiter bestows them with confidence in their own importance, a happy life, and great vitality.

Astrological portrait of Pisces

Pisces closes the Zodiac. This sign is a mirror of all the others, with a focus on their strengths and weaknesses. Pisces is a self-redeemer who is able to purify others by taking on the negativity. That is Pisces's greatest mission. Empathy, compassion, and the ability to reflect the qualities of any other sign with detachment are her main traits. "I feel, therefore I am" is Pisces's motto. However, in their negative manifestations, Pisces are ambivalent, unreliable, and prone to betrayal at any time. They make big promises and hardly ever follow through. They seek their own benefits and are very dishonest. Pisces always reflect their environment, which will determine their behavior. They are easily influenced by others, though this is usually unconscious. Without even realizing it, they take on the feelings and thoughts of whomever they are talking to. They can get carried away and simply go with the flow like water, not trying to change their own destiny. Pisces lack willpower and the ability to stand on their own two feet or have the inner core they need to resist the influence of others. Pisces is symbolized by two fish swimming in opposite directions. One fish is living, while the other is depicted as dead. This is Pisces – the living fish is in harmony with God and one with the cosmos. The dead Pisces is illusions, speculation of one's own weakness, opportunism, and chaos. At their worst, Pisces are capable of showing the vile human traits, only to be tormented by remorse afterward.

Pisces is a wise sign, with an understanding of others' suffering. They are capable of sacrificing themselves to help others. They are humane, merciful, and optimistic. But they are also overly sensitive and feel others' pain as their own. Pisces make good psychologists, and they are drawn to that which is hidden. They like to wrap their lives in mystery and express themselves symbolically. They tend to fantasize a lot. Others may not always understand Pisces, which causes her to suffer. She hates arguments and scandal but would rather tolerate evil and injustice than actually fight them. She has a good sense of humor, is friendly, humble, and calm. This draws many people in and opens doors. Pisces wants financial well-being but is rarely able to gain it on her own. As Pisces ages, she is eventually able to achieve peace and prosperity.

Pisces's great task is to carry divine love into the world, have compassion for her neighbors, and help them in their spiritual development. Nearly all Pisces are creative – many are musicians, artists, writers, performers, psychologist, or mystics.

How to recognize Pisces by appearances

Pisces is a sign that is constantly changing. Their appearance is a reflection of their inner state. Pisces tend to have large, deep, and alluring eyes, with an inward or wandering gaze that makes them look mysterious and almost absent. Pisces hardly ever look others in the eye. Their eyelids often appear red and irritated. Their skin is soft, pale, and almost transparent. Their hair is thin rather than thick, and their hands are small and soft, even in men. Pisces tend to gain weight, but they keep an eye on their figure.

Charting Pisces's Fate

Pisces's life path is often difficult and full of ups and downs. If she is not guided by someone else's strong hand, she may not achieve success. Pisces needs something or someone to stimulate and inspire her, especially among men. Female Pisces are often strong-minded, strong-willed individuals who forge their own path in life and are very successful in all of their endeavors.

A Guide to The Moon Cycle and Lunar Days

Since Ancient times, people have noticed that the moon has a strong influence on nature. Our Earth and everything living on it is a single living being, which is why the phases of the moon have such an effect on our health and mental state, and therefore, our lives. Remember Shakespeare and his description of Othello's jealousy in his famous tragedy:

"It is the very error of the moon, She comes more nearer Earth than she was wont And makes men mad."

If our inner rhythm is in harmony with that of the cosmos, we are able to achieve much more. People were aware of this a thousand years ago. The lunar calendar is ancient. We can find it among the ancient Sumerians (4000-3000 BC), the inhabitants of Mesopotamia, Native Americans, Hindus, and ancient Slavs. There is evidence that the Siberian Yakuts had a lunar calendar, as did the Malaysians.

Primitive tribes saw the moon as a source of fertility. Long before Christianity, the waxing moon was seen as favorable for planting new crops and starting a new business, for success and making money, while the waning moon was a sign that business would end.

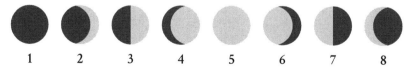

1   2   3   4   5   6   7   8

What are The Phases of The Moon?
- Phase 1 – new moon
- Phase 2 – waxing crescent moon
- Phase 3 – first quarter moon
- Phase 4 – waxing gibbous moon
- Phase 5 – full moon
- Phase 6 – waning gibbous moon
- Phase 7 – third quarter moon
- Phase 8 – waning crescent moon

To simplify things, we can divide the month into two phases:
- Waxing crescent moon – before the full moon
- Waning crescent moon – after the full moon

New Moon

We cannot see the new moon, as it is hidden. People might complain about feeling weak, mental imbalance, and fatigue. During this time, we want to avoid taking on too much or overdoing things. Generally, people are not very responsive and react poorly to requests, which is why it is best to look out for yourself, while not keeping your plate too full.

The new moon is a bad time for advertising – it will go unnoticed. It is not worth preparing any presentations, parties, or loud gatherings. People are feeling constrained, not very social, and sluggish.

This is also a less than ideal time for surgery, as your recovery will be slow, and the likelihood of medical error is high.

It is also difficult to get an accurate diagnosis during the new moon – diseases might seem to be hidden, and doctors might not see the real underlying cause of what ails you.

The new moon is also a bad time for dates, and sexual encounters may be dissatisfying and leave you feeling disappointed. Ancient astrologers did not advise planning a wedding night during the new moon.

Waxing Crescent Moon

It is easy to identify a waxing crescent moon. If you draw an imaginary line between the two "horns", you should see the letter P. The waxing moon is then divided into one and two quarters.

During the first quarter moon, we need to focus on planning – setting goals and thinking of how we will set about achieving them. However, it is still a good idea to hold back a bit and not overdo things. Energy levels are still low, though they are growing along with the moon. It is still a good idea to avoid any medical procedures during this time.

The second quarter is a time for bold, decisive action. Things will come easy, and there is a greater chance of a lucky break. This is a good time for weddings, especially if the moon will be in Libra, Cancer, or Taurus. Nevertheless, it is a good idea to put off any advertising activities and public speaking until closer to the full moon, if you can.

Full Moon

During the full moon, the Earth is located between the sun and the moon. During this time, the moon is round and fully illuminated. This takes place during days 14-16 of the lunar cycle.

During the full moon, many people feel more vigorous than usual. They are emotional, sociable, and actively seeking more contact, so this may be a good time for any celebrations.

However, be careful not to drink too much – you can relax to the point that you lose control, and the consequences of that can be very unpleasant. If you are able to stick to moderation, there is no better time for a party!

The full moon is also the best time for advertising, as not only will your campaign be widely seen, people will be apt to remember it.

The full moon is also a favorable time for dates, and during this time, people are at their most open, romantic, and willing to tell each other something important that might take their relationship to the next level of trust and understanding.

Moreover, during the full moon, people feel a surge of energy, which may lead to hyperactivity, restlessness, and insomnia.

It will be harder to keep your emotions in check. You might face conflicts with friends, disasters, and accidents. During the full moon, any surgeries are **not a good idea**, as the risk of complications and bleeding is on the rise. Plastic surgery is also a bad idea, as swelling and bruises might be much worse than in another lunar phase. At the same time, the full moon is a good time to get an accurate diagnosis.

During this time, try to limit your calories and liquid intake (especially if you deal with bloating and excess weight), as your body is absorbing both calories and liquids faster during the full moon, and it can be very difficult to get rid of the weight later on.

Waning Crescent Moon

The full moon is over, and a new phase is beginning – the waning moon. This is a quieter time, when all of the jobs you started earlier are being partly or entirely completed (it all depends on the speed and scale).

Surgery will turn out much better if it is performed during the waning moon. Your recovery will be faster, and the likelihood of complications is much lower. If you have any plans to lose weight, the waning moon is the best time to do that. This is also a good time for quitting bad habits, such as smoking or cursing.

The waning moon can also be divided into the third and fourth quarters.

Third quarter - this is a favorable period, and you are able to resolve a lot of problems without conflict. People are calming down and ready to listen and take in information, while still being active. However, this is not the best time to begin any major projects, especially if you are unsure if you will be able to complete them by the start of the new lunar month.

The third quarter is a good time to get married, especially if the moon is in Cancer, Taurus, or Libra.

Fourth quarter – This is the most passive period of the lunar cycle. You are not as strong as usual. Your energy is lagging. You will be tired until reaching a new beginning. The best thing you can do as the lunar cycle comes to an end is to get things in order, and avoid anything that might get in your way at work or in personal relationships. Examine your successes and failures.

Now, let's discuss the lunar days in greater detail. For centuries, people around the world have described the influence of lunar days, and modern astrologers only add to this work, as they compare old texts to modern life.

The 1ˢᵗ lunar day

The first lunar day is extremely important for the rest of the lunar month. This is a much-needed day to carefully plan your activities and lay the groundwork for the rest of the lunar month. Remember that the first lunar day is not a good day for major activities, but rather for sitting down and planning things.

Avoid conflicts on this day, unless you want them to overshadow the rest of the month. Try to see the positive side of things and imagine that the lunar month will bring you good things both at work and in love. The more vividly you can imagine this, the sooner your desires will come to fruition. Perhaps it would be a good idea to jot down plans that will bring you closer to achieving your dreams. This is the best time for both manifesting and making wishes!

This is also a favorable day when it comes to seeking a new job or starting an academic program.

It is fine to go out on a date on the first lunar day, but limit any sexual contact, as your energy levels are low, and you are likely to end up disappointed.

Getting married on the first lunar day is not recommended.

Avoid getting a haircut – there are many indications that cutting your hair on the first lunar day will have a negative effect on your health and life expectancy.

Under no circumstances should you undergo any major cosmetic procedures, including plastic surgery. Energy levels are low, your skin is dull and almost stagnant. The results will not live up to your expectations, and in the worst-case scenario, you will end up looking worse than before. It is common for cosmetic procedures performed on this day to be disappointing or even useless. Even the best surgeons are less capable.

Your good dreams on the first lunar day foretell happiness and joy. Bad ones usually do not come true.

The 2nd lunar day

This is considered a lucky day, and is symbolized by a cornucopia. It is not an exaggeration to say that the second lunar day is a favorable time for both work and love. It is a time for action, and a great period to work on yourself, look for a new job, start something new, or complete any financial transaction, whether a sale or purchase. This is also a great time for creative and scientific insights, and a good time for any meeting – whether political or romantic.

Any romantic dates or sexual encounters during the second lunar day are unlikely to disappoint. This is also a good day for weddings or taking a trip with someone special.

During the second lunar day, the moon is beginning its waxing phase, which is a good time for anything you might to do nourish and restore your skin. This is a great time for any cosmetic procedures aimed at preservation, though it is best to put off any plastic surgery until the waning moon. If that is not possible, then the second lunar day is acceptable, if not ideal, and you will not run into any complications.

Folklore tells us that this is not a good day for a haircut, as that may lead to arguments with a loved one.

This is the best time for exercise – your body is in good shape, and you are able to handle new exercise regimens. If the moon happens to be in Scorpio, though, be careful.

This is a good day for anything positive, but avoid any conflicts, discussions about the status of your relationship, or litigation.

Dreams of the second lunar day are usually not prophetic.

Third 3rd day

On this day, we are usually able to make out a thin sliver of the lunar crescent. It is a longstanding tradition to show money during the new month – it is believed that as the moon grows, so will your savings.

However, astrological systems around the world consider this an unlucky, unfavorable day. It is not a good idea to travel, begin any new business, or give into your bad mood.

You might run into many a lot of problems at work on this day, which will cause you a lot of anxiety. However, it is a good day to take a step back and identify and set about fixing any flaws and shortcomings. Remember that everything tends to look worse on this day than it actually is.

It is not the time to ask management for anything – you are likely to walk away disappointed, and end up unfairly reprimanded rather than receiving a promotion or raise. Instead, focus on areas of work that need to be smoothed over or studied further. It will be clear what problems you are facing, and you will easily be able to find a remedy.

Do not rush to criticize your loved ones – things may not be as they appear. "Measure twice and cut once" is your motto on this day.

This is not a good day to get married, as the couple is likely to have a turbulent, short-lived marriage.

You can schedule a cosmetic procedure for this day, but only if it is relatively minor. Plastic surgery should wait.

Do exercises as usual, without overdoing it or adding any new routines.

Dreams on this day do not mean anything.

The 4th lunar day

These are relatively neutral days, in that they are unlikely to bring anything bad, but they also will not bring you any windfalls. The fourth lunar day is symbolized by a tree of paradise, the tree of knowledge, and the choice between good and evil. Things ultimately depend on us and our final decisions.

This is a great day for anything money-related – signing contracts, agreements, or even taking on credit. There are also a lot of contradictions on this day – on one hand, we are likely to receive money, which is a good thing, but on the other, we will have to give some of it away, which is never particularly fun or pleasant. There is good reason to consider all of your opportunities and possibilities before acting.

It is not a good day to get married, as the wedding will not be as fun as you had hoped. However, the fourth lunar day is, in fact, a good day for sex and conceiving a healthy child.

Be careful on this day if you happen to engage in any physical exercise, as it is not a good idea to overeat or abuse alcohol. Take care of yourself. Any illnesses which began on this day may be extremely dangerous, if they are not dealt with immediately.

Cosmetic procedures are not contraindicated, as long as they are to preserve your appearance. Plastic surgery can be performed if you truly feel it is necessary.

However, avoid getting a haircut, as it is unlikely to grow back healthily, and will become brittle and dull. However, if the moon is in Leo, you can disregard this advice.

Dreams may turn out to be real.

The 5ᵗʰ lunar day

Traditionally, the fifth lunar day is one of the worst of the lunar month. It is symbolized by a unicorn. Unicorns need to be tamed, but only a virgin is capable of doing so. Many people will feel drained on this day, or frustrated with themselves, those around them, and life in general.

Try to avoid arguments- any conflicts are likely to drag out for a long time, and then you may be overcome with guilt. This advice is relevant for both work and love.

Sexual encounters may be pleasant, but this is not a good day to plan a wedding, as it is likely to lead to a marriage full of unpleasant incidents.

Do not start any new businesses, or ask those around you for favors- you may be misunderstood and rejected.

It is fine to engage in physical exercise, but if you overdo it on this day, you may injure yourself.

Your energy levels are low. Cosmetic procedures may not be effective, and avoid any plastic surgeries.

It is good if you dream something connected with the road, trips or with movement in general. A bad dream might be a sign of a health problem which should be addressed.

The 6th lunar day

The symbol of the sixth lunar day is a cloud and a crane. This is a philosophical combination that suggests that it is not worth rushing things on these days. This is a very positive, lucky day for both work and love. Creative work will be especially successful, as will any attempts at opening a new business in your field.

The sixth lunar day is a good time for resolving any financial matters. There is one limitation, however – do not give anyone a loan, as they may not pay it back. But you can certainly sponsor and support those who are more vulnerable than you.

This day is a good time to go on a trip, whether close to home or far away.

This is also a good day for dates, weddings, and marriage proposals. Remember that energy is more romantic than sexual, so it is better to give the gift of roses and a bottle of champagne than hot, passionate sex.

It is a good idea to get some exercise, but do not overdo things, though you will probably not want to, either.

Cosmetic procedures will be successful, and you can even have plastic surgery performed, so long as the moon is not in Scorpio.

It is still a good idea to avoid getting your hair cut, as you might "cut off" something good in addition to your hair.

It is better to not discuss dreams as they are usually true. Your dreams of this day can remind you of something that needs to be completed as soon as possible.

The 7ᵗʰ lunar day

This is also a favorable lunar day, and it is symbolized by a fighting cock, which is an Avestan deity. Avoid any aggression on this day, and instead work on yourself, spend time at home or in nature. Avoid discussing the status of your relationship with anyone, arguing, or wishing bad things on anyone. Everything will come back to haunt you, remember, silence is golden.

Business negotiations and contracts will be successful. You can find support, sponsors, and people ready to help you in both words and deeds.

Lighten up with your colleagues and subordinates. Pay attention not only to their shortcomings, but also to their skills. This is a good day for reconciliation and creating both political and romantic unions.

The seventh lunar day is good for traveling, no matter how near or far from home.

It is also a favorable time for love and marriage.

Exercise moderately, and any plastic surgeries will go very smoothly, as long as the moon is not in Scorpio.

Dreams of this day may become a reality.

The 8ᵗʰ lunar day

The symbol for this day is a Phoenix, which symbolizes eternal rebirth and renewal, because this day is a great time for changes in all areas of your life. Your energy is likely to be high, and you want to do something new and unusual. This is a good time to look for a new job or begin studying something. Any out-of-the-box thinking is welcome, along with shaking things up a bit in order to improve your life.

However, avoid any financial transactions, as you may incur losses.

Avoid aggression. You can share your opinion by presenting well-founded arguments and facts, instead.

The phoenix rises from the ashes, so this is a good time to be careful with electrical appliances and fire in general. The risk of housefires is high.

Avoid any major financial transactions on the eighth day, as you may end up facing a series of complications. You can pay people their salaries, as this is unlikely to be a large sum.

This is a good day for weddings, but only if you and your future spouse are restless, creative souls and hope to achieve personal development through your marriage.

Any cosmetic procedures and plastic surgeries will go well today, as they are related to rebirth and renewal. Surgeons may find that they are true artists on this day!

You can try to change your hairstyle and get a fashionable haircut on this day.

You can trust your dreams seen on this day.

The 9th lunar day

The ninth lunar day is not particularly auspicious, and is even referred to as "Satan's" day. You may be overcome with doubt, suspicions, even depression and conflicts.

Your self-esteem will suffer, so don't overdo things physically, and avoid overeating or abusing alcohol.

This is a negative day for any business deals, travel, or financial transactions.

This is a particularly bad day for any events, so keep your head down at work and avoid any new initiatives.

It is better to avoid getting married on "Satan's" day, as the marriage will not last very long. Avoid sex, as well, but you can take care of your partner, listen them, and support them however they need.

Any cosmetic procedures will not have a lasting effect, and avoid any plastic surgery. A haircut will not turn out as you hoped.

Dreams of this day are usually prophetic.

The 10th lunar day

This is one of the luckiest days of the lunar month. It is symbolized by a spring, mushroom, or phallus. This is a time for starting a new business, learning new things, and creating.

The 10th lunar day is particularly lucky for business. Networking and financial transactions will be a success and bring hope. This is an ideal time for changing jobs, shifting your business tactics, and other renewals.

This is a perfect time for people in creative fields and those working in science, who may come up with incredible ideas that will bring many successful returns.

This is a very successful day for building a family and proposing marriage. This is a good time for celebrations and communication, so plan parties, meet with friends, and plan a romantic date.

One of the symbols for this day is a phallus, so sexual encounters are likely to be particularly satisfying.

The 10th lunar day is the best time to begin repairs, buying furniture, and items for home improvement.

You can exercise vigorously, and cosmetic procedures and plastic surgery will be very effective.

Dreams of this day will not come true.

The 11th lunar day

This is one of the best lunar days, and seen as the pinnacle of the lunar cycle. People are likely to be energetic, enthusiastic, and ready to move forward toward their goals.

The 11th lunar day is very successful for any financial transactions or business deals and meetings.

You might actively make yourself known, approach management to discuss a promotion, or look for a new job. This is an auspicious time for advertising campaigns, performances, and holding meetings.

Any trips planned will be a great success, whether near or far from home.

Romantic relationships are improving, sex is harmonious, and very desired.

Weddings held on this day will be fun, and the marriage will be a source of joy and happiness.

Exercise is a great idea, and you might even beat your own personal record.

This is an ideal time for any cosmetic procedures, but any more serious plastic surgeries might lead to a lot of bruising and swelling.

A haircut will turn out as you had hoped, and you can experiment a bit with your appearance.

You can ignore dreams of this day – usually they do not mean anything.

The 12th lunar day

This day is symbolized by the Grail and a heart. As we move closer to the full moon, our emotions are at their most open. During this time, if you ask someone for something, your request will be heeded. This is a day of faith, goodness, and divine revelations.

For business and financial transactions, this is not the most promising day. However, if you help others on this day, your good deeds are sure to come back to you.

This is a day for reconciliation, so do not try to explain your relationships, as no one is at fault, and it is better to focus on yourself, anyway.

Avoid weddings and sex on this day, but if you want to do what your partner asks, there is no better time.

Many may feel less than confident and cheerful during this day, so take it easy when working out. Avoid overeating, stay hydrated, and avoid alcohol.

The 12th lunar day is not the best for getting married or having sex, but the stars would welcome affection and a kind word.

Avoid getting a haircut, or any plastic surgeries. This is a neutral day for minor cosmetic procedures.

Nearly all dreams will come true.

The 13th lunar day

This day is symbolized by Samsara, the wheel of fate, which is very erratic and capable of moving in any direction. This is why the 13th lunar day is full of contradictions. In Indian traditions, this day is compared to a snake eating its own tail. This is a day for paying off old debts and returning to unfinished business.

Avoid beginning any new business on this day. It is preferable to finish old tasks and proofread your work. Information you receive on this day may not be reliable and must be verified.

It is worth resolving financial problems very carefully, and avoid arguments and conflict.

Do not change jobs on this day or go to a new place for the first time. Do not sit at home alone, though, go see old friends, parents, or older family members.

Minor cosmetic procedures are welcome on this day, but avoid any plastic surgery, as you may experience major swelling and bruising. Avoid any haircuts, too.

As a rule, all dreams will come true.

The 14th lunar day

It's a full moon! The 14th lunar day is one of the happiest, and it is symbolized by the trumpet. Pay attention – you may run into new, much-needed information. Networking will be successful, and you can confidently sign agreements, meet with people, and attend fun gatherings or other leisure activities. This is one of the best days for advertising, performances, and concerts, and those working in creative professions should keep this in mind, as should those who work in politics. Do not sit in place on this day – you need to get out and see others, make new connections, and try to be visible.

This is one of the best days for communication with and making requests from management, as your initiatives will be noticed and welcome. You might talk about a promotion, raise, or something similarly related to professional growth.

Couples will see their relationship is moving along well on this day, and it is also a good day for getting married.

Any sex on this day will be vigorous and memorable for a long time. The full moon is the best time for conceiving a child.

Any cosmetic procedures will be effective, but avoid any major changes to your appearance, as there is a high likelihood of bleeding and bruising. A haircut will turn out well.

Your dreams of this day will be more or less doubtful.

The 15ᵗʰ lunar day

It's a full moon! This day is symbolized by a serpent of fire. This is the energy peak of the entire lunar cycle, and a lot will depend on where you are focusing your energy.

You might face a lot of temptations on this day, for example, you might tell someone else's secret or your own to others, and come to regret it for a long time. The stars suggest exercising restraint in both your words and actions, as the 15ᵗʰ day of the lunar cycle is a day of deception and weaknesses.

This is a very active time, and many people might take unnecessary risks. This is not the best day for signing any agreements or contracts. For any performances, concerts, or advertising, however, this is one of the best days of the month.

You can get married on the 15ᵗʰ day, but only if you know each other well and have carefully considered your partnership, without any hasty decisions. This is also a favorable day for a second marriage.

Your romantic relationship is looking wonderful – you are on cloud 9, writing poetry, and deeply convinced of how right your partner is for you – and they feel the same way. It is important that this does not suddenly lead to an abrupt disappointment.

Avoid getting any haircuts on the 15ᵗʰ day of the month, as you may end up with a headache.

Conservative cosmetic procedures and creams will be very effective, but avoid any injections or plastic surgery today. Bleeding, swelling, and bruising are all but guaranteed.

Dreams on the 15th day nearly always come true.

The 16th lunar day

This day is symbolized by a dove. The full moon is over, and the moon is now in its waning phase. Usually, after the turbulent days of the full moon, people feel a bit under the weather. They are not cheerful, and want to avoid excess worry and give themselves a chance to breathe.

Don't ignore your body's wishes, take it easy with physical activities, and take some time for yourself. You might spend time in nature, in the forest, or at a country home.

The 16th day of the lunar month is a time for moderation in all areas – your behavior, eating, and even in your clothes. If you overate during the full moon period, now is the time to diet a bit or at least avoid fatty foods and meat.

This is not a promising day for resolving any financial matters. Keep your documents in order and get ready for any future meetings, instead. If you help a loved one, your good deed will come back 100 times over.

Avoid getting married today, as well as sex.

Cosmetic procedures are likely to be a success, especially if they are related to cleansing your skin, but it is best to avoid any plastic surgery or injections. Your body is not ready to accept them. A haircut will turn out as you hoped.

Any dreams are likely to come true, but that also depends on a correct interpretation.

The 17th lunar day

This day is represented by a vine and bell. It is a happy day and both successful and fun-filled. It is also a good time for negotiations, concluding small business deals, shaking up staffing, and creativity. However, you should keep in mind that the 17th day is only favorable for minor business, and you should avoid starting any major events.

Avoid any major financial transactions on this day. Do not give anyone money as a loan or borrow anything yourself, either.

Any travel, whether for business or pleasure, is likely to be a success.

The 17th day is a great time to get married, and an ideal day for dates. Any sexual encounters will bring you happiness and joy.

Avoid getting your hair cut on this day, but cosmetic procedures and plastic surgery will be a success. Women will look better than usual.

Your dreams are likely to come true in three days.

The 18th lunar day

This day is represented by a mirror. It is a difficult, and generally unpromising day, too. Just as the mirror reflects our imperfections back to us, we need to remember that moderation and modesty are key.

The 18th day is not a favorable time for any business meetings or financial transactions. You can, however work on jobs you already began. It is, however, a positive day for those who work in research or the creative fields.

Your motto of the day is to keep a cool head when it comes to your opportunities and the opportunities of those around you. This is relevant for both work and romantic relationships. It is not a good time to criticize others – any conflicts or arguments may lead to lasting consequences, which you do not need.

Avoid getting married on this day, as well as sexual encounters, which are likely to be disappointing. It is a good time to take a trip together, which will only be good for your relationship.

Avoid getting your hair cut, though this is a relatively neutral day for a haircut, which might turn out well, and though it will not exceed your expectations, it will also not leave you upset. Avoid any plastic surgeries.

Dreams on this day will come true.

The 19th lunar day

This is a very difficult day and it is represented by a spider. The energy is complicated, if not outright dangerous. Don't panic or get depressed, though – this is a test of your strength, and if you are able to hold onto all you have achieved. This is relevant for both work and love. On the 19th day, you should avoid taking any trips.

The energy of the 19th lunar day is very unfavorable for beginning any major projects, and business in general. Work on what you started earlier, get your affairs in order, think over your ideas and emotions, and check to make sure that everything you have done hitherto is living up to your expectations. Do not carry out any financial transactions or take out any loans – do not loan anyone else money, either. Do not ask your managers for anything as they are unlikely to listen to what you have to say, and make judgments instead.

This is a day when you might face outright deception, so do not take any risks and ignore rumors. Do not work on anything related to real estate or legal matters.

This is a very hard time for people with an unbalanced psyche, as they may experience sudden exacerbations or even suicidal ideations.

This is a very unlucky day to get married. Sexual encounters might be disappointing and significantly worsen your relationship.

Avoid any haircuts or cosmetic procedures or surgeries.

Your dreams of this day will come true.

The 20th lunar day

This is also a difficult day, though less so than the 19th. It is represented by an eagle. This is a good time to work on your own development and spiritual growth, by speaking to a psychologist or astrologer.

Avoid pride, anger, arrogance, and envy.

The 20th lunar day is a good time for people who are active and decisive. They will be able to easily overcome any obstacles, flying over them just like an eagle. If you have to overcome your own fears, you will be able to do so – don't limit yourself, and you will see that there is nothing to be afraid of. It is a good day for any financial transactions, signing contracts, and reaching agreements, as well as networking.

The 20th lunar day is a favorable time for those who work in the creative fields, as they will be able to dream up the idea that will open up a whole host of new possibilities. Avoid conflicts – they may ruin your relationship with a lot of people, and it will not be easy to come back from that.

This is a lucky day for getting married, but only if you have been with your partner for several years, now. Sexual encounters will not be particularly joyful, but they also will not cause you any problems.

Avoid getting your hair cut, but you can certainly get it styled. The 20th lunar day is a good day for those who are looking to lose weight. You will be able to do so quickly, and it will be easy for you to follow a diet.

Cosmetic procedures will be a success, as will any plastic surgeries.

Pay attention to dreams of this day as they are likely to come true.

The 21st lunar day

This is one of the most successful days of the lunar month, and it is symbolized by a herd of horses – imagine energy, strength, speed, and bravery. Everything you think up will happen quickly, and you will be able to easily overcome obstacles. A mare is not only brave but also an honest animal, so you will only experience this luck if you remember that honesty is always the best policy.

This is also a favorable day for business. Reaching new agreements and signing contracts, or dealing with foreign partners – it is all likely to be a success. Any financial issues will be resolved successfully.

Those in the creative world will be able to show off their talent and be recognized for their work. Anyone involved in the performing arts can expect success, luck, and recognition. A galloping herd of horses moves quickly, so you might transition to a new job, move to a new apartment, or go on a business trip or travel with your better half.

The 21st lunar day is one of the best to get married or have a sexual encounter.

This is a great time for athletes, hunters, and anyone who likes adventurous activities.

But for criminals and thieves, this is not a lucky or happy day – they will quickly be brought to justice.

Any haircuts or cosmetic procedures are likely to be a huge success and bring both beauty and happiness. You will recover quickly after any surgeries, perhaps without any swelling or bruising at all.

Dreams tend to not be reliable.

The 22nd lunar day

This day will be strange and contradictory. It is symbolized by the elephant Ganesha. According to Indian mythology, Ganesha is the patron saint of hidden knowledge. so this is a favorable day for anyone who is trying to learn more about the world and ready to find the truth, though this is often seen as a hopeless endeavor. This is a day for philosophers and wisemen and women. However, it is an inauspicious day for business, and unlikely to lead to resolving financial issues, signing contracts, agreements, or beginning new projects. You can expect trouble at work.

For creative people, and new employees, this is a successful day.

This is a good day for apologies and reconciliation.

Avoid getting married, though you can feel free to engage in sexual encounters.

For haircuts and cosmetic procedures, this is a fantastic day. Surgeries will also turn out, as long as the moon is not in Scorpio.

Dreams will come true.

The 23rd lunar day

This is a challenging day represented by a crocodile, which is a very aggressive animal. This is a day of strong energy, but it is also adventurous and tough. Your main task is to focus your energy in the right direction. There may be accidents, arguments, conflicts, fights, and violence, which is why it is important to strive for balance and calm.

Keep a close eye on your surroundings – there may be traitors or people who do not wish you well, so be careful.

However, this is still a favorable day for business – many problems will be resolved successfully. You are able to sign contracts and receive credit successfully, as long as you remain active and decisive in what you do.

This is not a day for changing jobs or working on real estate transactions or legal proceedings. This is not a favorable day for traveling, no matter how near or far you plan on going.

This is not a promising day to get married – things may end in conflict, if not an all-out brawl.

Sexual relations are not off the table, as long as the couple trusts one another.

Haircuts or cosmetic procedures will not turn out as you had hoped, so avoid them.

Dreams during this lunar day usually mean something opposite of what awaits you, so you can disregard them.

The 24ᵗʰ lunar day

This is a neutral, calm day that is symbolized by a bear. It is favorable for forgiveness and reconciliation.

This is also a good day for learning new things, reading, self-development, and taking time to relax in nature.

This is a great day for any type of financial activity, conferences, academic meetings, and faraway travel.

The 24ᵗʰ lunar day is a good time for love and getting married, as any marriage will be strong and lasting.

Cosmetic procedures and plastic surgery will be a success, and you can expect a speedy recovery.

Avoid getting a haircut on this day, however, as your hair will likely thin and grow back slowly.

Dreams of this lunar day are usually connected with your personal life.

The 25th lunar day

This is still another quiet day, symbolized by a turtle.

Just like a turtle, this is not a day to rush, and it is best to sit down and take stock of your life. This is a good time for resolving any personal problems, as the moon's energy makes it possible for you to calm down and find the right path.

This is also not a bad day for business. It is believed that any business you begin on this day is sure to be a success. This is especially the case for trade and any monetary activities.

The 25th lunar day is not a good day to get married, especially if the couple is very young.

This is a neutral day for sexual encounters, as the moon is waning, energy is low, so the decision is yours.

Avoid any cosmetic procedures, except those for cleansing your skin. This is not a favorable day for haircuts or plastic surgery – unless the moon is in Libra or Leo.

You can have a prophetic dream on this day.

The 26th lunar day

The 26th lunar day is full of contradictions and complicated. It is represented by a toad.

It is not time to start or take on something new, as nothing good will come of it. Avoid any major purchases, as you will later come to see that your money was wasted. The best thing you can do on this day is stay at home and watch a good movie or read a good book.

Avoid traveling on this day, as it may not turn out well.

The 26th lunar day is a negative day for any business negotiations and starting new businesses. Do not complete any business deals or financial transactions. Your colleagues may be arguing, and your managers may be dissatisfied. But if you have decided to leave your job, there is no better time to do so.

This is not a good day to get married, as both partners' expectations may fall flat, and they will soon be disappointed.

The waning moon carries a negative charge, so avoid any haircuts and surgeries, though you can get cosmetic procedures if they are relatively minor.

Your dreams will come true.

The 27th lunar day

The 27th lunar day is one of the best days of the month, and it is represented by a ship. You can boldly start any new business, which is sure to be promising. This is a great day for students, teachers, and learning new things. Any information that comes to you on this day may be extremely valuable and useful to you.

The 27th day is good for communication and travel, whether near or far from home, and no matter whether it is for work or pleasure.

This is also a good day for any professional activities or financial transactions. If there are people around you who need help, you must support them, as your good deeds will come back 100-fold.

Romantic dates will go well, though any weddings should be quiet and subdued. This is a particularly good day for older couples or second marriages.

The waning moon means that hair will grow back very slowly, but in general, you can expect a haircut to turn out well. This is a great day for plastic surgery or cosmetic procedures, as the results will be pleasing, and you will have a speedy recovery, without any bruising or swelling, most of the time.

However, beware if the moon is in Scorpio on this day – that is not a good omen for any plastic surgery.

Do not pay any attention to dreams on this day.

The 28ᵗʰ lunar day

This is another favorable day in the waning moon cycle, and it is represented by a lotus. This is a day of wisdom and spiritual awakening. If possible, spend part of the day in nature. It is important to take stock of the last month and decide what you need to do during its two remaining days.

This is a good time for any career development, changing jobs, conducting business, decision-making, and signing agreements, as well as going on a trip. You might conclude any business deal, hold negotiations, work with money and securities.

This is also a good day for any repairs or improvements around your home or apartment.

Anyweddingstodayshouldbesubduedandmodest,andrestrictedtofamily members only. A loud, raucous wedding might not turn out very well. Your hair will grow slowly, but any haircuts will turn out very elegant and stylish. Cosmetic procedures and surgeries are not contraindicated. You will recover quickly with little bruising and swelling.

Do not take any dreams too seriously.

The 29ᵗʰ lunar day

This is one of the most difficult days of the lunar month, and it is considered a Satanic day, unlucky for everyone and everything. It is symbolized by an octopus.

This is a dark day, and many will feel melancholy, depression, and a desire to simply be left alone. This is a day full of conflict and injuries, so be careful everywhere and with everyone. If you can, avoid any travel, and be particularly careful when handling any sharp objects. Do not engage in any business negotiations, sign any contracts, or take part in any networking.

Astrologers believe that anything you start on this day will completely fall apart. For once and for all, get rid of things that are impeding you from living your life. This is a good time to avoid people who you do find unpleasant.

This is also a time for fasting and limitations for everyone. Do not hold any celebrations, weddings, or have sexual relations – these events may not turn out as you hoped, and instead bring you nothing but suffering and strife.

Avoid getting a haircut, as well, as it will not make you look more beautiful and your hair will come back lifeless and dull. Cosmetic procedures can go ahead, but avoid any surgeries.

Dreams are likely to be true.

The 30th lunar day

There is not always a 30th lunar day, as some lunar months have only 29 days. This day is represented by a swan. The 30th lunar day is usually very short, and sometimes, it lasts less than an hour. This is a time for forgiveness and calm.

You might take stock of the last month, while also avoiding anything you do not need around you. Pay back loans, make donations, reconcile with those who recently offended you, and stop speaking to people who cause you suffering.

This is a good time for tying up loose ends, and many astrologers believe that it is also a good day to start new business.

However, avoid celebrations or weddings on this day. Spouses will either not live long, or they will quickly grow apart.

Do not get a haircut on this day, though cosmetic procedures are possible, as long as you avoid any surgeries.

Dreams promise happiness and should come true.

A Guide to Zodiac Compatibility

Often, when we meet a person, we get a feeling that they are good and we take an instant liking to them. Another person, however, gives us immediate feelings of distrust, fear and hostility. Is there an astrological reason why people say that 'the first impression is the most accurate'? How can we detect those who will bring us nothing but trouble and unhappiness?

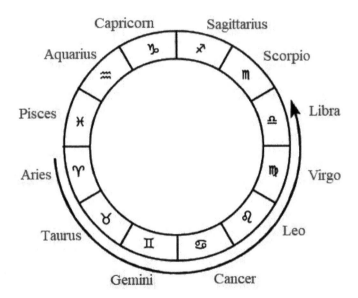

Without going too deeply into astrological subtleties unfamiliar to some readers, it is possible to determine the traits according to which friendship, love or business relationships will develop.

Let's begin with problematic relationships - our most difficult are with our **8ᵗʰ sign**. For example, for Aries the 8th sign is Scorpio, for Taurus it is Sagittarius and so on. Finding your 8th sign is easy; assume your own sign to be first (see above Figure) and then move eight signs counter clockwise around the Zodiac circle. This is also how the other signs (fourth, ninth and so on) that we mention are to be found.

Ancient astrologers variously referred to the 8th sign as the symbol of death, of destruction, of fated love or unfathomable attraction. In astrological terms, this pair is called 'master and slave' or 'boa constrictor and rabbit', with the role of 'master' or 'boa constrictor' being played by our 8th sign.

This relationship is especially difficult for politicians and business people.

We can take the example of a recent political confrontation in the USA. Hilary Clinton is a Scorpio while Donald Trump is a Gemini - her 8th sign. Even though many were certain that Clinton would be elected President, she lost.

To take another example, Hitler was a Taurus and his opponents – Stalin and Churchill - were both of his 8th sign, Sagittarius. The result of their confrontation is well known. Interestingly, the Russian Marshals who dealt crushing military blows to Hitler and so helped end the Third Reich - Konstantin Rokossovsky and Georgy Zhukov - were also Sagittarian, Hitler's 8th sign.

In another historical illustration, Lenin was also a Taurus. Stalin was of Lenin's 8th sign and was ultimately responsible for the downfall and possibly death of his one-time comrade-in-arms.

Business ties with those of our 8th sign are hazardous as they ultimately lead to stress and loss; both financial and moral. So, do not tangle with your 8th sign and never fight with it - your chances of winning are remote!

Such relationships are very interesting in terms of love and romance, however. We are magnetically attracted to our 8th sign and even though it may be very intense physically, it is very difficult for family life; 'Feeling bad when together, feeling worse when apart'.

As an example, let us take the famous lovers - George Sand who was Cancer and Alfred de Musset who was Sagittarius. Cancer is the 8th sign for Sagittarius, and the story of their crazy two-year love affair was the subject of much attention throughout France. Critics and writers were divided into 'Mussulist' and 'Sandist' camps; they debated fiercely about who was to blame for the sad ending to their love story - him or her. It's hard to imagine the energy needed to captivate the public for so long, but that energy was destructive for the couple. Passion raged in their hearts, but neither of them was able to comprehend their situation.

Georges Sand wrote to Musset, *"I don't love you anymore, and I will always adore you. I don't want you anymore, and I can't do without you. It seems that nothing but a heavenly lightning strike can heal me by destroying me. Good-bye! Stay or go, but don't say that I am not suffering. This is the only thing that can make me suffer even more, my love, my life, my blood! Go away, but kill me, leaving."* Musset replied only in brief, but its power surpassed Sand's tirade, *"When you embraced me, I felt something that is still bothering me, making it impossible for me to approach another woman."* These two people loved each other passionately and for two years lived together in a powder keg of passion, hatred and treachery.

When someone enters into a romantic liaison with their 8th sign, there will be no peace; indeed, these relationships are very attractive to those who enjoy the edgy, the borderline and, in the Dostoevsky style, the melodramatic. The first to lose interest in the relationship is, as a rule, the 8th sign.

If, by turn of fate, our child is born under our 8th sign, they will be very different from us and, in some ways, not live up to our expectations. It may be best to let them choose their own path.

In business and political relationships, the combination with our **12th sign** is also a complicated one.

We can take two political examples. Angela Merkel is a Cancer while Donald Trump is a Gemini - her 12th sign. This is why their relations are strained and complicated and we can even perhaps assume that the American president will achieve his political goals at her expense. Boris

Yeltsin (Aquarius) was the 12th sign to Mikhail Gorbachev (Pisces) and it was Yeltsin who managed to dethrone the champion of Perestroika.

Even ancient astrologers noticed that our relationships with our 12th signs can never develop evenly; it is one of the most curious and problematic combinations. They are our hidden enemies and they seem to be digging a hole for us; they ingratiate themselves with us, discover our innermost secrets. As a result, we become bewildered and make mistakes when we deal with them. Among the Roman emperors murdered by members of their entourage, there was an interesting pattern - all the murderers were the 12th sign of the murdered.

We can also see this pernicious effect in Russian history: the German princess Alexandra (Gemini) married the last Russian Tsar Nicholas II (Taurus) - he was her 12th sign and brought her a tragic death. The wicked genius Grigory Rasputin (Cancer) made friends with Tsarina Alexandra, who was his 12th sign, and was murdered as a result of their odd friendship. The weakness of Nicholas II was exposed, and his authority reduced after the death of the economic and social reformer Pyotr Stolypin, who was his 12th sign. Thus, we see a chain of people whose downfall was brought about by their 12th sign.

So, it makes sense to be cautious of your 12th sign, especially if you have business ties. Usually, these people know much more about us than we want them to and they will often reveal our secrets for personal gain if it suits them. However, the outset of these relationships is, as a rule, quite normal - sometimes the two people will be friends, but sooner or later one will betray the other one or divulge a secret; inadvertently or not.

In terms of romantic relationships, our 12th sign is gentle, they take care of us and are tender towards us. They know our weaknesses well but accept them with understanding. It is they who guide us, although sometimes almost imperceptibly. Sexual attraction is usually strong.

For example, Meghan Markle is a Leo, the 12th sign for Prince Harry, who is a Virgo. Despite Queen Elizabeth II being lukewarm about the match, Harry's love was so strong that they did marry.

If a child is our 12th sign, it later becomes clear that they know all our secrets, even those that they are not supposed to know. It is very difficult to control them as they do everything in their own way.

Relations with our 7th **sign** are also interesting. They are like our opposite; they have something to learn from us while we, in turn, have something to learn from them. This combination, in business and personal relationships, can be very positive and stimulating provided that both partners are quite intelligent and have high moral standards but if not, constant misunderstandings and challenges follow. Marriage or co-operation with the 7th sign can only exist as the union of two fully-fledged individuals and in this case love, significant business achievements and social success are possible.

However, the combination can be not only interesting, but also quite complicated.

An example is Angelina Jolie, a Gemini, and Brad Pitt, a Sagittarius. This is a typical bond with a 7th sign - it's lively and interesting, but rather stressful. Although such a couple may quarrel and even part from time to time, never do they lose interest in each other.

This may be why this combination is more stable in middle-age when there is an understanding of the true nature of marriage and partnership. In global, political terms, this suggests a state of eternal tension - a cold war - for example between Yeltsin (Aquarius) and Bill Clinton (Leo).

Relations with our 9th **sign** are very good; they are our teacher and advisor - one who reveals things we are unaware of and our relationships with them very often involve travel or re-location. The combination can lead to spiritual growth and can be beneficial in terms of business.

Although, for example, Trump and Putin are political opponents, they can come to an understanding and even feel a certain sympathy for each other because Putin is a Libra while Trump is a Gemini, his 9th sign.

This union is also quite harmonious for conjugal and romantic relationships.

We treat our **3rd sign** somewhat condescendingly. They are like our younger siblings; we teach them and expect them to listen attentively. Our younger brothers and sisters are more often than not born under this sign. In terms of personal and sexual relationships, the union is not very inspiring and can end quickly, although this is not always the case. In terms of business, it is fairly average as it often connects partners from different cities or countries.

We treat our **5th sign** as a child and we must take care of them accordingly. The combination is not very good for business, however, since our 5th sign triumphs over us in terms of connections and finances, and thereby gives us very little in return save for love or sympathy. However, they are very good for family and romantic relationships, especially if the 5th sign is female. If a child is born as a 5th sign to their parents, their relationship will be a mutually smooth, loving and understanding one that lasts a lifetime.

Our **10th sign** is a born leader. Depending on the spiritual level of those involved, both pleasant and tense relations are possible; the relationship is often mutually beneficial in the good times but mutually disruptive in the bad times. In family relations, our 10th sign always tries to lead and will do so according to their intelligence and upbringing.

Our **4th sign** protects our home and can act as a sponsor to strengthen our financial or moral positions. Their advice should be heeded in all cases as it can be very effective, albeit very unobtrusive. If a woman takes this role, the relationship can be long and romantic, since all the spouse's wishes are usually met one way or another. Sometimes, such couples achieve great social success; for instance, Hilary Clinton, a Scorpio is the 4th sign to Bill Clinton, a Leo. On the other hand, if the husband is the 4th sign for his wife, he tends to be henpecked. There is often a strong sexual attraction. Our 4th sign can improve our living conditions and care for us in a parental way. If a child is our 4th sign, they are close to us and support us affectionately.

Relations with our **11th sign** are often either friendly or patronizing; we treat them reverently, while they treat us with friendly condescension. Sometimes, these relationships develop in an 'older brother' or 'high-ranking friend' sense; indeed, older brothers and sisters are often our 11th sign. In terms of personal and sexual relationships, our 11th sign is always inclined to enslave us. This tendency is most clearly manifested in such alliances as Capricorn and Pisces or Leo and Libra. A child who is the 11th sign to their parents will achieve greater success than their parents, but this will only make the parents proud.

Our **2nd sign** should bring us financial or other benefits; we receive a lot from them in both our business and our family life. In married couples, the 2nd sign usually looks after the financial situation for the benefit of the family. Sexual attraction is strong.

Our **6th sign** is our 'slave'; we always benefit from working with them and it's very difficult for them to escape our influence. In the event of hostility, especially if they have provoked the conflict, they receive a powerful retaliatory strike. In personal relations, we can almost destroy them by making them dance to our tune. For example, if a husband doesn't allow his wife to work or there are other adverse family circumstances, she gradually becomes lost as an individual despite being surrounded by care. This is the best-case scenario; worse outcomes are possible. Our 6th sign has a strong sexual attraction to us because we are the fatal 8th sign for them; we cool down quickly, however, and often make all kinds of demands. If the relationship with our 6th sign is a long one, there is a danger that routine, boredom and stagnation will ultimately destroy the relationship. A child born under our 6th sign needs particularly careful handling as they can feel fear or embarrassment when communicating with us. Their health often needs increased attention and we should also remember that they are very different from us emotionally.

Finally, we turn to relations with **our own sign**. Scorpio with Scorpio and Cancer with Cancer get along well, but in most other cases, however, our own sign is of little interest to us as it has a similar energy. Sometimes, this relationship can develop as a rivalry, either in business or in love.

There is another interesting detail - we are often attracted to one particular sign. For example, a man's wife and mistress often have the same sign. If there is confrontation between the two, the stronger character displaces the weaker one. As an example, Prince Charles is a Scorpio, while both Princess Diana and Camilla Parker Bowles were born under the sign of Cancer. Camilla was the more assertive and became dominant.

Of course, in order to draw any definitive conclusions, we need an individually prepared horoscope, but the above always, one way or another, manifests itself.

Love Description of Zodiac Signs

We know that human sexual behavior has been studied at length. Entire libraries have been written about it, with the aim of helping us understand ourselves and our partners. But is that even possible? It may not be; no matter how smart we are, when it comes to love and sex, there is always an infinite amount to learn. But we have to strive for perfection, and astrology, with its millennia of research, twelve astrological types, and twelve zodiac signs, may hold the key. Below, you will find a brief and accurate description of each zodiac sign's characteristics in love, for both men and women.

Men

ARIES

Aries men are not particularly deep or wise, but they make up for it in sincerity and loyalty. They are active, even aggressive lovers, but a hopeless romantic may be lurking just below the surface. Aries are often monogamous and chivalrous men, for whom there is only one woman (of course, in her absence, they can sleep around with no remorse). If the object of your affection is an Aries, be sure to give him a lot of sex, and remember that for an Aries, when it comes to sex, anything goes. Aries cannot stand women who are negative or disheveled. They need someone energetic, lively, and to feel exciting feelings of romance.

The best partner for an Aries is Cancer, Sagittarius, or Leo. Aquarius can also be a good match, but the relationship will be rather friendly in nature. Partnering with a Scorpio or Taurus will be difficult, but they can be stimulating lovers for an Aries. Virgos are good business contacts, but a poor match as lovers or spouses.

TAURUS

A typical Taurean man is warm, friendly, gentle, and passionate, even if he doesn't always show it. He is utterly captivated by the beauty of the female body, and can find inspiration in any woman. A Taurus has such excess physical and sexual prowess, that to him, sex is a way to relax and calm down. He is the most passionate and emotional lover of the Zodiac, but he expects his partner to take the initiative, and if she doesn't, he will easily find someone else. Taureans rarely divorce, and are true to the end – if not sexually, at least spiritually. They are secretive, keep their cards close, and may have secret lovers. If a Taurus does not feel a deep emotional connection with someone, he won't be shy to ask her friends for their number. He prefers a voluptuous figure over an athletic or skinny woman.

The best partners for a Taurus are Cancer, Virgo, Pisces, or Scorpio. Sagittarius can show a Taurus real delights in both body and spirit, but they are unlikely to make it down the aisle. They can have an interesting relationship with an Aquarius – these signs are very different, but sometimes can spend their lives together. They might initially feel attracted to an Aries, before rejecting her.

GEMINI

The typical Gemini man is easygoing and polite. He is calm, collected, and analytical. For a Gemini, passion is closely linked to intellect, to the point that they will try to find an explanation for their actions before carrying them out. But passion cannot be explained, which scares a Gemini, and they begin jumping from one extreme to the other. This is why you will find more bigamists among Geminis than any other sign of the Zodiac. Sometimes, Gemini men even have two families, or divorce and marry several times throughout the course of their lives. This may be because they simply can't let new and interesting experiences pass them by. A Gemini's wife or lover needs to be smart, quick, and always looking ahead. If she isn't, he will find a new object for his affection.

Aquarians, Libras, and Aries make good partners for a Gemini. A Sagittarius can be fascinating for him, but they will not marry before he reaches middle age, as both partners will be fickle while they are younger. A Gemini and Scorpio are likely to be a difficult match, and the Gemini will try to wriggle out of the Scorpio's tight embrace. A Taurus will be an exciting sex partner, but their partnership won't be for long, and the Taurus is often at fault.

CANCER

Cancers tend to be deep, emotional individuals, who are both sensitive and highly sexual. Their charm is almost mystical, and they know how to use it. Cancers may be the most promiscuous sign of the Zodiac, and open to absolutely anything in bed. Younger Cancers look for women who are more mature, as they are skilled lovers. As they age, they look for someone young enough to be their own daughter, and delight in taking on the role of a teacher. Cancers are devoted to building a family and an inviting home, but once they achieve that goal, they are likely to have a wandering eye. They will not seek moral justification, as they sincerely believe it is simply something everyone does. Their charm works in such a way that women are deeply convinced they are the most important love in a Cancer's life, and that circumstances are the only thing preventing them from being together. Remember that a Cancer man is a master manipulator, and will not be yours unless he is sure you have throngs of admirers. He loves feminine curves, and is turned on by exquisite fragrances. Cancers don't end things with old lovers, and often go back for a visit after a breakup. Another type of Cancer is rarer – a faithful friend, and up for anything in order to provide for his wife and children. He is patriotic and a responsible worker.

Scorpios, Pisces, and other Cancers are a good match. A Taurus can make for a lasting relationship, as both signs place great value on family and are able to get along with one another. A Sagittarius will result in fights and blowouts from the very beginning, followed by conflicts and breakups. The Sagittarius will suffer the most. Marriage to an Aries isn't off the table, but it won't last very long.

LEO

A typical Leo is handsome, proud, and vain, with a need to be the center of attention at all times. They often pretend to be virtuous, until they are able to actually master it. They crave flattery, and prefer women who comply and cater to them. Leos demand unconditional obedience, and constant approval. When a Leo is in love, he is fairly sexual, and capable of being devoted and faithful. Cheap love affairs are not his thing, and Leos are highly aware of how expensive it is to divorce. They make excellent fathers. A Leo's partner needs to look polished and well-dressed, and he will not tolerate either frumpiness or nerds.

Aries, Sagittarius, and Gemini make for good matches. Leos are often very beguiling to Libras; this is the most infamous astrological "master-slave" pairing. Leos are also inexplicably drawn to Pisces – this is the only sign capable of taming them. A Leo and Virgo will face a host of problems sooner or later, and they might be material in nature. The Virgo will attempt to conquer him, and if she does, a breakup is inevitable.

VIRGO

Virgo is a highly intellectual sign, who likes to take a step back and spend his time studying the big picture. But love inherently does not lend itself to analysis, and this can leave Virgos feeling perplexed. While Virgo is taking his time, studying the object of his affection, someone else will swoop in and take her away, leaving him bitterly disappointed. Perhaps for that reason, Virgos tend to marry late, but once they are married, they remain true, and hardly ever initiate divorce. In bed, they are modest and reserved, as they see sex as some sort of quirk of nature, designed solely for procreation. Most Virgos have a gifted sense of taste, hearing, and smell. They cannot tolerate pungent odors and can be squeamish; they believe their partners should always take pains to be very clean. Virgos usually hate over-the-top expressions of love, and are immune to sex as a mean s of control. Many Virgos are stingy and more appropriate as husbands than lovers. Male Virgos tend to be monogamous, though if they are unhappy or disappointed with their partner, they may begin to look for comfort elsewhere and often give in to drunkenness.

Taurus, Capricorn, and Scorpio make the best partners for a Virgo. They may feel inexplicable attraction for Aquarians. They will form friendships with Aries, but rarely will this couple make it down the aisle. With Leos, be careful – this sign is best as a lover, not a spouse.

LIBRA

Libra is a very complex, wishy-washy sign. They are constantly seeking perfection, which often leaves them in discord with the reality around them. Libra men are elegant and refined, and expect no less from their partner. Many Libras treat their partners like a beautiful work of art, and have trouble holding onto the object of their affection. They view love itself as a very abstract concept, and can get tired of the physical aspect of their relationship. They are much more drawn to intrigue and the chase- dreams, candlelit evenings, and other symbols of romance. A high percentage of Libra men are gay, and they view sex with other men as the more elite option. Even when Libras are unhappy in their marriages, they never divorce willingly. Their wives might leave them, however, or they might be taken away by a more decisive partner.

Aquarius and Gemini make the best matches for Libras. Libra can also easily control an independent Sagittarius, and can easily fall under the influence of a powerful and determined Leo, before putting all his strength and effort into breaking free. Relationships with Scorpios are difficult; they may become lovers, but will rarely marry.

SCORPIO

Though it is common to perceive Scorpios as incredibly sexual, they are, in fact, very unassuming, and never brag about their exploits. They will, however, be faithful and devoted to the right woman. The Scorpio man is taciturn, and you can't expect any tender words from him, but he will defend those he loves to the very end. Despite his outward control, Scorpio is very emotional; he needs and craves love, and is willing to fight for it. Scorpios are incredible lovers, and rather than leaving them tired, sex leaves them feeling energized. They are always sexy, even if they aren't particularly handsome. They are unconcerned with the ceremony of wooing you, and more focused on the act of love itself.

Expressive Cancers and gentle, amenable Pisces make the best partners. A Scorpio might also fall under the spell of a Virgo, who is adept at taking the lead. Sparks might fly between two Scorpios, or with a Taurus, who is perfect for a Scorpio in bed. Relationships with Libras, Sagittarians, and Aries are difficult.

SAGITTARIUS

Sagittarian men are lucky, curious, and gregarious. Younger Sagittarians are romantic, passionate, and burning with desire to experience every type of love. Sagittarius is a very idealistic sign, and in that search for perfection, they tend to flit from one partner to another, eventually forgetting what they were even looking for in the first place. A negative Sagittarius might have two or three relationships going on at once, assigning each partner a different day of the week. On the other hand, a positive Sagittarius will channel his powerful sexual energy into creativity, and take his career to new heights. Generally speaking, after multiple relationships and divorces, the Sagittarian man will conclude that his ideal marriage is one where his partner is willing to look the other way.

Aries and Leo make the best matches for a Sagittarius. He might fall under the spell of a Cancer, but would not be happy being married to her. Gemini can be very intriguing, but will only make for a happy marriage after middle age, when both partners are older and wiser. Younger Sagittarians often marry Aquarian women, but things quickly fall apart. Scorpios can make for an interesting relationship, but if the Sagittarius fails to comply, divorce is inevitable.

CAPRICORN

Practical, reserved Capricorn is one of the least sexual signs of the Zodiac. He views sex as an idle way to pass the time, and something he can live without, until he wants to start a family. He tends to marry late, and almost never divorces. Young Capricorns are prone to suppressing their sexual desires, and only discover them later in life, when they have already achieved everything a real man needs – a career and money. We'll be frank – Capricorn is not the best lover, but he can compensate by being caring, attentive, and showering you with valuable gifts. Ever cautious, Capricorn loves to schedule his sexual relationships, and this is something partners will just have to accept. Women should understand that Capricorn needs some help relaxing – perhaps with alcohol. They prefer inconspicuous, unassuming women, and run away from a fashion plate.

The best partners for a Capricorn are Virgo, Taurus, or Scorpio. Cancers might catch his attention, and if they marry, it is likely to be for life. Capricorn is able to easily dominate Pisces, and Pisces-Capricorn is a well-known "slave and master" combination. Relationships with Leos tend to be erratic, and they are unlikely to wed. Aries might make for a cozy family at first, but things will cool off quickly, and often, the marriage only lasts as long as Capricorn is unwilling to make a change in his life.

AQUARIUS

Aquarian men are mercurial, and often come off as peculiar, unusual, or aloof, and detached. Aquarians are turned on by anything novel or strange, and they are constantly looking for new and interesting people. They are stimulated by having a variety of sexual partners, but they consider this to simply be normal life, rather than sexually immoral. Aquarians are unique – they are more abstract than realistic, and can be cold and incomprehensible, even in close relationships. Once an Aquarius gets married, he will try to remain within the realm of decency, but often fails. An Aquarian's partners need uncommon patience, as nothing they do can restrain him. Occasionally, one might encounter another kind of Aquarius – a responsible, hard worker, and exemplary family man.

The best matches for an Aquarius are female fellow Aquarians, Libras, and Sagittarians. When Aquarius seeks out yet another affair, he is not choosy, and will be happy with anyone.

PISCES

Pisces is the most eccentric sign of the Zodiac. This is reflected in his romantic tendencies and sex life. Pisces men become very dependent on those with whom they have a close relationship. Paradoxically, they are simultaneously crafty and childlike when it comes to playing games, and they are easily deceived. As a double bodied sign, Pisces rarely marry just once, as they are very sexual, easily fall in love, and are constantly seeking their ideal. Pisces are very warm people, who love to take care of others and are inclined toward "slave-master" relationships, in which they are the submissive partner. But after catering to so many lovers, Pisces will remain elusive. They are impossible to figure out ahead of time – today, they might be declaring their love for you, but tomorrow, they may disappear – possibly forever! To a Pisces, love is a fantasy, illusion, and dream, and they might spend their whole lives in pursuit of it. Pisces who are unhappy in love are vulnerable to alcoholism or drug addiction.

Cancer and Scorpio make the best partners for a Pisces. He is also easily dominated by Capricorn and Libra, but in turn will conquer even a queen-like Leo. Often, they are fascinated by Geminis – if they marry, it will last a long time, but likely not forever. Relationships with Aries and Sagittarians are erratic, though initially, things can seem almost perfect.

Women

ARIES

Aries women are leaders. They are decisive, bold, and very protective. An Aries can take initiative and is not afraid to make the first move. Her ideal man is strong, and someone she can admire. But remember, at the slightest whiff of weakness, she will knock him off his pedestal. She does not like dull, whiny men, and thinks that there is always a way out of any situation. If she loves someone, she will be faithful. Aries women are too honest to try leading a double life. They are possessive, jealous, and not only will they not forgive those who are unfaithful, their revenge may be brutal; they know no limits. If you can handle an Aries, don't try to put her in a cage; it is best to give her a long leash. Periodically give her some space – then she will seek you out herself. She is sexual, and believe that anything goes in bed.

Her best partners are a Sagittarius or Leo. A Libra can make a good match after middle age, once both partners have grown wiser and settled down a bit. Gemini and Aquarius are only good partners during the initial phase, when everything is still new, but soon enough, they will lose interest in each other. Scorpios are good matches in bed, but only suitable as lovers.

TAURUS

Taurean women possess qualities that men often dream about, but rarely find in the flesh – they are soft, charming, practical, and reliable – they are very caring and will support their partner in every way. A Taurus is highly sexual, affectionate, and can show a man how to take pleasure to new heights. She is also strong and intense. If she is in love, she will be faithful. But when love fades away, she might find someone else on the side, though she will still fight to save her marriage, particularly if her husband earns good money. A Taurus will not tolerate a man who is disheveled or disorganized, and anyone dating her needs to always be on his toes. She will expect gifts, and likes being taken to expensive restaurants, concerts, and other events. If you argue, try to make the first peace offering, because a Taurus finds it very hard to do so – she might withdraw and ruminate for a long time. Never air your dirty laundry; solve all your problems one-on-one.

Scorpio, Virgo, Capricorn, and Cancer make the best matches. A relationship with an Aries or Sagittarius would be difficult. There is little attraction between a Taurus and a Leo, and initially Libras can make for a good partner in bed, but things will quickly cool off and fall apart. A Taurus and Aquarius make an interesting match – despite the difference in signs, their relationships are often lasting, and almost lifelong.

GEMINI

Gemini women are social butterflies, outgoing, and they easily make friends, and then break off the friendship, if people do not hold their interest. A Gemini falls in love hard, is very creative, and often fantasizes about the object of her affection. She is uninterested in sex without any attachment, loves to flirt, and, for the most part, is not particularly affectionate. She dreams of a partner who is her friend, lover, and a romantic, all at once. A Gemini has no use for a man who brings nothing to the table intellectually. That is a tall order, so Geminis often divorce and marry several times. Others simply marry later in life. Once you have begun a life together, do not try to keep her inside – she needs to travel, explore, socialize, attend events and go to the theater. She cannot tolerate possessive men, so avoid giving her the third degree, and remember that despite her flirtatious and social nature, she is, in fact, faithful – as long as you keep her interested and she is in love. Astrologists believe that Geminis do not know what they need until age 29 or 30, so it is best to hold off on marriage until then.

Leo and Libra make the best matches. A relationship with a Cancer is likely, though complex, and depends solely on the Cancer's affection. A Gemini and Sagittarius can have an interesting, dynamic relationship, but these are two restless signs, which might only manage to get together after ages 40-45, once they have had enough thrills out of life and learned to be patient. Relationships with a Capricorn are very difficult, and almost never happen. The honeymoon stage can be wonderful with a Scorpio, but each partner will eventually go their own way, before ending things. A Gemini and Pisces union can also be very interesting – they are drawn to each other, and can have a wonderful relationship, but after a while, the cracks start to show and things will fall apart. An Aquarius is also not a bad match, but they will have little sexual chemistry.

CANCER

Cancers can be divided into two opposing groups. The first includes a sweet and gentle creature who is willing to dedicate her life to her husband and children. She is endlessly devoted to her husband, especially if he makes a decent living and remains faithful. She views all men as potential husbands, which means it is dangerous to strike up a relationship with her if your intentions are not serious; she can be anxious and clingy, sensitive and prone to crying. It is better to break things to her gently, rather than directly spitting out the cold, hard truth. She wants a man who can be a provider, though she often earns well herself. She puts money away for a rainy day, and knows how to be thrifty, for the sake of others around her, rather than only for herself. She is an excellent cook and capable of building an inviting home for her loved ones. She is enthusiastic in bed, a wonderful wife, and a caring mother.

The second type of Cancer is neurotic, and capable of creating a living hell for those around her. She believes that the world is her enemy, and manages to constantly find new intrigue and machinations.

Another Cancer, Virgo, Taurus, Scorpio, and Pisces make the best matches. A Cancer can often fall in love with a Gemini, but eventually, things will grow complicated, as she will be exhausted by a Gemini's constant mood swings and cheating. A Cancer and Sagittarius will initially have passionate sex, but things will quickly cool off. A relationship with a Capricorn is a real possibility, but only later in life, as while they are young, they are likely to fight and argue constantly. Cancer can also have a relationship with an Aries, but this will not be easy.

LEO

Leos are usually beautiful or charming, and outwardly sexual. And yet, appearances can be deceiving – they are not actually that interested in sex. Leo women want to be the center of attention and men running after them boosts their self-esteem, but they are more interested in their career, creating something new, and success than sex. They often have high-powered careers and are proud of their own achievements. Their partners need to be strong; if a Leo feels a man is weak, she can carry him herself for a while- before leaving him. It is difficult for her to find a partner for life, as chivalrous knights are a dying breed, and she is not willing to compromise. If you are interested in a Leo, take the initiative, admire her, and remember that even a queen is still a woman. Timid men or tightwads need not apply. Leos like to help others, but they don't need a walking disaster in their life. If they are married and in love, they are usually faithful, and petty gossip isn't their thing. Leo women make excellent mothers, and are ready to give their lives to their children. Their negative traits include vanity and a willingness to lie, in order to make themselves look better.

Sagittarius, Aries, and Libra make the best matches. Leos can also have an interesting relationship with a Virgo, though both partners will weaken each other. Life with a Taurus will lead to endless arguments – both signs are very stubborn, and unwilling to give in. Leos and Pisces are another difficult pair, as she will have to learn to be submissive if she wants to keep him around. A relationship with a Capricorn will work if there is a common denominator, but they will have little sexual chemistry. Life with a Scorpio will be turbulent to say the least, and they will usually break up later in life.

VIRGO

Virgo women are practical, clever, and often duplicitous. Marrying one isn't for everyone. She is a neat freak to the point of annoying those around her. She is also an excellent cook, and strives to ensure her children receive the very best by teaching them everything, and preparing them for a bright future. She is also thrifty – she won't throw money around, and, in fact, won't even give it to her husband. She has no time for rude, macho strongmen, and is suspicious of spendthrifts. She will not be offended if you take her to a cozy and modest café rather than an elegant restaurant. Virgos are masters of intrigue, and manage to outperform every other sign of the Zodiac in this regard. Virgos love to criticize everyone and everything; to listen to them, the entire world is simply a disaster and wrong, and only she is the exception to this rule. Virgos are not believed to be particularly sexual, but there are different variations when it comes to this. Rarely, one finds an open-minded Virgo willing to try anything, and who does it all on a grand scale – but she is rather the exception to this general rule.

The best matches for a Virgo are Cancer, Taurus, and Capricorn. She also can get along well with a Scorpio, but will find conflict with Sagittarius. A Pisces will strike her interest, but they will rarely make it down the aisle. She is often attracted to an Aquarius, but they would drive each other up the wall were they to actually marry. An Aries forces Virgo to see another side of life, but here, she will have to learn to conform and adapt.

LIBRA

Female Libras tend to be beautiful, glamorous, or very charming. They are practical, tactical, rational, though they are adept at hiding these qualities behind their romantic and elegant appearance. Libras are drawn to marriage, and are good at imagining the kind of partner they need. They seek out strong, well-off men and are often more interested in someone's social status and bank account than feelings. The object of their affection needs to be dashing, and have a good reputation in society. Libras love expensive things, jewelry, and finery. If they are feeling down, a beautiful gift will instantly cheer them up. They will not tolerate scandal or conflict, and will spend all their energy trying to keep the peace, or at least the appearance thereof. They do not like to air their dirty laundry, and will only divorce in extreme circumstances. They are always convinced they are right and react to any objections as though they have been insulted. Most Libras are not particularly sexual, except those with Venus or the Moon in Scorpio.

Leos, Geminis, and Aquarians make good matches. Libra women are highly attracted to Aries men - this is a real case of opposites attract. They can get along with a Sagittarius, though he will find that Libras are too proper and calm. Capricorn, Pisces, and Cancer are all difficult matches. Things will begin tumultuously with a Taurus, before each partner goes his or her own way.

SCORPIO

Scorpio women may appear outwardly restrained, but there is much more bubbling below the surface. They are ambitious with high self-esteem, but often wear a mask of unpretentiousness. They are the true power behind the scenes, the one who holds the family together, but never talk about it. Scorpios are strong-willed, resilient, and natural survivors. Often, Scorpios are brutally honest, and expect the same out of those around them. They do not like having to conform, and attempt to get others to adapt to them, as they honestly believe everyone will be better off that way. They are incredibly intuitive, and not easily deceived. They have an excellent memory, and can quickly figure out which of your buttons to push. They are passionate in bed, and their temperament will not diminish with age. When she is sexually frustrated, a Scorpio will throw all of her energy into her career or her loved ones. She is proud, categorical, and "if you don't do it right, don't do it at all" is her motto. Scorpio cannot be fooled, and she will not forgive any cheating. Will she cheat herself? Yes! But it will not break up her family, and she will attempt to keep it a secret. Scorpios are usually attractive to men, even if they are not particularly beautiful. They keep a low profile, though they always figure out their partner, and give them some invisible sign. There is also another, selfish type of Scorpio, who will use others for as long as they need them, before unceremoniously casting them aside.

Taurus is a good match; they will have excellent sexual chemistry and understand each other. Scorpio and Gemini are drawn to each other, but are unlikely to stay together long enough to actually get married. Cancer can be a good partner as well, but Cancers are possessive, while Scorpios do not like others meddling in their affairs, though they can later resolve their arguments in bed. Scorpio and Leo are often found together, but their relationship can also be very complicated. Leos are animated and chipper, while Scorpios, who are much deeper and more stubborn, see Leos as not particularly serious or reliable. One good example of this is Bill (a Leo) and Hillary (a Scorpio) Clinton. Virgo can also make a good partner, but when Scorpio seemingly lacks emotions, he will look for them elsewhere. Relationships with Lira are strange and very rare. Scorpio sees Libra as too insecure, and Libra does not appreciate Scorpio's rigidity. Two Scorpios together make an excellent marriage! Sagittarius and Scorpio are unlikely to get together, as she will think he is shallow and rude. If they do manage to get married, Scorpio's drive and persistence is the only thing that will make the marriage last. Capricorn is also not a bad match, and while Scorpio finds Aquarius attractive, they will rarely get married, as they are simply speaking different languages! Things are alright with a Pisces, as both signs are emotional, and Pisces can let Scorpio take the lead when necessary.

SAGITTARIUS

Sagittarius women are usually charming, bubbly, energetic, and have the gift of gab. They are kind, sincere, and love people. They are also straightforward, fair, and very ambitious, occasionally to the point of irritating those around them. But telling them something is easier than not telling them, and they often manage to win over their enemies. Sagittarius tends to have excellent intuition, and she loves to both learn and teach others. She is a natural leader, and loves taking charge at work and at home. Many Sagittarian women have itchy feet, and prefer all kinds of travel to sitting at home. They are not particularly good housewives – to be frank, cooking and cleaning is simply not for them. Their loved ones must learn to adapt to them, but Sagittarians themselves hate any pressure. They are not easy for men to handle, as Sagittarians want to be in charge. Sagittarius falls in love easily, is very sexual and temperamental, and may marry multiple times. Despite outward appearances, Sagittarius is a very lonely sign. Even after she is married with children, she may continue living as if she were alone; you might say she marches to the beat of her own drum. Younger

Sagittarians can be reckless, but as they mature, they can be drawn to religion, philosophy, and the occult.

Aries and Leo make the best matches, as Sagittarius is able to bend to Leo's ways, or at least pretend to. Sagittarians often end up with Aquarians, but their marriages do not tend to be for the long haul. They are attracted to Geminis, but are unlikely to marry one until middle age, when both signs have settled down. Sagittarius and Cancer have incredible sexual chemistry, but an actual relationship between them would be tumultuous and difficult. Capricorn can make a good partner- as long as they are able to respect each other's quirks. Sagittarius rarely ends up with a Virgo, and while she may often meet Pisces, things are unlikely to go very far.

CAPRICORN

Capricorn women are conscientious, reliable, organized, and hardworking. Many believe that life means nothing but work, and live accordingly. They are practical, and not particularly drawn to parties or loud groups of people. But if someone useful will be there, they are sure to make an appearance. Capricorn women are stingy, but not as much as their male counterparts. They are critical of others, but think highly of themselves. Generally, they take a difficult path in life, but thanks to their dedication, perseverance, and willingness to push their own limits, they are able to forge their own path, and by 45 or 50, they can provide themselves with anything they could want. Capricorn women have the peculiarity of looking older than their peers when they are young, and younger than everyone else once they have matured. They are not particularly sexual, and tend to be faithful partners. They rarely divorce, and even will fight until the end, even for a failed marriage. Many Capricorns have a pessimistic outlook of life, and have a tendency to be depressed. They are rarely at the center of any social circle, but are excellent organizers. They have a very rigid view of life and love, and are not interested in a fling, as marriage is the end goal. As a wife, Capricorn is simultaneously difficult and reliable. She is difficult because of her strict nature and difficulty adapting. But she will also take on all the household duties, and her husband can relax, knowing his children are in good hands.

Taurus, Pisces, and Scorpio make good matches. Aries is difficult, once things cool off after the initial honeymoon. When a Capricorn meets another Capricorn, they will be each other's first and last love. Sagittarius isn't a bad match, but they don't always pass the test of time. Aquarius and Capricorn are a difficult match, and rarely found together. Things are too dull with a Virgo, and while Leo can be exciting at first, things will fall apart when he begins showing off. Libra and Aquarius are both difficult partners for Capricorn, and she is rarely found with either of them.

AQUARIUS

A female Aquarius is very different from her male counterparts. She is calm and keeps a cool head, but she is also affectionate and open. She values loyalty above all else, and is unlikely to recover from any infidelity, though she will only divorce if this becomes a chronic trend, and she has truly been stabbed in the back. She is not interested in her partner's money, but rather, his professional success. She is unobtrusive and trusting, and will refrain from listening in on her partner's phone conversations or hacking into his email. With rare exceptions, Aquarian women make terrible housewives. But they are excellent partners in life – they are faithful, never boring, and will not reject a man, even in the most difficult circumstances. Most Aquarians are highly intuitive, and can easily tell the truth from a lie. They themselves only lie in extreme situations, which call for a "white lie" in order to avoid hurting someone's feelings.

Aquarius gets along well with Aries, Gemini, and Libra. She can also have a good relationship with a Sagittarius. Taurus often makes a successful match, though they are emotionally very different; the same goes for Virgo. Aquarius and Scorpio, Capricorn, or Cancer is a difficult match. Pisces can make a good partner as well, as both signs complement each other. Any relationship with a Leo will be tumultuous, but lasting, as Leo is selfish, and Aquarius will therefore have to be very forgiving.

PISCES

Pisces women are very adaptable, musically inclined, and erotic. They possess an innate earthly wisdom, and a good business sense. Pisces often reinvent themselves; they can be emotional, soft, and obstinate, as well as sentimental, at times. Their behavioral changes can be explained by frequent ups and downs. Pisces is charming, caring, and her outward malleability is very attractive to men. She is capable of loving selflessly, as long as the man has something to love. Even if he doesn't, she will try and take care of him until the very end. Pisces' greatest fear is poverty. They are intuitive, vulnerable, and always try to avoid conflict. They love to embellish the truth, and sometimes alcohol helps with this. Rarely, one finds extremely unbalanced, neurotic and dishonest Pisces, who are capable of turning their loved ones' lives into a living Hell!

Taurus, Capricorn, Cancer, and Scorpio make the best matches. She will be greatly attracted to a Virgo, but a lasting relationship is only likely if both partners are highly spiritual. Any union with a Libra is likely to be difficult and full of conflict. Pisces finds Gemini attractive, and they may have a very lively relationship – for a while. Occasionally, Pisces ends up with a Sagittarius, but she will have to fade into the background and entirely submit to him. If she ends up with an Aquarius, expect strong emotional outbursts, and a marriage that revolves around the need to raise their children.

Tatiana Borsch